ed in Education

Donald L. MacMillan

DEPARTMENT OF EDUCATION
UNIVERSITY OF CALIFORNIA • RIVERSIDE

Behavior Modification in Education

The Macmillan Company • New York
Collier-Macmillan Publishers • London

Copyright © 1973, Donald L. MacMillan

Printed in the United States of America

All rights reserved. No part of this book may be reproduced or transmitted in any form or by any means, electronic or mechanical, including photocopying, recording, or any information storage and retrieval system, without permission in writing from the Publisher.

The Macmillan Company
866 Third Avenue, New York, New York 10022

Collier-Macmillan Canada, Ltd., Toronto, Ontario

Library of Congress catalog card number: 72-90539

Printing:　　2 3 4 5 6 7 8　　　Year:　3 4 5 6 7 8 9

To Mom and Dad and
the memory of their grandson,
Walter M. Trumbull III

Preface

This book was written in an attempt to meet what I perceived to be a need for a book that encompasses the principles of learning on which behavior modification practices are based, and ways in which these principles have been translated into educational practice. Such a need became apparent when, in preparing a course on behavior modification, I began searching for an adequate text for preservice teacher-training candidates. What became readily apparent was that no source was available that included both the principles and practices; rather, one could find introductory learning texts with strong experimental learning psychology orientation or books of readings on behavior modification. In the first instance, it was necessary to put the principles into some educational context, since most examples were from studies with infrahuman subjects. The books of readings, while appropriate for one with a background in learning theory, included articles from journals whose readers are assumed to understand that a certain practice reflects a certain principle of learning. Thus, the present book represents an attempt to bridge the gap for preservice or in-service teachers with a limited background in learning theory, in that principles are presented in an educational context, and practices are presented as reflecting the principles.

For organizational purposes, Part I deals primarily with

principles of learning, with a strong emphasis on operant conditioning. The decision to include such a heavy emphasis on principles of learning dimensions is based on the fact that these principles should guide practice. In my own experience observing in classrooms where a "behaviorist orientation" is professed but where inappropriate practices exist, it has usually been a situation in which the teacher fails to understand the principles of learning. Instead of letting principles guide the practice, the teacher adopts a program reported in the literature "lock, stock, and barrel" for his class, despite the fact that the program was used with children who in no way resemble his class. A second reason for the emphasis on principles stems from a bias of the author. Books of readings and journal articles include how others have seen fit to translate principles of learning into practice, but by no means exhaust the possible ways in which these principles might be used to guide practice. It therefore seems restricting to present what has been done and thereby imply that these are the only ways in which these principles can be used. I have seen too often that preservice teacher-training candidates see many alternative ways in which these principles can be used, and once they comprehend the principles of learning, they well may see new ways of making use of them.

Part II contains practices in education that have been derived from behavior modification. In Chapter 5 the role of the teacher as a behavior analyst is discussed together with a description of the step-by-step ways in which the effectiveness of various interventions would be evaluated. Chapter 6 discusses how a teacher would go about establishing a token economy in a classroom. Included is a discussion of the kinds of children for whom a token economy would be appropriate. Chapter 7 examines the ways in which a regular class teacher, with children for whom the very contrived token economy would be inappropriate, can translate the principles of learning into practice. Concluding the book is a chapter that explores the areas of controversy surrounding behavior modification with some attempt to ascertain the role of behavior modification in the larger context of education.

In Part I some decisions had to be made regarding which principles to include and which to exclude. In coming to this decision, I attempted to include those principles on which present practices are based and those principles on which practice could be based. Any errors in judgment regarding these decisions are assumed fully by me. It is hoped, however, that the principles and concepts provided herein will be adequate for the reader to be able subsequently to read critically the professional literature in the various journals, as the rate at which practices are evolving is impressive.

At this point, I would like to take the opportunity to thank those individuals who have exerted considerable influence on my educational and professional career. From my public school experiences are a group of educators, in the best sense of the word, including Russell Hobart, William Kingzett, Dorothy and Jerry Krasovec, Michael Palermo, and Charles Schlaff. From my undergraduate program at Western Reserve University, I wish to thank Dean C. Henley Cramer for his guidance and assistance, and Robert Lautenschleger, my master teacher while I was student teaching. And finally, from my graduate program at the University of California, Los Angeles, there are several individuals who greatly influenced me then, and have done so since completion of my doctoral program: specifically, Frank M. Hewett, Ph.D.; Wendell Jeffrey, Ph.D.; Reginald Jones, Ph.D.; Barbara Keogh, Ph.D.; and George Tarjan, M.D.

I am also indebted to certain individuals for their assistance in the preparation of this manuscript by reacting to ideas and reviewing drafts. These include Richard Eyman, Ph.D., Pacific State Hospital; Robert Lennan, California School for the Deaf, Riverside; C. Edward Meyers, Ph.D., University of Southern California; Arthur Silverstein, Ph.D., Pacific State Hospital; Howard Spicker, Ph.D., Indiana University; Annette Tessier, Ed.D., California State University, Los Angeles; and Bonnie Wolf, Riverside

Unified School District. Special thanks are due Steven R. Forness, Ed.D., with whom I have worked closely since our graduate days, and whose counsel and expertise are greatly appreciated. Also, I wish to thank Barbara Keogh, Ph.D., for her constant support and advice. She is the kind of teacher from whom one never ceases learning. For their valiant efforts at deciphering my handwriting and typing of the manuscript, I will always be grateful to my mother, Mrs. Arline MacMillan, and to Mrs. Betty Medved.

Finally, I want to express my gratitude to my family for their constant support of my career—particularly to my wife, Dianne, whose contributions have been too numerous to mention. To my sons, Andrew and John, I would like to acknowledge their timely interruptions which made completion of this book much longer than was necessary, but which made life more enjoyable during the time of the writing.

D. L. M.

Contents

PART I
Principles of Behavior Modification 1

1 BEHAVIOR MODIFICATION: AN ALTERNATIVE 3
   Medical Model 4
   Psychological Model 7
   The History of Behavior Modification 11
   Early 1900s 14
   1930s and 1940s 18
   1950s 23
   1960s 28

2 LEARNING CONCEPTS AND MODELS 41
   Concepts 42
   Explanations of Behavior 42
   Environmental Determinants of Behavior 44
   Concepts of Responses and Stimuli 46
   Responses 46
   Stimuli 47
   Contingencies 48

CONTENTS

    Learning Models   49
      Respondent Conditioning   50
      Operant Conditioning   54
      Contingency Management   57
      Modeling   57

3 MODIFICATION OF OPERANT BEHAVIOR   63

    Stimulus Control of Operants   63
      Unconditioned and Conditioned Reinforcers   66
    Weakening Operants   69
      Extinction   69
      Counterconditioning   72
      Satiation   73
      Punishment   76
      Summary   79
    Strengthening or Building Operants   79
      Contingency Management   81
      Chaining   82
      Shaping   85
      Modeling   89
      Summary   89

4 REINFORCEMENT REVISITED   93

    Schedules of Reinforcement   93
      Continuous Reinforcement   95
      Ratio Schedules   96
      Interval Schedules   97
      Fixed and Variable Schedules   97
      Fixed-Ratio (FR) Schedules   99
      Fixed-Interval (FI) Schedule   101
      Variable-Ratio (VR) Schedule   104
      Variable-Interval (VI) Schedule   107
    A Continuum of Reinforcers   110

PART II
Translating Principles into Practice 117

5 LEARNING THEORY AND TEACHING 119
  What's New About Behavior Modification? 121
  The Teacher as a Behavior Analyst 124
    Selection of Target Behavior 126
    Selection of Goal Behavior 127
    Recording Target Behavior 129
    Identification and Recording of Antecedents 132
    Identification and Recording of Consequences 133
    Intervention Program 134
    Reversal of Contingencies 136
  Behavior Modification in the Context of Education 138

6 BEHAVIOR MODIFICATION IN THE SPECIAL CLASS: A TOKEN ECONOMY 145
  Population 147
  Environment to Which Children Will Move 149
  The Token Economy 150
    Selection of Tokens and Backup Reinforcers 152
  Implementing a Token System in a Classroom 154
    Introduction of System to the Class and Establishment of Token Value 154
    Acquisition Stage 156
    Maintenance Stage 160
  Individualization 165
  Some Additional Considerations 166
  Critique of Token Economies 169

7 BEHAVIOR MODIFICATIONS IN THE REGULAR CLASS 175
  Population 177

General Classroom Procedures 178
   Strengthening Behavior 180
   Developing New Behaviors 189
   Weakening or Eliminating Behaviors 193
Contracting 200

8 CONTROVERSIES SURROUNDING BEHAVIOR MODIFICATION 207
Popularity 208
Limitations of the Model 209
   Human Learning 210
   Motivation 212
   Reinforcement 216
Problems in the Application of the Model 219
   Goals 219
   Overkill 221
   When to Use Behavior Modification 222
Ethical Considerations 222
Conclusion 224

GLOSSARY 227
INDEX 233

PART I
Principles of Behavior Modification

CHAPTER 1

Behavior Modification: An Alternative

CHILDREN whose behavior is considered inappropriate have posed a problem to educators for centuries. It is interesting to note, however, the number of points of view proposed to account for such misbehavior, and how each position thrusts the teacher into a slightly different role. Hewett (1968) suggested that the three major frameworks within which behavior problems are considered are the psychoanalytic, sensory-neurological, and behavior modification approaches. The point that bears mention concerning these three positions is that each would suggest that the *causes* of the misbehavior are in altogether different areas of study. For example, the psychoanalytic proponents contend that such behavior stems from faulty personality development. The sensory-neurological advocates look to structural damage to account for the behavior, while the behavior modifiers contend that such behavior results from learning to behave in an inappropriate manner, or the failure to learn these behaviors.

An outgrowth of these different ways of conceptualizing the causes of the problem is the fact that each approach indicates a different role for the teacher in dealing with behavior problems. Hewett (1968) contended that the psychoanalytic approach places the teacher into the role of an *educational therapist* and thereby relegates the teaching of academic tasks to a position of secondary importance. The sensory-neurological approach places the teacher in a role of *diagnostician* wherein the teacher attempts to identify sensory and/or neurological deficits and to program materials in order to circumvent those areas of weakness. Finally, the behavior modification approach places the teacher in the role of a *learning specialist,* in which the teacher arranges consequences in order to facilitate the learning of appropriate behavior and unlearning of inappropriate behavior. For a detailed account of programs representative of the psychoanalytic approach, one should consult Bettelheim (1950), Redl and Wineman (1952), or Rabinow (1960). For the sensory-neurological approach, several good accounts are available, including Cruickshank (1961), Kephart (1960), or Delacato (1959).

Historically speaking, the educator has conceptualized problem behavior in frameworks borrowed from the medical profession. That is to say, when the child misbehaves the misbehavior is seen as a symptom (behavioral manifestation) of some underlying problem. If such a view is assumed, then it becomes meaningless to deal with the symptom since all one does in treating symptoms is to delay the necessity of treating the "cause" which underlies the problem. Treatment of one symptom will simply lead to the appearance of another symptom until at last the underlying "cause" is cured. Several of the approaches for working with children with behavior problems reflect this medical model. Ullmann and Krasner (1965), Bandura (1969), and Hewett (1968) discussed in considerable detail the implications of using such a model in treating or educating children with behavioral problems.

MEDICAL MODEL

Both the psychoanalytic and sensory-neurological approaches are derived from medical approaches to the treatment of illness. As noted by MacMillan (1969) the data collected by persons operating from such a perspective may be interesting and valid, yet typically these data are of little help to the educator in search of the educational prescription needed by a particular child. That is to say, the teacher may be glad to know that a particular child is suffering from premature narcissistic dethronement, minimal cerebral dysfunction, dyslexia, or some other "illness," yet this information provides little direction to the teacher in determining how to get the child to read to grade level or to solve math problems at the appropriate level. This is not meant to minimize the importance of these data or concepts for the psychiatrist or neurologist. However, each discipline defines parameters that are relevant to their particular discipline; these parameters are not necessarily relevant for the educator. Yet many of the categories used by educators are borrowed from disciplines whose concerns are different from those of the educator. For example, emotionally disturbed (psychological or psychiatric), socially disadvantaged (sociological), brain damaged (neurological) are all borrowed from other professions or disciplines. Once the child is categorized, we, as educators, apparently feel more comfortable in dealing with him. However, I would submit that these categories are based on surfacing characteristics that have little or no direct bearing on the learning needs of the child. In addition, categorization tends to lead those charged with instructing these children with the false impression that they are a homogeneous group which ignores the within-category variability.

Ullmann and Krasner (1965) discussed in some detail the impact of the concepts of the medical model on conceptualization of maladaptive behavior. The basic premise underlying the medical model is that the individual's behavior is considered abnormal, diseased, or sick *because* of some underlying cause. There are several by-products of this notion. First, one cannot deal with the maladaptive behaviors directly because they are simply manifestations of the cause. Second, any change in the behavior, as such, is insignificant because the real cause has gone untreated. Therefore, attempts to treat "symptoms" will simply mask the behavior, but the fact that the cause still is untreated will result in symptom substitution, or the appearance of other behaviors symptomatic of the existence of some underlying "pathology."

The fears arising in response to the notion of symptom substitution seem somewhat unfounded. To quote Ullmann and Krasner (1965), "The first argument against the theory of symptom substitution is that there is little, if any, evidence for it." In addition, Eysenck (1959), one of the leading clinicians using behavior modification, reported that an extensive review of the literature revealed no substantial evidence to support these fears. This is not to imply that maladaptive behavior, once altered, will never return; however, alternative explanations seem more reasonable in explaining this phenomenon than that of symptom substitution.

There has also been growing dissatisfaction with the medical model within educational circles on grounds other than those presented above. First of all, it has led to the grouping of children on the basis of etiology rather than on the basis of learning needs —for example, all children "diagnosed" as emotionally disturbed, brain injured, and socially disadvantaged. Yet educators have come to realize that within each of these groups are children with vastly different learning needs, and the overlap between groups is considerable. It is almost analogous to grouping in wards of a hospital, cases of broken legs according to *how* the leg was broken: in Ward A are those who broke them skiing; in Ward B are those who fell off barstools, etc.

Another basis for concern centers around what has come to be referred to as the "self-fulfilling prophecy." One will note that almost all the labels and categories used by educators (with the exception of the gifted) imply a deficit or deficiency. The question that arises is how that deficit label affects how the individual so labeled feels about himself and how the attachment of that label affects how others respond toward that individual. The expectancies of the child for success and failure and those of the significant others in their environment (e.g., parents, teachers, and peers) might well alter the levels achieved by a particular child. This phenomenon is probably a very complex interaction and not nearly as simplistic as might be inferred from some of the popularized accounts in the educational literature.

In summary, then, educators' growing dissatisfaction with the medical model as a conceptual tool for considering maladaptive behavior seems to have developed for several reasons:

1. The data typically collected are of little help to the teacher in planning an educational program for the child.
2. The teacher is thrust into a role which he is ill prepared to play.
3. Grouping on the basis of etiology has not resulted in educationally homogeneous groups and has led to treatment of such groups as if they were homogeneous.
4. Categories evolved have been basically deficit oriented and there is growing concern about the possibility of a "self-fulfilling prophecy."

PSYCHOLOGICAL MODEL

The past decade has seen more and more practice in education based on a psychological, rather than medical, model. Such practice has probably been most prominent in the field of special education; however, other subfields within education have also felt the impact, such as counseling, school psychology, and regular classroom practice. This psychological model has come to be referred to in common parlance as *behavior modification*. The choice of the term behavior modification may not be a fortunate selection since alternative approaches purport to, and do in fact, modify behavior.

The major difference between behavior modification and therapies or programs based on the medical model is that behavior modification concerns itself only with the behavior manifested. That is to say, the rationale does not assume underlying causes for the behavior or that the behavior is symptomatic of some more obscure force. One of the most basic assumptions underlying the behavior modification rationale is that all behavior, good and bad, is learned. If one accepts this premise, it follows that all behavior is subject to change according to the principles of learning. Hence one can rely on a vast amount of information regarding learning that has accumulated in university and private laboratories for decades as a guide for determining a program for altering a certain behavior. One consequence of this approach is that one starts with the concepts and principles of learning upon which the program for behavior change is based. Hence, one can start with any of a number of learning theories (see Hilgard, 1956) such as the Pavlovian model of classical conditioning, Hull's theory, Guthrie's theory, or Skinner's model of operant conditioning. Programs of therapy have been developed based on each of the above (see Ullmann and Krasner, 1965; Krasner and Ullmann, 1965, for examples of each). However, after surveying the literature in education it strikes this author that the overwhelming majority of behavior modification work done in the context of education has been based on the works of Skinner, and therefore this book will deal with his model. This is in no way meant to reflect the *best* theory or the most parsimonious, but simply to present the rationale on which most educational work is based and therefore to familiarize the reader with the concepts underlying that approach.

Ullmann and Krasner (1965, p. 2) defined behavior modification as "the application of the results of learning theory and experimental psychology to the problem of altering maladaptive behavior." The authors went on to point out that the focus is on overt behavior. From the operant perspective, one might say that the focus is on the relationship between the behavior of the individual and his environment; with the study of the variations in that behavior as a result of the consequences of that behavior.

The teacher employing the behavioristic approach might follow the three questions suggested by Ullmann and Krasner (1965, pp. 1–2) for analyzing behavior judged to be inappropriate.

1. What behavior is maladaptive; that is, what subject behaviors should be increased or decreased?
2. What environmental contingencies currently support the subject's behavior (either to maintain his undesirable behavior or to reduce the likelihood of his performing a more adaptive response)?
3. What environmental changes, usually reinforcing stimuli, may be manipulated to alter the subject's behavior?

In attempts to answer these questions, the teacher should be cautioned to be as precise as possible in describing the behavior. That is to say, avoid terms like "acting out," "hyperactive," "brain injured," and "aggressive" which may mean different things to different people and therefore cloud the issue by failing to specify the exact behavior that is to be modified. Rather, one is advised to describe the behavior in such terms as "John kicks other children," "Bob was out of his seat without permission six times during a 60-minute period," "Carol does not speak with her peers during free play." Such descriptions describe the actual behavior rather than using a global term encompassing the precise behavior plus a host of other behaviors.

An answer to the second question represents an attempt to identify what environmental events or consequences are supporting the behavior judged to be inappropriate. The teacher tries to stop the payoff for misbehaving, which reflects the notion that people do things because of their consequences. Children in classrooms perform certain acts because of the positive consequences (teacher smiles at him, peers laugh, teacher gives him an "A" which increases his status in the class) or to avoid noxious consequences (e.g., child throws a book in order to be sent to the office and thus misses the math exam where he would demonstrate an inability). If the payoff is under the direct control of the teacher (e.g., the teacher's attention), then the teacher can be careful to ignore the misbehavior. If the child doesn't get the payoff over a long period of time, the behavior should terminate.

Finally, the teacher turns to devising ways in which potential payoffs can be used systematically in order to change the behavior. In the foregoing paragraph, it was shown how the teacher might withhold the attention the child wanted in order to terminate misbehavior. Conversely, if for a given child the teacher's attention is a potent consequence, then the teacher can use it (the attention) when, and only when, the child exhibits desirable behavior. Most educational attempts to answer this third question have led to the adoption of token economies, check mark systems, or other systems using arbitrary rewards that are redeemable for candy, toys, or free time. This state of affairs will be discussed later in the book.

One further question has been suggested by MacMillan (1969); that is, what takes place just before the inappropriate behavior is exhibited by the child? All too often, one finds that a given child misbehaves principally during a particular time of the day (e.g., just before lunch or just before school is dismissed). Information of this type enables the teacher to anticipate misbehavior and to prevent it, as opposed to simply focusing on the consequences that follow the misbehavior.

Then the behavior modification approach conceptualizes behavior as having been learned, and therefore subject to change according to the principles of learning. As a result, the teacher is placed in the role of the learning specialist. This role is far more compatable with the preparation of teachers and their competences than were either of the roles assigned to teachers by the psychoanalytic or sensory-neurological approaches. In the behavior modification strategy, the teacher attempts to analyze the relationship between behavior and environmental events, and subsequently to modify the latter in order to change the former.

As noted by Hewett (1968), many individuals feel uneasy about operant conditioning in that it conjures up images of laboratory research with pigeons and rats, or the use of electric shock, or maybe just the discomfort over "manipulating" other people's behavior against their will. Might individual teachers misuse the techniques for their own convenience but to the disadvantage of the children in their class? Using the cattle prod to control behavior of children may violate the human dignity of man. Ethical issues are definitely involved in the use of behavior modification, and should not be casually dismissed. Certain of these issues will be discussed in Part II of this book. However, a very promising technique should not be discarded because of its potential misuse by insensitive teachers. Behavior modification is a delivery system and can be used for good or ill. In the course of the book, an attempt will be made to provide guidelines that will sensitize the reader to the can's and can'ts of the technique.

Another response to behavior modification is that it is nothing new, and that teachers have been using such techniques since the beginning of time. Such a contention is probably true; and the major thrust of behavior modification is to make the use of learning principles *more systematic,* and to focus on altering behavior in the setting in which it occurs rather than in an artificial setting such as the counselor's office.

THE HISTORY OF BEHAVIOR MODIFICATION

Behavior modification as an approach to altering maladaptive behavior has an extensive and rich history. While the practice of developing techniques consistent with theory or principles of learning is a relatively recent development, an *ad hoc* analysis of treatment procedures used much earlier indicates that many procedures were, in fact, consistent with the learning principles of the present day. In a selected history of behavior modification, Forness and MacMillan (1970) were able to trace procedures that are consistent with learning principles back to the temple psychiatry of the Greeks.*

Schwitzgebel (1970) placed behavior modification in perspective when he stated that wisdom was not born yesterday. Any idea has a history, and behavior modification is no exception. In the *Republic* Plato suggested that children take lessons in the form of play, whereas Erasmus related the story of a father

---

* This section relies heavily on the article cited. The author wishes to express his appreciation to Dr. Steven R. Forness for his permission to use the article so extensively.

who presented Greek and Latin letters to his sons in the form of delicious biscuits cut into the letters. Zilboorg and Henry (1941) told of the early Roman aversive for alcoholism which consisted of putting eels in the wine cup. Schwitzgebel (1970, p. 1) related treatments of disordered people including, "For a man who thought he had no head, a physician prescribed that he wear a lead helmet for a week; another physician treated a woman who thought she had swallowed a snake by giving her an emetic and then deftly placing a snake in the receptacle."

In 1871 a French practitioner, Anton Mesmer, was able to relax the inhibiting responses of certain hysterical diseases. Although his claims were found to be largely unscientific as a result of an investigation led by Benjamin Franklin, among others, and were later discarded, his influence continued for decades. He believed that there was a constant flow of magnetic fluid in the universe, the imbalance of which in the human organism caused disease to appear. He appeared to reinstate this balance through stroking patients with a wandlike device. He effected dramatic "cures" of what were obviously psychosomatic diseases resembling St. Vitus dance, rheumatism, and the like. It is likely the cures resulted from the relaxation of the muscles induced by the stimulus of the stroking and the concomitant seance-like atmosphere surrounding the treatment (Zilboorg and Henry, 1941).

In the same era, the more responsible physician, Phillippe Pinel, introduced the concept of Moral Treatment. When appointed to head the Bicêtre, he found the insane in that institution treated as animals and chained in their cells. Pinel hypothesized that the insane needed not to be treated as diseased and dangerous but as normal human beings who, when treated normally, would respond in like manner. He applied for and gained from the Commune, at considerable risk to his professional career, permission to release his charges from their chains. Following Dacquin's dictum that the answers to mental illness must be gained from the mentally ill, he initiated the practice of spending considerable time with his patients and keeping records of their progress. It was the positively reinforcing aspect of this social approval which was perhaps the most effective aspect of his Moral Treatment (Zilboorg and Henry, 1941).

In the well-known work of Jean Itard in 1800, we have one of the earliest documented uses of positive and negative reinforcement in the educational practice. Itard's work with Victor is legendary (Boyd 1914), but his use of reinforcement techniques is largely overlooked and it is evident that he employed such techniques in much the same way that sophisticated researchers do presently. For example, in attempting to teach Victor to spell the word for milk, Itard would point to the word on the board and pronounce it, rewarding Victor with a drink of the milk when he was able to repeat the word correctly. Eventually, after several demonstrations, Victor was able to unscramble the mixed letters of the word and spell it correctly, upon which he was again rewarded with a drink of milk (or positively reinforced). Victor's outbreaks of temper were usually mitigated by compliance, up to a point. Once during a lesson, Victor became enraged and scattered his word cards about the room. Since they happened to be on the fourth floor at the time, Itard picked the boy up by the seat of the pants and held him out the window (aversive stimulus), whereupon Victor seemed to gain renewed respect for his teacher's wishes and when returned to the room began meekly to pick up the cards.

In 1803 the German psychiatrist Johan Christian Reil employed what he called "non-injurious torture" in treating the insane. He hypothesized that sudden shock or trauma would bring a patient to his senses (Zilboorg and Henry, 1941). The noise of firing cannons and dunking in cold water were commonly prescribed treatments. One of his more effective treatments with catatonic patients was to infect them with scabies, which made motor responses reinforcing.

Edward Seguin (Boyd, 1914), a disciple of Itard, published the results of his work with the mentally retarded in 1837. He also was committed to certain techniques of reinforcement, giving numerous examples of their use in his work. One of the more obvious was his use of positive reinforcement as a means of inhibiting future incorrect responses. As a part of his physical training scheme, students were required to lower themselves rung by rung from an inclined ladder to improve coordination and perception. However, their hands would often be bruised and scraped by the time they reached the bottom. To prevent them from forming an aversion to the task, Seguin's teachers were instructed to place an apple in each of the pupil's hands. Thus the cooling sensation on the burning surface plus the positive reinforcement of two apples was deemed sufficient to overcome any tendencies toward the maladaptive response of not performing the task the next time.

The work of A. A. Liebault in 1866 and the subsequent presentation of a paper on the subject presented to the Academy of Science by Charcot (Zilboorg and Henry, 1941), laid the foundation for hypnotism as a method of treatment. Liebault was a physician in Nancy, France, who treated the poor through hypnosis and was effective with disorders similar to those encountered by Mesmer. His work is only mentioned here since it represents a forerunner of the work by Wolpe and others who believed that the acting out of acceptable behavior in a relaxed state was a necessary antecedent to modification.

To summarize, the *ad hoc* analysis of practices used by physicians, educators, and others in working with behavior-disordered individuals during this time period reflects the principles of learning. This is not to suggest that they were behaviorists in the present-day use of the word. Rather, they used "what worked," but their procedures were not derived from learning theory. Instead, it is only by applying learning theory to their procedures that one is able to say that the changes in behavior reported can be explained in terms of learning theory.

Early 1900s

It was actually toward the end of the nineteenth century and the beginning of the twentieth century that the theories of Charles Darwin and William James and the experimentation of Ebbinghaus, Pavlov, and Thorndike paved the way for the behavior modification movement. Hence theories of learning were being proposed and principles of learning identified in laboratories throughout the world. At this point, the earliest attempts are seen in which the procedures are derived from the theories and principles of learning.

The work of J. B. Watson (1920) at Johns Hopkins University is classic in the field of behavior modification since it was the first time that a human emotional reaction was conditioned in an experimental setting. Watson proceeded on the basis of four assumptions: that the emotional response of fear could be conditioned, that it would transfer to stimuli other than the initial stimulus which evoked the fear, that the fear would last over a period of time, and that it could be unlearned.

For his subject, Watson chose an eleven-month-old infant, Albert, who was especially noted for his robust health and his apparent lack of fearful responses. As the conditioned stimulus, Watson chose a harmless white rat to which Albert had previously shown no fear. As the unconditioned stimulus, Watson struck a large steel bar with a hammer directly behind the subject's head. When the rat was first presented, Albert showed no fear and reached for it, but when it touched his hand, the unconditioned stimulus was paired with the conditioned stimulus, causing Albert to whimper. After two trials, the experiment was discontinued and resumed one week later, at which time fear of the white rat alone was conditioned after six pairings. After five days the conditioned response was still evident, and Albert's fear of the white rat was found to generalize to a rabbit, a dog, a fur coat, and cotton. The fear did not generalize to wooden blocks or to the experimental room. Although Watson was not able to carry through the last phase of his planned experiment, he did offer suggestions for reconditioning similar to those later used by Mary Cover Jones (1924).

His findings received support indirectly in the same year in a report by James Haberman (1917), who discussed the development of a conditioned response of vomiting in a schoolchild. The child was rushed through breakfast one morning and upon reaching school vomited because of anxiety that had been generated over breakfast and being late for school. The next morning, although there was no rushing, the child again vomited upon reaching school because of the pairing of stimuli which occurred the previous day. Haberman also discussed the case of a man who attended the opera immediately after suffering a bilious attack and became dizzy when leaning over the balcony. He eventually had to give up his balcony seat when, through a similar pairing of stimuli, he became dizzy several times after that even though not physically predisposed to dizziness. In both instances we find examples of contiguous learning of maladaptive behavior.

In 1924 Mary Cover Jones, at Columbia University, attempted to take up where Watson left off. She worked with some 70 children, ages 3 months to 7 years, in an institution for temporary care. She arrived at seven different methods by which children's fears are eliminated.

1. Elimination through disuse (fear will die out if left alone).
2. Verbal appeal (persuasion, usually by an adult).
3. Negative adaptation (familiarity breeds indifference).
4. Repression (the child tries not to show his fear).
5. Distraction (presence of an adult near the fear stimulus).
6. Direct conditioning (pleasant stimulus, e.g., food in presence of the negative stimulus).
7. Social imitation (children who are not fearful serve as models).

Through her observations she concluded that the last two methods were the most effective. She reported their use with a boy named Peter who, at the age of 3 years, was for all intents and purposes a grown-up Albert. He was afraid of a white rabbit. She attempted a type of desensitization by presenting the rabbit in the far corner of the room while Peter was eating. She gradually was able to move the rabbit (aversive stimulus) closer and closer until finally the rabbit was placed on the same tray of food from which Peter was eating (pleasant stimulus). This, coupled with Peter's exposure to children who found pleasure in playing with the rabbit, soon overcame the fear. The implications were obvious: not only is fear learned, but it can be systematically unlearned as well.

In the same year a short article appeared (Moss, 1924) which discussed the conditioning of food aversion in two children which, although not as sophisticated, still added support to Watson's hypothesis. But it was the major work by William Burnham (1924) at Clark University that helped to codify much of the research which had been done to date. He attempted to bridge the gap between research and educational application.

Burnham felt that the essence of education was the setting of a task to be done, a meaningful plan of action devised to complete the task, and lastly, freedom to complete the task according to plan. He felt that absence of any of the three led to the development of maladaptive behavior. He further felt that adaptive behavior should be trained so that maladaptive responses wouldn't have a chance to occur, or that the training of dominant purposeful responses was a preventative of fear. Burnham foresaw the principles of programmed instruction in his insistence on the use of small increments of learning with little chance for failure on the part of the student. He believed that discipline was a systematic attempt to develop conditioned responses to the tasks of school and life. His chapter "Inhibition of the Inhibitions" lists such reinforcing stimuli as electric shock, the use of drugs, the atmosphere of an organized, goal-directed group, and a sense of humor as means of dealing with maladaptive responses that prevent full use of one's capacities. Although Burnham included no systematic research upon which to validate his assumptions, he presented several case studies and a valuable review of the literature from which he drew his conclusions.

In 1929 a case study by William English added further evidence to the work of previous authors. He presented a case study on the development of a fear response in a natural home setting that replicated Watson's research in the laboratory. He related the case of Joan, who was mistakenly offered a stuffed toy by her parents while at the same time an older sister (the toy's owner) howled in protest. Joan became frightened by the howl, refused to touch the toy, and on subsequent occasions, whimpered when it was presented. The parents were able, through a process of systematic desensitization similar to that employed by Jones, to overcome the child's fear in a relatively short time.

The works of Watson and Jones were the major studies in which it was demonstrated that (1) fears are learned, and (2) fears can be unlearned by reversing the process whereby they are learned initially. The other studies reported here replicated the Watson and Jones works but were not seminal in the behavior modification movement. For the educator these two studies have particular importance in that the model used has served as the same model employed in helping children unlearn school-related fears, such as school phobia, fear of certain subjects, and fear of authority figures.

1930s and 1940s

The next two decades witnessed a refinement of technique and a widening of application of the principles established in the 1920s. The studies herein would appear to be prototypes of later work which emphasized aversive conditioning and the use of negative practice.

In 1930 a Russian researcher, N. Kantorovich, reported the use of conditioning techniques with twenty confirmed alcoholics at the Leningrad Psychiatric Institute. He discussed the development of alcoholism as an associative process leading to a pathological reflex. He felt that if the previously conditioned stimulus of alcohol were paired with a negative reinforcement, a stable defensive response would develop. He presented glasses of alcohol, bottles, and word cards such as "vodka" and "drunk" and paired them with strong electric shocks, whereas other word cards such as "sober" were followed with no shock. The observable responses were withdrawal of hands and body and certain miniosomatic reactions of repugnance. Kantorovich reported favorable results with few trials required for actual conditioning, and the defensive responses continued to be stable for a number of months after the initial treatment with no apparent symptom substitution. The study is one of the first in which character disorders were treated successfully with behavior therapy.

It was in the same year, at Johns Hopkins University, that Loretta Bender and Paul Schilder (1930) used electric shock as a negative stimulus to reinforce movement in catatonic stuporific patients. Cases were reported at 16 adults with varying degrees of involvement. The apparatus included a device in which the subject's hand served as the conductor between two electric circuits; when the palm of the hand was placed on one end, the fingers touched the other, completing the electric circuit. A light served as the conditioned stimulus and was turned on when the subject's hand was in place; a split second later, the electric current was turned on. Only several subjects were conditioned successfully to respond to the light. Responses ranged from movement of the entire arm and shoulder to localized squirming of the fingers and arching of the hand. It was interesting to note that sometimes a complete return to the stimulus was a common feature in several cases, almost as if the patient wished to negate having moved in the first place. In one instance, conditioning was complete after one trial, but in two patients no conditioned response was established after as many as 50 trials. In most cases, the use of an aversive stimulus was seen as a base from which to establish contact and shape future social responses.

In a study primarily concerned with children's fear, A. R.

Jersild and Frances B. Holmes (1935) arrived at conclusions similar to those of Jones (1924) and were able to elaborate on some of the earlier findings. At Columbia University the researchers compiled 153 case records and other supplementary source materials on 139 subjects from ages 3 months to 6 years. The case records contained periodic observations over a 21-day period. As an aside, the researchers found that young children feared (1) animals, (2) the dark, (3) high places, (4) strange people, and (5) loud noises, in that order. Furthermore, they found Watson's thesis on how fear develops as a decided over-simplification and thought that fear developed from a sudden novel stimulus for which the child had no adequate response.

Jersild and Holmes (1935) arrived at the following methods of preventing and overcoming fear responses in children. To prevent fear from developing, one should take care to avoid the use of fearful stimuli in such activities as teasing or as a disciplinary measure. Promoting skills to cope with fear, such as rough-and-tumble games, dodge ball, and the like would build stimulus-response associations in which the response would later generalize to fearful stimuli. In overcoming fear, the authors suggested such things as aiding the child to escape, verbal explanation, instruction in methods of coping with fear, gradual habituation, counterstimuli, and promotion of experience through social prompting.

A remarkable study by Krasnogorski (1930) demonstrated the development of a neurosis under laboratory conditions. The experiment was actually carried out by a co-worker, Panferov, who trained a six-year-old boy to give a motor response to a metronome beat of 144 per minute. The child was trained to make differential responses (inhibited responses) to beats of 92 and 120. However, as the difference was decreased, the subject showed emotional responses and disliked coming to the laboratory. When the beat requiring a differential response was increased to 132, the subject "broke down" and became disobedient, cried, became excited, and even went to sleep. When the differential was increased and the beat was lowered to 120, a stimulus to which the boy had responded earlier, he didn't seem to be able to respond, and it was only when the beat was lowered to 92 that he was able to relearn the response. This study indicated that the concept of discrepancy between the child's capacity to behave and the demands of the environment is what accounts for the development of many learning disorders.

Work begun by Knight Dunlap some years earlier was summarized and clarified in a subsequent article in 1942. Dunlap's contributions centered around the concept of negative practice in dealing with stammering and tics. He felt that practicing the stammer or tic led to its control and subsequently to its inhibition. He cautioned, however, against viewing the response acquired through negative practice as being the response that was eventually unlearned, since the latter response is in a different ideational and emotional context and considerable transfer must occur.

An example of the technique can be found in a study by Bernice Rutherford (1940) on cerebral palsied children, specifically the extraneous facial and body movements that athetoid subjects make when attempting to speak. She felt that the primary movements of the athetoid were due to subcortical lesion and thus impossible to control; however, the secondary movements observed in speaking had developed because the energy to speak had been incorrectly channeled into these extraneous movements and when finally associated with speaking had become habit patterns, reminiscent of the superstitious behavior observed in animals by Skinner. Her treatment centered about redirecting the muscles to get them to perform in a prescribed manner through the following procedures:

1. Identification—child watches his face in the mirror while the teacher records his movements.
2. Recognition—child responds verbally when he observes certain movements.

PRINCIPLES OF BEHAVIOR MODIFICATION

3. Attack on the purpose—the child gains understanding of the relative value of the movement.
4. Analysis—step-by-step examination of the sequence of the response.
5. Imitation—practicing the sequence of movements and bringing it under conscious control, often fooling even the examiner.

Rutherford found considerable success in working with children six years of age and older; and though complete success was impossible in all cases, she felt a decrease in the awkward behavior helped to raise the subjects' self-confidence considerably.

The final study of significance in this era exemplifies the use of operant conditioning of behavior using positive reinforcement. Paul Fuller (1949) was able to establish a learned response in a vegetative human organism, an eighteen-year-old profoundly retarded boy who was dismissed by attending physicians as being incapable of even the simplest learning. The subject lay on his back unable to move save for random movement of the arms and head and was totally speechless. Fuller used a syringe filled with sugar-milk solution to reinforce and shape movement in one arm. In two sessions he was able to raise the rate of response from 0.67 per minute to over 3 responses per minute and also observed anticipatory responses such as opening the mouth to receive the reinforcement. Fuller felt that experimenters had long established a preference for the less variable behavior of subhuman organisms in laboratory research and that research on the particular form of human organism which he had used would serve to bridge the gap from animal studies to the study of man.

One can see from the foregoing the refinement in manipulanda and measurement that occurred during this period in time. Accompanying this period of refinement, animal research in psychological laboratories was expanding the understanding of learning processes. It should be noted how the Jersild and Holmes (1935) study revealed the complexity of how fear develops, and their findings expanded the understanding beyond what had come of the Watson research. In addition, the work of Rutherford (1940) with cerebral palsied children and that of Fuller (1949) with the profoundly retarded set the stage for the activities of the 1950s in the extensive work with extremely deviant, heretofore unreachable, subjects. The research remained, however, in the clinical laboratory setting during the 1930s and 1940s—just one step from the learning laboratories using infrahuman organisms.

1950s

The theoretical work of B. F. Skinner, at Harvard University, helped to lay the foundations for the upsurge of both the intensity and quality of research seen in the 1950s. The sophistication of techniques led to larger studies on a variety of subjects. Skinner's work will be discussed in detail in subsequent chapters; however, it should be mentioned here that his research provided a major impetus for much of the work in behavior modification.

In 1951 Joseph Sheehan, at UCLA, applied certain principles of reinforcement to the behavior of stutterers. He hypothesized that stuttering occurs because it is reinforced, the point of reinforcement being that at which the stutterer is allowed to go on to the next word. Therefore, the instrumental act of stuttering which eventually terminates the sequence is reinforced instead.

He studied twenty stutterers who served as their own controls on two passages of 200 words each. In the control segment of the study, the subjects read the passage as they normally would with stuttering not interfered with. In the experimental segment, the subjects read the passage, but whenever they stuttered, they were not allowed to continue until they pronounced the word once without stuttering; thus the stuttering which is instrumental was further removed from the reinforcement. There was reinforcement taking place for "attacking" the word as well. In both segments, five trials were given, followed by a sixth in which the subjects read without interference, and a seventh which took place after a 30-minute interval.

Sheehan's results indicated a lower frequency of stuttering under the experimental condition, and an examination of the interpassage quadrants showed a significant decline in stuttering within each passage as trials increased. The theory of extinction through nonreinforcement proved to be a particularly effective technique both here and in subsequent studies (Williams, 1959; Zimmerman and Zimmerman, 1962).

The work of Joseph Wolpe, of Johannesburg, South Africa (1954), is perhaps the most well known in behavior therapy. Wolpe's principles are based on hullian theory in that he believed that if a response to a stimulus (situation, event, or person) results in drive reduction, then learning will occur. If drive reduction does not occur, then the response will be extinguished. Wolpe held that neurotic behavior is unadapted learned behavior which is acquired in an anxiety-producing situation: the unadaptive response must be inhibited by replacing it with another stronger response.

In systematic desensitization, the patient and the therapist arrive at a list of stimuli which seem to elicit fear in the patient's case and arrange them in order of most to least fearful. When the patient decides this stimulus is no longer producing anxiety, he moves up the list to the next, and so on. Thus a bus driver who had an anxiety reaction to blood from an accident he had experienced was asked to imagine, first, a blood-stained bandage lying in a wastebasket. The stimuli became more and more intense until, at the end of the treatment, he was able literally to imagine a roomful of carnage without undue anxiety. On the day prior to termination, he actually was instrumental in saving the life of a man injured in a motorcycle accident by stopping the man's bleeding. Wolpe's (1954) technique actually represented variations of the work of Mary Cover Jones some thirty years earlier.

In 1955 L. A. Liversedge and J. Sylvester used a variation of negative practice in treating writer's cramp, a motor neurosis.

BEHAVIOR MODIFICATION: AN ALTERNATIVE

He used a metal plate with ½- to ⅛-inch holes in which the patient attempted to place a metal stylus attached to an electric circuit. As the patient gained control over the larger holes, he moved to the smaller, thereby gaining finer and finer control over hand movements. Liversedge also used strips of curved tape simulating normal writing patterns which the subjects traced, being negatively reinforced with shock if the stylus left the pattern. He also employed a special pen which gave an electric shock if there were any spasm flexions of the thumb. In six cases, treatment was given 30 minutes per day for anywhere from 6 to 15 days. There were no symptom substitutions for three and four months later, indicating that pathological muscle responses can be extinguished effectively.

An interesting method of inhibiting stammering known as the Cherry-Sayers method was developed initially by these British researchers in 1956. In studies on normal subjects, it was discovered that stammering could be developed by playing an auditory feedback of the subject's voice on a one-fifth-second delay; thus, it was hypothesized that screening out or distracting the auditory feedback stimulus in stutterers would inhibit the stuttering response. The authors experimented with several distracting stimuli. In "shadowing," the stutterer reads another person's lips as he reads aloud and says the words along with him, thus screening out the sound of his own choice. In "simultaneous reading," the stutterer reads from the same text as the reader and say the words simultaneously. But it was found that when the reader switched to another paragraph, the stutterer continued to read for several lines in the original paragraph, indicating that the crucial variable was not the distraction but the perceptual auditory variable. They found that both whispering and a high tone stimulus to screen out bone conduction resulted in no stammering.

In research with 54 stammerers, some as young at 2½ years, Colin Cherry and Bruce Sayers (1956) found that training with these techniques resulted in nearly total inhibition, some effective up to six months at the time of writing, with and without retraining. It would appear also that the so-called elimination of the symptom led to an overall lowering of anxiety and improved adjustment.

In 1956 Nathan H. Azrin and Ogden R. Lindsley were able to condition cooperation between young children with operant conditioning. The subjects were 20 boys and girls from 7 to 12 years of age, in a normal classroom setting, who volunteered for the experiment. Subjects were matched for sex and age and were placed at a special table with a screen in the middle and told they could "play a game" with the apparatus. Each subject had a stylus which, when placed into a hole opposite his partner's, would result in reinforcement with a jelly bean if his partner placed his stylus opposite as well. No instructions were given; but during the first reinforcement period of 15 minutes, subjects usually learned to cooperate within 10 minutes. Leadership patterns often developed. During an extinction period, there was a gradual decline in cooperation which was more variable in rate; but in the second reinforcement period, it increased quickly to the preextinction rate. The implications here seem to be that cooperative social behavior could be controlled by reinforcing contingencies and could be developed without verbal instructions.

Donald Baer and his co-workers, at the University of Chicago and later at the University of Washington, have done considerable work in determining the nature of social reinforcers (Gewirtz and Baer, 1958). Baer hypothesized that social reinforcers would be sensitive to the effects of deprivation and satiation. Using 102 middle-class, primary-grade subjects, he studied three types of conditions. In the deprivation condition, the subjects were brought from their classroom, singly, by E (a young woman) who interacted only minimally with the subjects along the way and left them alone in the experimental room for 20 minutes. E then returned with a game in which the child was instructed to place marbles in two holes while E verbally reinforced (after a baseline period) the correct choice. In the nondeprived condition, E reacted in a similar manner, but began the game immediately on arriving in the experimental room. In the satiation period, E showed lively interest along the way to the room and interacted in a lively manner with the subjects for 20 minutes, but played the game in the same manner as before. An analysis of correct responses (number of marbles) for each group confirmed Baer's hypothesis. Thus it would seem that not only were social reinforcers sensitive to deprivation-satiation conditions, but their effectiveness could be enhanced in predictable ways.

In 1959 Arnold A. Lazarus extended Wolpe's (1954) techniques to children's therapy with considerable success. In one particular study at Johannesburg (1959), Lazarus reported work with 18 subjects ranging in age from 3½ years to 10 years. In one case in which a child had a phobia of cars resulting from a previous auto accident, Lazarus used desensitization coupled with positive reinforcement to overcome the child's fear. He began with reinforcing the child with chocolates for each time he mentioned cars in a positive way and later reinforced the child for sitting in, and eventually riding in, a car. Another subject with a phobia of animals was presented with different animals while under tranquilizing medication, and the amount of the dosage was gradually decreased each session until the child reacted without aversive responses. A conditioned avoidance response was used to overcome another child's fear of sleeping alone. He was told to imagine his mother's bed and was given a mild electric shock which terminated when he said the words "my bed." This procedure was reported 14 times in a 10-minute period; and a week later the boy reported he had not slept in his mother's bed since the initial treatment. On follow-up, the response continued in effect, and positive changes in his attitude and that of his mother were reported. It is evident that some of the foregoing techniques could be used effectively when adapted to a school situation.

In the same year Carl D. Williams (1959), at the University of Miami, reported a case of the elimination of tantrum behavior through extinction. The subject was a 21-month-old child whose tantrum behavior developed after a long illness and would occur when he was being put to bed. He would scream and rage if the parent left the room too soon after he was put to bed, and these sessions often lasted for two hours, with the result that the parents were reinforcing the behavior by remaining in the room. At Williams' suggestion, the parents were instructed not to reinforce the behavior but to put the child in bed in a casual and loving manner and simply leave the room, shutting the door behind them. In the first session, the child's tantrum behavior lasted for 45 minutes; but the second night (possibly due to the exhaustion in the first session) the child went immediately to sleep. Tantrum behavior reappeared for 10 minutes in the third session, but was totally extinguished by the tenth, with no adverse maladjustment or symptom substitution reported after a year and a half.

In summary, the 1950s saw the major thrust of behaviorism into a variety of areas. The work of Wolpe (1954) and Lazarus (1959) in clinical work has been the cornerstone on which such practice has grown until today when it represents one of the major models for clinical practice. In Sheehan's (1951) work one sees how the principles of learning were applied to a population (stutterers) whose problem lent itself to this rationale. The work of Lindsley (1964) is of particular importance to educators. He was a pioneer in the application of behavior modification principles to educational settings with atypical children. Finally, the contribution of Baer, first in his work with Gewirtz (1958) and later at the University of Washington, began sensitizing the field to the power of social reinforcers—a tool used by educators but one that was not being used as systematically as possible. All in all, the 1950s saw the field turn the corner by applying techniques based on learning theory to a wider variety of types of subjects and in differing settings.

1960s

In the present decade the work begun in a therapy setting in the previous decade was applied with considerable success in hospital settings with more severely disturbed subjects. Shaping and modeling techniques were applied on a much larger scale, and it is evident that this heralded a systematic approach to the previously fragmented and haphazard techniques employed in many large institutions.

In the early 1960s Theodoro Ayllon (1962) pioneered the use of behavior modification techniques in the psychiatric ward. Ayllon's work centered around the psychiatric nurse as the source of immediate and constant contact and, therefore, the source of reinforcement for patients.

Ayllon is perhaps most well known for his study in Saskatchewan, Canada, involving the shaping of behavior with the use of food. On the wards of Saskatchewan Hospital, many patients had to be coaxed to the cafeteria at mealtime, and several who refused to go were unwittingly reinforced for this behavior by being fed in their rooms. The response of going to the cafeteria was reinforced by the following procedure. The cafeteria was opened only for 30 minutes at mealtimes, and anyone who failed to arrive during that time was not allowed to eat. The time was gradually decreased to 5 minutes, with all 32 patients eventually meeting criterion. When criterion was met, patients were further required to obtain a token from the nurses and drop it in a slot in order to enter the cafeteria. Later, patients were also taught cooperation in obtaining tokens using a method somewhat similar to Lindsley's (discussed earlier). This shaping of behavior has endless possibilities for shaping school behaviors as well.

In 1962, at Indiana University, Charles Ferster and M. K. DeMeyer developed a technique for analyzing reinforcers with autistic children. Ferster used a specially designed room containing several types of reinforcing devices ensuring that at least one of the devices would be relevant to the current deprivation condition of the child. Subjects obtained a coin by pressing a lever in one device and used the coin to obtain reinforcement in one of the other dispensers. The other dispensers of reinforcement included a pinball machine, an electric organ, a phonograph, a picture viewer, an electric train, a food vendor, a compartment in which a trained monkey would perform when his cage was lighted, and a trinket vendor. Initial research indicated that the candy and trinket vendors were the reinforcers that accounted for most of the behavior of the three subjects studied (aged 3½, 10, and 11 years). However, when the reinforcers were dispensed on varying intermittent schedules and when lights over the machines indicated when machines were not dispensing reinforcement, more complex repertoires could be developed, such as the ability of delaying gratification (coin saving). Subjects were also taught discrimination learning through a matching device over the coin dispenser. The indications were that normal learning processes in autistics were at a very basic level but could be gradually shaped through an almost totally automatic environment, implying that the same potential would exist in the social milieu if the proper conditions could be generated.

By 1962 Albert Bandura had performed a number of experiments at Stanford University with modeling techniques. He felt that in some cases, operant conditioning was laborious and inefficient in developing new repertoires. He noticed that when rhesus monkeys were trained through operant techniques to solve various problems and then were used as models for naive monkeys, the naive monkeys solved 76 percent of the problems through this no-trial imitative behavior. One experiment with children revolved around Piaget's concept of the development of moral judgment. In the first 7 years, children tend to judge an act as morally wrong in terms of material damages involved. After this age, they tend to judge an act by its intent. By using adults who made evaluative statements contrary to this developmental scheme, it was found that children could be taught to judge in terms of intent at younger ages.

Bandura presented films to different groups of young children in which models for aggressive responses were portrayed. Children who viewed a film of adults or cartoon characters performing aggressive acts reacted with imitative-aggressive responses when placed in a frustrating situation, while controls didn't. In the same type of experiment, children who had viewed films in which the model was punished for his aggressiveness tended to respond with fewer aggressive acts. There were indications that the use of certain catharsis techniques in dealing with aggression, that is, viewing films and TV programs of aggressive content, may actually be teaching aggression through reinforcement.

At the University of Illinois, Herbert Quay (Quay *et al.*, 1966) pioneered much of the systematic inquiry in behavior modification techniques as adapted for use in the classroom. He placed considerable emphasis on viewing problem behavior in terms of external observable events which could be modified through the use of discriminative stimuli and response-reinforcement contingencies. He stressed immediate contingency. He experimented with a classroom of five subjects, roughly 6 to 10 years of age, whose behavior problems were of the unsocialized aggressive variety.

One method of shaping involved a small box with a flashing light on the desk of each student. The light would flash whenever the child was observed attending to the teacher; each child was reinforced on a fixed interval basis at the end of the lesson with the candy he had earned. At the end of the conditioning period, the rate of attending behaviors increased significantly. Another method took into consideration the problem of instructing subjects who were at varying levels of proficiency in basic skills. Programmed instruction in reading was offered with immediate candy reinforcement. This was later shifted to poker chips which were traded at lunchtime for candy. Thus, the subjects were taught both to work for symbolic reward and to delay gratification—abilities necessary for success in a regular classroom.

Quay also used modeling techniques in teaching social skills. An adult model demonstrated how to approach, greet, and initiate play activity with a peer. The subject then imitated this behavior and was reinforced with candy. Then another child, previously known to be accepting, interacted with the subject, who was reinforced for the appropriate social behavior. Gradually, this behavior is shaped so that eventually the subject actually seeks out a child of his own age on the playground and applies the techniques he has learned in class.

At approximately the same time, Elaine and Joseph Zimmerman, of Butler University in Indiana (1962), reported another example of altering classroom behavior by manipulating its consequences. They discussed the case of one boy who appeared to have difficulty in spelling and, when called on, would flounder and have to be urged and prodded by the teacher. The teacher's response (giving attention) was viewed as actually reinforcing the inability to spell. Therefore the teacher attempted to ignore the boy unless he spelled correctly. The maladaptive response (misspelling) decreased and was gradually replaced by the adaptive response (spelling achievement), which was reinforced by the teacher's smiling, chatting, and physical proximity.

By 1964 Ogden Lindsley, mentioned earlier, and now at the University of Kansas, was developing and encouraging the use of several means of tailoring the environment for the retarded, the brain damaged, and the emotionally disturbed (Lindsley, 1964). Lindsley felt that retardation was not inherent in the ability of the child but was part of the educator's inability to design a suitable environment for such a child. He speaks of such an environment as a prosthetic device for the higher-order deficits of the retarded as physical therapists speak of artificial limbs, ramps, and elevators for amputees. Lindsley advocated the use of operant techniques because they represented a fresh theoretical approach to educating the retarded, were amenable to experimental description and evaluation, and offered individualized prescriptions for a prosthetic environment.

Lindsley's scheme called for the prosthetic design of stimuli, prosthetic response devices, and prosthetic reinforcers, as in the following examples:

Stimuli: Multiple-sense bulletin boards (with lights and sound)
Expanded auditory narrations (slow speed recordings)
Response-controlled narration (tape switches off individually when the subject has a seizure so he doesn't "lose time")
Response devices: Arm-operated water faucets (like those used by surgeons)
More easily manipulated clothes fasteners
First-key typewriters for cerebral palsied children
Rate switches for turning off machines when the subject becomes distracted
Reinforcers: Individualized social consequences (consideration of the retarded child's greater need for social reinforcement)
Generalized conditioned reinforcers (such as tokens)
Compressed narrations (recordings of the compressed human voice were found to be reinforcing with retardates)
Exaggerated social reinforcers (cartoons, exaggerated smiles and approval)

It was implied that these exaggerated prosthetic devices would be gradually diminished until they began to approximate the normal environment.

In 1964 Ralph Schwitzgebel reported his work with juvenile delinquents in Boston in which he used operant techniques in the delinquent's own environment. His "street-corner research" was an operation in which he used contingency management, arranging positive reinforcers to encourage behaviors that would be socially rewarding later.

Schwitzgebel chose only subjects with a notable police record. He went to the subjects' own neighborhood and offered them a dollar per hour to speak into a tape recorder about their own experiences as a juvenile offender. Most were suspicious at first but were intrigued by the opportunity for "easy money." They usually showed up late but began to arrive earlier when paid extra for arriving on time at the given location. Most, feeling an obligation to talk the full hour, began to fill in the gaps of conversation with apparent cathartic material. They were also reinforced for positive, socially oriented material; but reinforcement was operant and nonverbal. Subjects usually went through a stage of hostility toward their parents, peers, and the experimenter, but this hostility later turned inward and moved to a stage of insight and reorientation.

In a 3-year follow-up, the subjects had a 50 percent reduction in arrests and incarceration when compared with controls. It would appear that shaping techniques can be used to develop attitudes and desirable behavior in a subject's natural environment as well as in the laboratory and school setting.

In 1965 Gerald Patterson, at the University of Oregon, reported his work in controlling hyperactive behavior with operant techniques. The subject was a nine-year-old boy, Earl, with minimal brain damage. He was hyperactive, academically retarded, and aggressive. Patterson felt that environmental stimuli conditioned hyperactivity and that one should be able to arrange the environment so as to strengthen the associations among stimuli in the classroom and certain interfering responses for the hyperactivity. Patterson's apparatus consisted of a light on Earl's desk which was controlled by the experimenter. Each time the light went on, Earl was told, he would be rewarded with a penny. The class was also told that the light was part of a "magic machine" that would teach Earl to sit still so he could learn and that they would share in his earnings. Earl was rewarded immediately at first with candy each time he attended to relevant stimuli (his book or the teacher) and later rewarded with delayed reinforcement.

There was a significant decline in Earl's hyperactive behavior due, perhaps, in no small part to the "bootleg reinforcement" by his classmates, who dropped by his desk at intervals to see how he was doing and to compliment him on his behavior.

He was also reported to be much quieter at home. Thus it was illustrated that behavior, even with a supposedly organic basis, could be controlled in the classroom.

In 1965 O. Ivar Lovaas observed that autistic children seldom showed signs of fear or anxiety. Since a person's discomfort is a basic condition for his improvement, Lovaas speculated that the failure of the autistic to improve might somehow be due to this apparent lack of discomfort. He was concerned, then, with the use of pain as a reinforcer, particularly the response toward a person associated with the removal of pain, which may be the basis for a child's love of his parents. In a room equipped with a grid wired for electroshock, autistic subjects were placed between two experimenters. The grid was turned on and one experimenter coaxed the child to come to him. The child either went or, if necessary, was pushed to the experimenter, whereupon the shock was terminated, and the child was reinforced with verbal reassurance and physical contact. Another portable device was used in reinforcing generalized responses to the ward nurses, as well. In the experimental sessions, punishment was also used to reinforce the subject's response to the command "No." This stimulus command was found to have a greater effect on lever-pressing behavior which had been learned before the experimental sessions than on lever-pressing that followed the experiment.

Although Lovaas felt that the use of punishment was more efficient in some circumstances than food reinforcers, he did not feel that a more widespread use of shock would lead to even better outcomes. He felt that punishment was useful only as an initiating stimulus.

That same year, another researcher at UCLA, Frank Hewett (1964), used operant conditioning to teach reading to an autistic boy, Jimmy. Jimmy was 13 years old and had literally no speech to begin with. When Jimmy entered the classroom, the experimenter "reinforced" him away from hyperactive behaviors and over to his desk with gumdrops. Hewett had devised an upright board with two levels onto which word and picture cards could be placed and arranged for matching. Beginning with concrete objects matched to picture cards, Jimmy was eventually taught to match the picture cards to the appropriate words. For example, the word "ball" was placed on the left of the board and Jimmy learned to slide the word card under the appropriate picture and receive his gumdrop reinforcer which appeared behind a glass door on the right. This also reinforced the lateral sequence involved in reading. Hewett was able to teach a 55-word sight vocabulary to Jimmy, as well as an understanding of basic principles of classification, the letters of the alphabet, and the writing of basic phrases. One day when the gumdrops ran out, Jimmy continued to perform, indicating that the teacher had become a reinforcing stimulus.

In recent years, while work has continued in the area of clinical research, behavior modification principles have been successfully applied to several special education classroom settings. Representative of the various programs are the Experimental Education unit at the University of Washington for children with learning disorders (Haring, 1967); the Rainer School, also in Washington, for retarded children (Birrbrauer et al., 1965); the Children's Rehabilitation Unit at the University of Kansas Medical Center for emotionally disturbed children (Whelan and Haring, 1966); the Juniper Gardens Project in Kansas City for culturally disadvantaged children (Hall et al., 1968), and the Santa Monica City Schools Project for the educationally handicapped (Hewett, 1968). Countless other programs are operating in university, hospital, and public school settings as testimony to the effectiveness of the behavior modification strategy.

During the 1960s behavior modification "came of age" as a methodology with applications in a variety of fields including nursing, clinical psychology, social work, and education. Probably the greatest impetus for the expansion of its use came from the work of Ayllon (1962) involving many patients in a psychiatric ward. This work demonstrated the use of a token economy with application for many subjects simultaneously—a situation more like classes of children than the previous work which was done typically on a one-to-one basis. The work of Quay, Lindsley, Hewett, and Patterson showed how the principles of learning could be used as a basis for organizing entire classrooms of children, or to focus on one child in the context of an entire classroom. Throughout the decade, the work of Bandura has refined further the modeling rationale which more recently has led to applications of this rationale to the classroom setting. Although during the early years of the 1960s the educational programs were situated in hospital or university settings, the latter half of the decade saw these programs being field tested in public school classrooms.

Historians of special education will perhaps look upon the closing decade as a turning point for the behavior modification movement. As the programs above bear evidence, behavior modification adherents have begun to move from examination of the ingredients of learning and reinforcement toward incorporation of those ingredients into coherent programs for exceptional children. The coming decade should indicate whether or not the synthesis has been favorable.

REFERENCES

Ayllon, T., and Houghton, E. Control of the behavior of schizophrenics by food. *J. Exp. Anal. Behav.*, 5:343–52, 1962.

Azrin, N. H., and Lindsley, O. R. The reinforcement of cooperation between children. *J. Abnorm. Psychol.*, 52:100–102, 1956.

Bandura, A. Behavior modification through modeling procedures. In L. Krasner and L. P. Ullmann (eds.) *Research in Behavior Modification*. New York: Holt, Rinehart and Winston, Inc., 1965, 310–40.

Bandura, A. *Principles of Behavior Modification*. New York: Holt, Rinehart and Winston, Inc., 1969.

Bender, L., and Schilder, P. Unconditioned and conditioned reactions to pain in schizophrenia. *Am. J. Psychiatry*, 10:365–84, 1930.

Bettelheim, B. *Love Is Not Enough*. Glencoe: The Free Press, 1950.

Birnbrauer, J., Bijou, S., Wolf, M., and Kidder, J. Programmed instruction in the classroom. In L. Ullmann and L. Krasner (eds.) *Case Studies in Behavior Modification.* New York: Holt, Rinehart and Winston, Inc., 1965.

Boyd, W. *From Locke to Montessori.* New York: Henry Holt and Co., 1914.

Burnham, W. *The Normal Mind.* New York: Appleton, 1924.

Cherry, C., and Sayers, B. Experiments upon the total inhibition of stammering by external controls and some clinical results. *J. Psychosom. Res.,* 1:233–46, 1956.

Cruickshank, W., Bentzen, F., Ratzburg, F., Tannhauser, M. *A Teaching Methodology for Brain-Injured and Hyperactive Children.* Syracuse: Syracuse University Press, 1961.

Delacato, C. H. *Treatment and Prevention of Reading Problems: Neuro-psychological Approach.* Springfield, Ill.: Charles C Thomas, Publishers, 1959.

Dunlap, K. Technique of negative practice. *Am. J. Psychol.,* 55:270–73, 1942.

English, W. Three cases of conditioned fear response. *J. Abnorm. Psychol.,* 24:221–25, 1929.

Eysenck, H. J. Learning theory and behavior therapy. *J. Ment. Sci.,* 105:61–75, 1959.

Ferster, C. B., and DeMeyer, M. K. A method for the experimental analysis of the behavior of autistic children. *Am. J. Orthopsychiatry,* 32:89–98, 1962.

Forness, S. R., and MacMillan, D. L. The origins of behavior modification with exceptional children. *Except. Child.,* 37:93–100, 1970.

Fuller, P. Operant conditioning of a vegetative human organism. *Am. J. Psychol.,* 62:587–90, 1949.

Gewirtz, J. L., and Baer, D. J. Deprivation and satiation of social reinforcers as drive conditions. *J. Abnorm. Psychol.,* 57:165–72, 1958.

Haberman, J. Probing the mind, normal and subnormal. *Med. Rec.,* 92:927–33, 1917.

Hall, R. V., Lund, D., and Jackson, D. Effects of teacher attention on study behavior. *J. Appl. Behav. Anal.,* 1:1–12, 1968.

Haring, N. and Lovitt, T. Operant methodology and educational technology in special education. In N. Haring and R. Schiefelbusch (eds.) *Methods in Special Education.* New York: McGraw-Hill Book Company, 1967.

Hewett, F. M. Teaching reading to an autistic boy through operant conditioning. *Read. Teach.,* 17:613–18, 1964.

Hewett, F. M. *The Emotionally Disturbed Child in the Classroom.* Boston: Allyn & Bacon, Inc., 1968.

Hilgard, E. R. Theories of Learning, 2nd ed., New York: Appleton-Century-Crofts, 1956.
Jersild, A. T., and Holmes, F. B. Methods in overcoming children's fears. *J. Psychol.*, 1:75–104, 1935.
Jones, M. C. The elimination of children's fears. *J. Exp. Psychol.*, 7:382–90, 1924.
Kantorovich, N. An attempt at associative reflex therapy in alcoholism. *Psychol. Abstr.*, 4:493, 1930.
Kephart, N. C. *The Slow Learner in the Classroom*. Columbus, Ohio: Charles E. Merrill Publishers, 1960.
Krasner, L., and Ullmann, L. *Research in Behavior Modification*. New York: Holt, Rinehart and Winston, Inc., 1965.
Krasnogorski. Conditioned reflex and childhood neurosis. *Am. J. Disturbed Child.*, 30:753–68, 1930.
Lazarus, A. A. The elimination of children's phobias by deconditioning. *S. Afr. Med. Proc.*, 5:261–65, 1959.
Lindsley, O. Direct measurement and prosthesis of retarded behavior. *J. Educ.*, 147:62–81, 1964.
Liversedge, L. A., and Sylvester, J. Conditioning techniques in the treatment of writer's cramp. *Lancet*, 1:1147–49, 1955.
Lovaas, O., Schaeffer, B., and Simmons, J. Building social behavior in autistic children by use of electric shock. *J. Exp. Res. Personal.*, 1:99–109, 1965.
MacMillan, D. L. Behavior modification: A teacher strategy to control behavior. *Report of the Proceedings of the Forty-fourth Meeting of the Convention of American Instructors of the Deaf*. Berkeley, Calif.: 1968, pp. 66–76.
Moss., F. Note building likes and dislikes in children. *J. Exp. Psychol.*, 7:475–78, 1924.
Patterson, G. R. An application of conditioning techniques to the control of a hyperactive child. In L. Ullmann and L. Krasner (eds.) *Case Studies in Behavior Modification*. New York: Holt, Rinehart and Winston, Inc., 1965.
Quay, H., Werry, J., McQueen, M., and Sprague, R. Remediation of the conduct problem child in the special class setting. *Except. Child.*, 32:509–15, 1966.
Rabinow, B. A proposal for a training program for teachers of emotionally disturbed and the socially maladjusted. *Except. Child.*, 26:287–93, 1960.
Redl, F., and Wineman, D. *Controls from Within*. Glencoe: The Free Press, 1952.
Rutherford, B. Use of negative practice in speech therapy with children handicapped by cerebral palsy, athetoid. *J. Speech Hear. Disord.*, 5:259–64, 1940.

Schwitzgebel, R. *Streetcorner Research.* Cambridge: Harvard University Press, 1964.

Schwitzgebel, R. Behavior modification: Past, present, and future. In R. H. Bradfield (ed.) *Behavior Modification.* San Rafael, Calif.: Dimensions Publishing Co., 1971.

Sheehan, J. Modification of stuttering through non-reinforcement. *J. Abnorm. Psychol.,* 46:51–63, 1951.

Ullmann, L., and Krasner, L. *Case Studies in Behavior Modification.* New York: Holt, Rinehart and Winston, Inc., 1965.

Watson, J. B., and Rayner, R. Conditioned emotional reactions. *J. Exp. Psychol.,* 3:1–14, 1920.

Whelan, R., and Haring, N. Modification and maintenance of behavior through systematic application of consequences. *Except. Child.,* 32:281–89, 1966.

Williams, C. D. The elimination of tantrum behavior by extinction procedures. *J. Abnorm. Psychol.,* 59:269, 1959.

Wolpe, J. Reciprocal inhibition as the main basis of psychotherapeutic effects. *Arch. Neurol.,* 72:205–26, 1954.

Zilboorg, G., and Henry, G. *History of Medical Psychology.* New York: W. W. Norton & Company, Inc., 1941.

Zimmerman, E., and Zimmerman, J. Alteration of behavior in a special classroom situation. *J. Exp. Anal. Behav.,* 5:59–60, 1962.

CHAPTER 2

Learning Concepts and Models

IN CHAPTER 1 several of the problems that have arisen from application of the medical model to educational situations were discussed. Furthermore, one of the noticeable trends in the historical evolution of behavior modification as a clinical and educational tool was the increasingly greater reliance on demonstrated principles of learning as guides to practice. That is to say, that while in ancient times practices existed which can now be seen to be consistent with learning principles, the practitioners did not employ the techniques with any awareness of the principles of learning. Instead, they used "what works" because there is no basis for predicting the successful and unsuccessful techniques. However, the present-day behavior modifier uses learning principles as guides for practice. If the practice is consistent with the principles of learning, the probability of that technique working is increased. Another way of saying it is that behavior modification is dependent on the principles of learning, and in the next three chapters the author will attempt to present the major concepts and principles on which are based most of the educational behavior modification practices.

Let us briefly review the assumptions underlying the psychological, or behavior modification, model. First, it is assumed that all behavior, good and bad, is learned. Second, if all behavior is learned, it follows that one can employ the principles of learning to bring about change in behavior. Furthermore, any person attempting to use behavior modification techniques as a means of changing behavior must be well grounded in principles of learning in order to analyze the behavior and plan an intervention for modifying that behavior.

In his book on reinforcement theory, Keller (1969) noted the various contexts in which the verb *to learn* is used. As an infant, we learn to distinguish the face of our mother from those of other people. We learn that some objects are hot, or sharp, or sticky. We learn to speak our native language. In school we learn to follow directions, to sit quietly, to read, to solve algebra problems. We learn to throw a curve, to shoot baskets, or to skate. We learn the value of money, to fear a rattlesnake, to feel ashamed in certain circumstances. Are these all alike, or is each characteristic of a different type of learning? How many kinds of learning are there? Keller (1969) concluded that no brief answer is possible at this time, since we are still learning about learning. While we may not be ready to answer the question "What is learning?" in a concise, definitive way, we are able to identify certain general laws and principles of learning which have emerged from research. Most of these laws and principles are easily understood; however, it is essential that one become familiar with them. Once this is done, one will have at his command a very useful tool for analyzing behavior and planning for changes in behavior deemed necessary.

CONCEPTS

Explanations of Behavior

In attempts to explain why individuals behave as they do we often provide incomplete and insufficient explanations. A teacher states that a child attends class because he *wants* to learn.

A child cheats on an examination because his superego is insufficiently developed. The child misbehaves in class because he needs the attention the misbehavior obtains for him. From the behavior modification perspective such explanations are unacceptable in that they do not specify the conditions under which the behavior has a high probability of occurring. Does the child *want* to learn the subject matter in all classes or only in certain cases? Does the second child *cheat* on all examinations or only on final exams in courses for which he has not studied? Does the third child *need* the attention of a certain teacher, all teachers, or the peer group?

Staats and Staats (1963) cautioned against the use of a descriptive term as a cause, and argued that one frequently finds oneself treating a descriptive term as a pseudo cause. These authors used the example of a group of behaviors: suspiciousness, envy, extreme jealousy, stubbornness, delusions of persecution, etc., which appear together in some cases. Such a syndrome has been clinically labeled paranoia. However, the behavior has not been explained; it has only been labeled. A similar case is exemplified in the oft-told anecdote about the teacher who explained to the psychologist that one of her children, Alex, was depressed on some occasions and euphoric on others. After much thought the psychologist informed the teacher that Alex was a manic-depressive. The teacher asked what that meant, whereupon the psychologist said, "Well, it means that on some occasions Alex will be depressed and on others he will be euphoric."

The circularity in logic is apparent and frustrating. When we ask the psychologist how he knows that Alex is manic-depressive, he tells us that he can tell by the way he behaves. Hence the behavior is explained in terms of the construct, while the concept is verified on the basis of the behavior. Skinner (1953, p. 202) discussed this phenomenon in a passage regarding traits:

> Trait-names usually begin as adjectives—"intelligent," "aggressive," "disorganized," "angry," "introverted," "ravenous," and

so on—but the almost inevitable linguistic result is that adjectives give birth to nouns. The things to which these nouns refer are then taken to be the active causes of the aspects. We begin with "intelligent behavior," pass first to "behavior which *shows* intelligence," and then to "behavior which is the *effect* of intelligence." Similarly, we begin by observing a preoccupation with a mirror which recalls the legend of Narcissus; we invent the adjective "narcissistic," and then the noun "narcissism," and finally we assert that the thing presumably referred to by the noun is the cause of the behavior with which we began. But at no point in such a series do we make contact with any event outside the behavior itself which justifies the claim of a causal connection.

Rather than explanations of behavior in terms of constructs which themselves need explaining, the behaviorists have opted for a functional analysis of behavior; that is, they determine the conditions that will reliably produce the behavior under consideration. Since the focus is on the relationship between the environment and behavior, the behaviorist studies the specific changes in the environment that will produce behavior and then experimentally demonstrates this relationship. Reynolds (1968, pp. 2–3) wrote, "Because explanation in operant conditioning requires the experimental production and manipulation of behavior, the actual control of behavior becomes an essential part of the process of explanation. In operant research, to understand behavior is to control it, and vice versa."

Environmental Determinants of Behavior

According to Reynolds (1968) there are two types of environmental determinants of behavior: contemporary and historical. An individual's behavior at any moment may be produced by the contemporary environment and/or the individual's past experiences with similar environmental conditions. When a child is told to stop talking by his teacher, he quits talking because that teacher told him to do so and because of his past experience with consequences applied by authority figures when he failed to obey. Another child may misbehave in order to obtain the attention of his teacher. This can be analyzed if the teacher will subsequently ignore the misbehavior, since then it can be determined if that environmental event (i.e., the teacher attending) was producing the misbehavior.

The historical determinants of behavior are more difficult to assess, since they involve experiences which have taken place over a longer period of time. However, this does not alter the need to analyze the behavior experimentally. For example, children who have experienced excessive failure in mathematics are often assumed to be "turned off" to math, which usually means that when presented with a math text the child exhibits behavior aimed at escaping from the situation they "know" will result in failure and will be painful. The teacher's task then is to get the child to attempt the problems, but first she must terminate the avoidance behaviors. She might try presenting mathematics in a form that does not at all resemble the situation the child has associated with failure and pain. For example, she may ask him to calculate the shooting percentages of two basketball teams from the morning paper, rather than giving him a math text. If this reduces the avoidance behavior, the teacher has *explained* his behavior. If this task does not reduce the avoidance behavior, she has made an incorrect supposition about the historical determinants of his behavior, and must try again.

The point to be made here is that the behavior modification approach rejects mere plausible speculations about the causes of behavior. Instead, it requires experimental demonstration of the contemporary and historical determinants of the behavior in question.

One point needs to be made before moving on, and that relates to the *probability* of a particular behavior occurring. Despite the oft expressed belief by teachers that a particular child "always" misbehaves, such is hardly ever the case. And conversely, even the best-behaved child sometimes misbehaves. Hence what is usually the case when specifying the environmental determinants of behavior is whether the *probability* of a behavior occurring is increased or decreased. If a behavior is produced every single time a particular environmental change occurs, we say it has a probability of 1.0; if it occurs half the time, then 0.5. Therefore, in this context *probability* refers to the frequency of occurrence of a behavior relative to a specified environmental event.

Concepts of Responses and Stimuli

The two major concepts in the behavior modification model are related to behavior and the environment, both of which are the focus of a functional analysis of behavior. Behavior is segmented into units that are called *responses*, while the environment is segmented into units called *stimuli*. Reynolds (1968) noted that both terms may be misleading in that neither, in the context of behavior modification, refers to what their everyday meanings suggest. Responses are not "replies" to the environment, and stimuli do not stimulate the organism in such a way as to force him to act. In fact, from the perspective of behavior modification, relatively few of the relationships between the environment and behavior are of this sort.

Responses

The units of behavior, responses, can be further classified into two types: *respondents* and *operants*. Keller (1969) described respondent behavior as involuntary or reflexive. Respondent behavior is drawn out of the organism by specific stimulus changes in the environment. A puff of air blown in the eye makes the individual blink, going from a dimly lit room into a brightly lit room makes the pupils of the eye contract, or putting one's hand into a bucket of ice water causes the blood vessels to constrict. These responses (i.e., blink, pupil contraction, blood vessel constriction) are not under the control of the individual, and are evoked by their own special stimuli. These stimuli elicit the same respondents from birth—they are not learned.

The other type of responses, operants, are emitted by the individual and are under his control because they are *not* responses to an environmental stimulus. Operant responses account for the overwhelming majority of human behavior. It includes all behaviors that have an effect on or do something to the environment—it is said to *operate* on the environment. Whenever one raises his hand in class, sharpens his pencil, or runs on the playground, he is exhibiting operant behavior. Some effects of the behavior on the environment are immediate and obvious, such as when the child sharpens his pencil. Others, however, are only understood when one considers the history of such behavior, such as when one talks to himself. No obvious stimulus evokes the operant behavior; rather, it is emitted by the individual of his own volition. If, when emitted, it leads to pleasant consequences it becomes more probable that it will again be emitted; if it leads to negative consequences, it becomes less probable.

Stimuli

The units of the environment, stimuli, can be divided into four classes on the basis of their function: eliciting stimuli, reinforcing stimuli, discriminative stimuli, and neutral stimuli.

Stimuli serving an *eliciting* function precede responses and elicit fixed and stereotyped responses. In so doing, they elicit the respondent type of responses only. If you recall the examples of respondents used earlier, the puff of air, the increase in light intensity, and the sudden decrease in temperature were the stimuli that evoked specific responses (eye blink, pupil contraction, and blood vessel constriction, respectively). If these stimuli were presented ten times in a row they would elicit virtually the same response.

Stimuli serving a *reinforcing* function follow responses and increase the probability of those responses they follow. Those responses that become more probable when followed by a reinforcing stimulus are the operants. In operant research with infrahuman subjects, food is a common reinforcing stimulus. In the classroom, several stimuli that are *assumed* by teachers to be reinforcing are grades, teacher approval, and peer approval which are thought to increase the probability of the responses they follow, an assumption that may be questioned in certain instances. The acid test of whether a particular stimulus is reinforcing to a given child is whether or not it increases the probability of a response it follows.

Discriminative stimuli precede and accompany operant responses but *do not* elicit them. They serve as cues to the organism, and their presence increases the probability of those operants which previously have been reinforced in the presence of the discriminative stimulus. For example, Miss Smith may turn off the classroom lights when the noise level gets too high. She expects her class to get quiet when the lights are turned off (discriminative stimulus). Over time, in Miss Smith's class, however, children learn that when the lights are turned off and they quiet down, Miss Smith is likely to approve and, conversely, if they continue being loud, she is likely to punish. Obviously, turning off the lights does not elicit quieting-down behavior. Similarly, telling the class to get quiet and to get in their seats (other forms of discriminative stimuli) do not elicit the appropriate behavior. Notice how many children who disregard such stimuli and continue with the activity. However, in the presence of these discriminative stimuli, quieting down is more likely to be reinforced than in the same behavior in the absence of such stimuli.

The final type of stimuli are *neutral* stimuli; they bring about no changes at all in behavior, whether they precede, accompany, or follow responses.

Contingencies

The final elementary concept that relates behavior and the environment is the nature of their relationship referred to by the concepts *dependency* and *contingency*. An environmental event is said to be *dependent* on behavior if that event must follow the behavior. For example, if a ball is kicked, it must be propelled; if a light switch is turned on, the light bulb must illuminate. An environmental event is said to be *contingent* upon behavior if the event does not necessarily have to follow, but in fact does follow it. For example, when a child gives a correct answer the teacher can smile (the smile is contingent upon the child giving the correct answer), but teachers do not *have* to smile when their students give the correct answers. The importance of contingencies will be seen later when we discuss the development of intervention programs.

LEARNING MODELS

As noted in the introduction to this chapter, the verb *to learn* encompasses a wide variety of situations, and no one paradigm or model can explain adequately all the different kinds of learning. However, certain models, which will be discussed subsequently, seem to accommodate a great proportion of the kinds of learning with which educators are concerned. These models can be superimposed on the behavior and provide answers for the question: *How did the child learn to behave in a given manner?* To carry this a step further, one must have a paradigm or model to explain *how* the child learned a bit of behavior in order to design an intervention to help the child unlearn that behavior considered maladaptive. Keep in mind the assumptions underlying the behavioristic approach: (1) All behavior is learned, and (2) if all behavior is learned, the principles of learning can be applied to alter such behavior. The question then confronting the teacher pertains to *how* a particular behavior was learned in order that he can arrange the environment in an attempt to modify that behavior.

Let us now turn to the consideration of the models that account for the ways in which schoolchildren learn most of the behavior with which we are concerned. Three models have been selected: respondent conditioning, operant conditioning, and modeling, since these paradigms appear to explain most parsimoniously the most common behaviors with which educators are concerned.

Respondent Conditioning

Behaviors learned through respondent conditioning are characterized by their involuntary nature. That is to say, behaviors elicited through the respondent paradigm are for all intents and purposes *not* under the control of the individual—they are automatic responses. For illustrative purposes, take the example of what happens when a puff of air is blown into one's eye. Immediately, the subject will blink. Furthermore, the subject will blink every time another puff of air is blown into his eye. In this case, the stimulus (puff of air) is said to *elicit* the response of blinking in that the subject requires no previous experience with that stimulus to make the response. Furthermore, through presenting another stimulus (ringing a bell) that has no eliciting power, just prior to the puff of air, it is possible to develop the bell as an eliciting stimulus through repeated pairings, despite the fact that the bell originally had no power to elicit the response of blinking. Most emotional learning occurs via respondent conditioning—fears, anxieties, affectionate responses. One person may know that it is silly to be afraid of a king snake —after all it is not poisonous, and it provides a balance in nature; but that is little consolation when one accidentally steps on one while hiking. Should this happen to a person who fears snakes, a number of involuntary responses are possible and some highly probable—screaming, perspiring, running, and/or jumping.

Two classical studies conducted during the early 1900s illustrate the respondent model nicely. They were described in the historical review, but will now be reconsidered by superimposing the respondent model upon them for illustrative purposes. In the case study by J. B. Watson and R. A. Raynor (1920), an eleven-month-old boy, Albert, was the subject. Like

LEARNING CONCEPTS AND MODELS

any other child, Albert startled at a sudden loud noise. Watson then paired a white rat, which Albert did not fear initially, with the loud noise. This was accomplished by presenting the white rat and when Albert touched the rat, the loud noise was presented by striking a large steel bar directly behind the child's head, which caused Albert to whimper. This model can be represented as follows:

Loud noise *(had eliciting power)* ⟶ Whimpering
White rat *(initially could not elicit)* ⟶

In this instance, the loud noise was able initially to elicit the stereotyped response of whimpering; however, the white rat was unable to elicit this response initially. Through pairing the white rat with the loud noise, it was found that the white rat acquired the eliciting power it initially lacked; that is, Albert "learned" to make the same response (whimpering) to a new stimulus (white rat).

Hewett (1968) described the case of Todd, a nonreading child who "froze" whenever books were placed in front of him and a request made of him to read. It was Hewett's (1968, p. 29) contention that Todd had learned to freeze in such situations. He wrote, "It is the result of previously neutral stimuli (books and reading) acquiring properties for automatically eliciting a response (fear and avoidance) due to repeated pairings with unpleasant and painful events (ridicule of other children, criticism of teacher and parents because of failure to learn to read)." Although ridicule can elicit avoidance and fear responses in most schoolchildren, for some children these stimuli have been specifically paired with stimuli like teachers, books, tests, mathematics, reading, or geography. Hence the child generally described as unmotivated or fearful may, in fact, have learned to fear or avoid particular subject matter, books, or teachers out of prior association of these stimuli with ridicule of peers, parents, or teachers.

DESENSITIZATION. The process whereby the child "unlearns" responses learned through respondent conditioning is commonly called "desensitization." In order to illustrate this process, let us turn to the second study from the early 1900s mentioned earlier. This is the study by Mary Cover Jones (1924) with three-year-old Peter who feared white rabbits. The Jones study is an extension of the work of Watson in that it reversed the process used by Watson to teach a fear to Albert. Assuming that Peter had associated the white rabbit with an effective unconditioned stimulus that elicited fear responses, Jones proceeded to "desensitize" Peter to the stimulus of the white rabbit—to make it lose its eliciting power. The approach she used was to present Peter in a chair with various pleasant stimuli (candy, ice cream) while the rabbit was presented in a far corner of the room. The following represents the conditioning program she designed for Peter:

Candy, ice cream *(had eliciting power)* ⟶ Enjoyment

White rabbit *(did not elicit initially)* ⟶

By pairing the feared stimulus (rabbit) with one known to elicit desired responses (enjoyment), might the rabbit take on the same eliciting function as the candy and ice cream? Gradually, the rabbit was moved closer and closer until finally Peter would allow it to be placed on the same tray from which he was eating. The message is clear: *If fear is learned, it can be systematically unlearned by reversing the respondent model.*

Another means of weakening the eliciting power of the conditioned stimulus (such as the rabbit in the example above) is to present it repeatedly in the absence of the stimulus that initially had the eliciting power. For example, keep exposing the child to the snake; make the child attend school; present him with books; but in the process be sure the stimulus that elicited the fear response initially (whatever it may be) is not present.

This approach has several inherent dangers such as the possibility that one does not know the original eliciting stimulus, and the procedure may actually intensify the emotional state.

The alternative is based on the technique of Jones (1924) in which one accelerates the detachment of the respondent from the eliciting stimulus by associating the conditioned stimulus with a pleasant event. Jones (1924) used eating candy and ice cream. In school one might teach arithmetic through calculation of batting averages in baseball or shooting percentages in basketball to a boy who enjoys athletics but fears arithmetic.

In keeping with the above, stimuli in a classroom which *could* become conditioned eliciting stimuli for fear or avoidance behaviors include: a specific teacher, books, tests, reading, mathematics, a particular classroom, or any number of objects in a classroom. MacMillan (1968) used as an example a child who avoids reading in a text. The teacher might have the child write his own stories, then have them typed. Hence the child is reading from a sheet of paper his own writing (unlike a text). The material he is reading is his own—not someone else's or something the teacher assigned. Only gradually would the teacher introduce reading in a form resembling that which was associated with failure and/or ridicule.

The process of desensitization is critical in dealing with children who have failed repeatedly in school and are "turned off" to learning in school. In much the same way as the individual runs from the snake, these children "run" from learning through belligerance, apathy, or any other technique that gets them away from the stimuli they have learned to fear. For the teacher the problem becomes one of teaching specific skills in a manner which does not resemble the format which has been associated with failure in the past.

Desensitization procedures have been used primarily in clinical work for treating fears of flying, heights, crowds, death, stuttering, and sex. To date very little has been done with desensitization procedures within the context of education. However, it would seem to be a promising technique in educational settings when children have been exposed to ridicule, reprimands, and other noxious events that elicit fear and/or withdrawal responses. The presence of anxiety in schoolchildren is apparent, and Blackham and Silberman (1971) noted that much of what is called anxiety is produced via a respondent conditioning model.

To conclude, Bijou and Baer (1961) made several points regarding characteristics of respondent behavior. First, they are responsive to stimuli which precede them, rather than those which follow them as in operants. Second, the response *always* follows the presentation of the eliciting stimulus, except under unusual circumstances. Third, if the conditioned stimulus (the one which originally could not elicit the behavior) is repeatedly presented alone, it will gradually lose its eliciting power. These points direct the teacher in ways in which maladaptive behavior, which has been learned and is respondent in nature, can be altered.

Operant Conditioning

A second paradigm or model, which accounts for probably the majority of behaviors which concern us as educators, is the operant model. It is this model that has served as the basis for the vast majority of behavioristic programs in the context of education. It is based on one of the best established principles of behavior which was called by Edward L. Thorndike the "Law of Effect." This law states that *an act may be altered in its strength by its consequences*. The term *act* refers to behavior or responses; the *strengthening* refers to an increase in the probability of the act occurring more frequently in the future; and *consequences* refers to the environmental events or stimuli which follow, or are contingent upon, the act. For example, if you walk down a street and say "hello" to the first five people you meet, and they smile and return the greeting (pleasant consequence),

LEARNING CONCEPTS AND MODELS

the probability is increased that you will say "hello" to the sixth person you encounter. Conversely, if the first five people you encountered scowl and ignore your greeting (unpleasant or neutral consequence), the chances are reduced that you will greet the sixth person. By the same token, children in school are subject to the Law of Effect. If the teacher provides pleasant consequences for children's academic achievement or deportment, such behaviors are more likely to recur than if they go unnoticed or are followed by unpleasant consequences.

Operant responses are *emitted* by the organism of his own free will, hence the frequency of a given operant is determined by its effect on the environment (i.e., its consequences). The effects of an operant on the environment may be the appearance of a stimulus or the disappearance of a stimulus. If the appearance of a stimulus results in an increased probability of that behavior, the stimulus is said to be a positive reinforcing stimulus, or positive reinforcer. For example, if after a child raises his hand in class the teacher smiles at him, if his hand-raising behavior (as opposed to just speaking out) is increased, then the teacher's smile is a positive reinforcer. Conversely, if the disappearance of a stimulus, as a consequence of a response, results in an increased probability of that response being made in the future, then the stimulus is called a negative reinforcer. This implies that the response leads to the termination of a stimulus that the individual finds *noxious,* or *aversive*. Negative reinforcement is exemplified by the situation of a group of children ridiculing (aversive stimulus) Walter on the playground and he finally spits (response) at one of the children resulting in the termination of the ridiculing. The termination of the teasing is negatively reinforcing, and Walter is more likely to exhibit the spitting behavior in the future when ridiculed. A third possible consequence of an operant is the appearance of a noxious or aversive stimulus, or *punishment* after the response. Note how negative reinforcers and punishments differ, and the effects on the probability of a response occurring in the future vary. Punishment reduces the likelihood of the response being made, whereas negative reinforcers increase the probability. The operant model can be represented:

$$\text{Response} \longrightarrow \text{Stimulus}$$

In this case, the individual emits some response that is followed by a consequence. The consequence can consist of:

1. Presentation of a pleasant stimulus, which increases the probability of that response recurring, and is called a *positive reinforcer*.
2. Termination of a noxious stimulus, which also increases the probability of that response recurring, and is called a *negative reinforcer*.
3. Presentation of a noxious stimulus, which decreases the probability of that response recurring, and is called *punishment*.

Both positive and negative reinforcers operate as follows: an operant is emitted and has an effect on the environment, and because of that effect the operant will more probably occur in the future. In the case of punishment, however, the operant is emitted and has an effect on the environment, and because of that effect the operant will less probably occur in the future.

It then follows from the foregoing that behavior that recurs for any given individual (good or bad) is currently supported by some consequence, either a positive or negative reinforcer. The child misbehaves in the classroom because there is some "payoff"; either he gets the attention of the teacher or his peers. Other children study for examinations in order to receive a high grade and to be recognized by their peers, parents, and teachers. Even teachers are subject to the Law of Effect. They attend workshops in order to move up the salary schedule. Were these consequences removed, one would expect children to stop misbehaving, others to stop studying, and even teachers to stop attending workshops.

Contingency Management

Once the teacher has identified the target behavior and the consequence believed to be supporting the misbehavior, several alternative tacks might be taken in order to change the behavior. Briefly, the teacher alters the contingency relating the behavior to the consequence. For example, if the teacher's attention was supporting talking out in class, then the teacher, in essence says, "If you want my attention you are going to have to be recognized prior to speaking; no longer will I attend to your talking out." Then teacher attention is contingent on being recognized, not on talking out. Hence the teacher no longer pays off on misbehavior. Another approach is to use the desired consequence contingent on some behavior that is incompatible with the behavior he is trying to decrease. For example, if the teacher's attention is supporting out-of-seat behavior, the teacher changes the contingency and makes his attention contingent on in-seat behavior. Notice, the child cannot be out of his seat if he is in his seat; and his in-seat behavior is what the teacher is positively reinforcing. In Part II of the book, the ways in which the operant model can be used to modify behavior will be considered in detail.

Modeling

One form of learning commonly observed in children is not adequately explained by either respondent or operant paradigms discussed previously. That form of learning is imitation or modeling. Particularly in young children, observation and subsequent imitation constitute a major learning form as they learn to talk, walk, master physical skills like throwing a ball, and some other behaviors parents often wish their children did not notice and subsequently imitate for an audience of friends. As the child gets older there are still cases where reliance on trial-and-error learning or operant conditioning procedures would be less efficient and, in some instances, dangerous. Bandura (1965) pointed out that in teaching a child to swim or in teaching an adolescent to drive an automobile, one does not wait to reinforce the correct response, since in these instances the student might be killed. Rather, the teacher demonstrates how to perform the task, the student observes, and then attempts to imitate the adult model. Bandura's (1969) work relied heavily on such a "no-trial learning" paradigm, with rather impressive results.

To summarize the above, that children learn a great deal through observation seems beyond question. What does seem in question is the explanation of this phenomenon at the theoretical level. The theoretical debate over what accounts for the modeling phenomenon is beyond the scope of this book; however, the interested reader should consult Holt (1931), Miller and Dollard (1941), and Bandura (1969) for a discussion of three differing explanations. For example, assume that a father wanted to teach his son to swing a baseball bat. He would probably take the bat, assume the proper stance, hold the bat up over his back shoulder, stride with the leg toward the imaginary pitcher, shift his weight from his back foot to his front foot, bring the bat around in a level swing, and follow through. That is a rather complex task to teach, and one which would take forever if one were to utilize an operant conditioning approach. However, if the father demonstrates and has his son watch him and then has the child imitate what he has done, there is often a close approximation to the complete behavioral pattern, which then needs only some refinement. This process can be represented as follows:

Father demonstrates batting ⟶ Son observes and then imitates

Bandura (1965) distinguished between learning and performance in his comparison of the relative efficiency of operant methods vs. modeling. He saw operant procedures as an efficient means of promoting performance, especially when an individual already has a response in his behavioral repertoire. Hence for strengthening and maintaining skills a student has but does not emit as frequently as the teacher might like, then the use of reinforcement for each occurrence of that behavior is advisable. Where Bandura (1965) advocates the use of modeling instead of operant conditioning is in the development of new behavioral responses, those which the individual does not possess, such as would be the case in teaching foreign languages. In teaching a foreign language, the teacher says a word in the foreign language; the student or the class as a whole then attempts to emulate the teacher's pronunciation.

It should be pointed out that modeling procedures are often coupled with operant procedures in very useful ways. Taking the example of the father teaching his son to swing a baseball bat, when the child approximates the entire behavioral chain, the father is likely to praise him (positive reinforcement). While reinforcement does appear helpful in increasing *performance* of those behaviors learned through modeling, it does not appear necessary for learning to take place. Recently, I noticed my three-year-old son watching a televised baseball game, fully attired in his baseball hat and with his plastic baseball bat. He seemed totally unaware that anyone was even watching him, but he proceeded to tip his hat, "dig in" to the carpeting, tap his bat on an imaginary home plate, swing, drop his bat, and run and slide safely into an end table. After observing that, it was decided that he should not be allowed to watch any television shows on which a child does violence to his father.

Bandura and his associates at Stanford University have conducted numerous studies dealing with variables that enhance or detract from the effectiveness of the model. Some of the variables that appear related to modeling effects are the sex of the model, the consequences applied to the model, and whether the models are live or filmed. In general, it has been shown that modeling is enhanced if the model is of the same sex as the child observing the model; and while live models work quite well, human subjects on films seem about equally effective. However, when nonhuman models are used on films the effects are diminished in direct relation to the extent to which the models deviate from reality (Bandura, 1965).

Furthermore, Bandura (1965) found that modeling can

affect three different classes of responses: (1) new or unique behaviors (modeling effect), (2) inhibiting or disinhibiting previously acquired responses (inhibitory or disinhibitory effect), and (3) trigger a response that has been rather dormant in the response repertoire of a child (response facilitation effect). The first type of response, modeling effects, are exemplified by young children's learning to speak or to throw a ball. These are responses they have not demonstrated before and it is through observation and imitation that they acquire these behaviors. The second class, inhibitory or disinhibitory effect, is demonstrated in a study by Bandura (1967) in which the subjects were children who all feared dogs. Four groups were created. In Group I the children observed a child who did not fear dogs play with a dog in a party setting; Group II children watched a child play with a dog but not in a party setting; Group III watched a dog in a party setting but without a child model playing with it; and Group IV children participated in party activities but were not exposed to a dog or child model. The children in Groups I and II who watched a child without fear interact with a dog lost their fear of dogs. This study demonstrates through observation the disinhibitory effect on their reticence to interact with dogs.

The third set of behaviors affected by modeling, response facilitation effect, is illustrated by another study by Bandura (1965). In that study, one group of children viewed a film of a model who was aggressive but punished for his aggression; another group watched an aggressive model rewarded; and a third group watched the aggressive model who received no consequence. In the subsequent evaluation, the groups that saw the aggressive model rewarded or receive no consequences exhibited more aggressive responses. In a follow-up, all children were offered incentives to imitate the model's behavior. In that case, all groups emitted more imitative behavior than they had when no incentive had been offered, and the group who saw the model punished showed as much imitation as the other two groups, indicating that the consequences for the model's behavior does not affect *learning* but does affect the willingness to imitate.

As teachers, the modeling paradigm should sensitize us to possible imitation of good and bad models in the classroom. For example, the teacher serves as a model, either yelling at children in an excited manner or quietly moving about the class. As an excited, frantic teacher one can expect an excited and frantic classroom full of children. Furthermore, we, as teachers, point out models for other children to notice with statements such as "John, sit down," or "I like how Alex is sitting quietly." In Part II of this book the ways in which individuals have seen fit to use the modeling paradigm in the classroom will be explored. However, the amount of educational research using a modeling approach is limited to date, and teachers should not be restricted to using exclusively what has been done, but rather be constantly on the alert for applications they see as consistent with this paradigm.

REFERENCES

Bandura, A. Behavior modification through modeling procedures. In L. P. Ullmann and L. Krasner (eds.) *Research in Behavior Modification*. New York: Holt, Rinehart and Winston, Inc., 1965.

Bandura, A. Behavioral psychotherapy. *Sci. Am.*, March, 1967, pp. 78–86.

Bandura, A. *Principles of Behavior Modification*. New York: Holt, Rinehart and Winston, Inc., 1969.

Bijou, S. W., and Baer, D. M. *Child Development*, Vol. I. New York: Appleton-Century-Crofts, 1961.

Blackham, G. J., and Silberman, A. *Modification of Child Behavior*. Belmont, Calif.: Wadsworth Publishing Co., Inc., 1971.

Buckley, N. K., and Walker, H. M. *Modifying Classroom Behavior*. Champaign, Ill.: Research Press, 1970.

Hewett, F. M. *The Emotionally Disturbed Child in the Classroom*. Boston: Allyn & Bacon, Inc., 1968.

Holt, E. B. *Animal Drive and the Learning Process*, Vol. I. New York: Holt, 1931.

Jones, M. C. A laboratory study of fear: The case of Peter. *Pedagog. Sem.*, **31**:310–11, 1924.

Keller, F. S. *Learning: Reinforcement Theory,* 2nd ed. New York: Random House, Inc., 1969.

MacMillan, D. L. Behavior modification: A teacher strategy to control behavior. *Report of the Proceedings of the Forty-fourth Meeting of the Convention of American Instructors of the Deaf.* Berkeley, Calif.: 1968, pp. 66–76.

Miller, N. E., and Dollard, J. *Social Learning and Imitation.* New Haven: Yale University Press, 1941.

Reynolds, G. S. *A Primer of Operant Conditioning.* Glenview, Ill.: Scott, Foresman and Company, 1968.

Skinner, B. F. *Science and Human Behavior.* New York: The Macmillan Company, 1953.

Staats, A. W., and Staats, C. K. *Complex Human Behavior.* New York: Holt, Rinehart and Winston, Inc., 1963.

Watson, J. B., and Raynor, R. A. Conditioned emotional reactions. *J. Exp. Psychol.,* 3:1–4, 1920.

CHAPTER 3

Modification of Operant Behavior

THE VAST MAJORITY of behavior that teachers want to modify is operant, as opposed to respondent. That is to say, it is emitted by the children, rather than being elicited by stimuli in the classroom. The problems posed to teachers generally can be categorized as (1) How can I help the child to stop emitting a particular behavior? (2) How can I help the child to emit a new behavior which he has not emitted yet? (3) How can I help the child to emit a behavior more frequently? In the present chapter, these questions will be considered in terms of how stimuli exert control over operant behavior, and then by considering the various approaches from which the teacher can select in order to weaken operant behaviors considered inappropriate, to increase the strength of behaviors that should occur more frequently, and to develop new or more complex behaviors. First, let us consider what controls operant behavior.

STIMULUS CONTROL OF OPERANTS

Even though operants are emitted by the child, rather than elicited from him, they are still, in a sense, controlled by stimuli that precede them and stimuli that follow them. These two kinds of stimuli are called discriminative stimuli (designated by the symbol S^D), those that precede the operant, and reinforcing stimuli (designated by the symbol S^r), those that follow the operant. The presentation of a discriminative stimulus does not ensure that the response will be made, as is the case with an eliciting stimulus in a respondent paradigm; however, it does exert some control over the response in that it *sets the occasion*, or cues the individual on *when* to emit the operant. A discriminative stimulus tells the individual, "If I make the response now I am likely to get reinforced," whereas if the discriminative stimulus is not present the individual knows that the likelihood of his being reinforced for emitting the same operant is quite low. For example, one is unlikely to recite the Pledge of Allegiance in the middle of a forest with no one nearby, or to say "hello" to a tree. Why? Because in the absence of certain discriminative stimuli one comes to learn that making certain responses does not lead to any consequence. The probability of these responses being made is high only in the presence of certain discriminative stimuli. Hence the probability of an operant response being emitted may be increased by presenting a discriminative stimulus, or decreased by removing or withholding a discriminative stimulus.

    How do stimuli come to function as discriminative stimuli, and how can one develop a particular stimulus to exert that kind of control over operant responses? The answer to both questions can be summed up by saying that in order to develop a stimulus as a discriminative stimulus one must reinforce the operant in the presence of that stimulus and not reinforce it in the absence of that stimulus. This is precisely the tack taken by parents in teaching a young child to call his father "daddy." When the child looks, or points, at his father and says "daddy" the parents praise him. Typically, problems occur in this process, as the child sees any man on the street and calls that man "daddy." This is an example of stimulus generalization, where the response becomes more likely in the presence of other stimuli somewhat like the original one. In such instances, the parents do not praise the child, and gradually the response "daddy" comes to be tied to only the child's actual father. Similar examples can be drawn from the classroom, such as when a child is first learning to read and when shown the word "sat" responds by saying "cat." The stimulus, in this case the printed word, is similar and the child generalizes, in this case inappropriately. The task is to get the child in either instance to discriminate between the stimuli that are similar. This can be done through selective, or differential, reinforcement: reinforcing the response in the presence of the discriminative stimulus, and withholding reinforcement of the response in the absence of the discriminative stimulus. Many discriminative stimuli used by teachers are verbal cues, such as "Let's all stand," or "Put away your materials and you may go to recess." When a child follows these directions promptly, the teacher often rewards him with a smile, compliment, or privilege. In other cases, a teacher's frown may serve as a cue to stop whatever is being done, in which case the teacher might praise him, or at least, not punish him. The ringing of a school bell signifies recess, lunch, or the end of school whereupon leaving one's seat is permitted. Note that in each case the stimulus (teacher's words, teacher's frown, or bell ringing) does not lead automatically to the behavior. The child has a choice, but he learns that in the presence of certain stimuli (S^D), certain responses are more likely to be rewarded.

The second type of stimuli exerting control over operant behaviors consist of the consequences that follow them. As noted earlier, the frequency of an operant is greatly influenced by the consequences it has on its environment. The types of environmental consequences, described earlier, are positive reinforcers, negative reinforcers, and punishments. For purposes of simplicity, the immediate discussion will focus on positive reinforcers. Positive reinforcers not only increase the frequency of the operants they follow but also increase the activity level of the individual, and increase the emission of other bits of behavior in addition to the specific bit of behavior being reinforced.

For example, you probably have noticed that when you praise (positive reinforcement) a child for giving a correct answer, it frequently becomes necessary to quiet him down soon after, as he gets overzealous in his further attempts to be correct. In addition, positive reinforcement affects the *topography* of the response; that is, the physical nature of the response, such as the forcefulness, the duration, and the exact form of the response. The effect of positive reinforcement on the topography of a response is vital to the building of new responses with operant conditioning, and will be shown later in this chapter in the section on shaping procedures.

Unconditioned and Conditioned Reinforcers

In discussing positive reinforcers it is necessary to consider how certain stimuli come to have the power to reinforce the behaviors they follow. Certain stimuli, such as food and water, have, from birth, the power to reinforce behavior they follow. These are not learned, but are necessary for survival. Such stimuli are called *primary*, or *unconditioned*, reinforcers. Other stimuli acquire the power to reinforce behavior only through the experiences of the child; that is, at first they will not serve as reinforcers but can become reinforcing through pairings with stimuli that are reinforcing. For example, one can smile all day at a newborn and smiling will not increase any behavior. Over time, however, if a mother smiles every time she feeds the child, and smiles when she relieves the child's discomfort (such as in changing a diaper), smiles are associated with these primary reinforcers and smiles acquire the power to reinforce. Praise, smiles, privileges, grades, and money are examples of stimuli that must be learned if they are to serve as reinforcers. These stimuli which come to have reinforcing properties through learning are called *secondary*, or *conditioned*, reinforcers.

It is with the conditioned reinforcers that teachers are most concerned, because primary reinforcers are seldom used in the context of education. In some cases, children have not learned that stars on papers, A and B grades, or even some social stimuli (e.g., teacher approval) are reinforcing. In such cases, it falls to the teacher to develop these stimuli as reinforcements; therefore, it becomes important to see how conditioned reinforcers acquire their power. Conditioned reinforcers acquire their reinforcing power through their association with other reinforcing stimuli: conditioned or unconditioned reinforcers (Skinner, 1953; Travers, 1963). Therefore, the list of potential conditioned reinforcers is endless, because virtually any stimulus can intentionally or accidentally be paired with an effective reinforcer, hence come to be a conditioned reinforcer. As a result, a smile, a touch, a star on a paper can all acquire conditioned reinforcing properties if they are systematically paired with a reinforcer that works for any particular child.

Some stimuli have been paired with a variety of other reinforcing stimuli (unconditioned and conditioned) and are called *generalized reinforcers*. However, not all secondary or conditioned reinforcers are generalized reinforcers. Money is a common example of a generalized reinforcer, since over time it is paired with a host of reinforcing stimuli for a given individual. As will be discussed later, check marks and tokens are common generalized reinforcers used in school programs utilizing operant principles. In the social reinforcement area, attention, approval, and affection serve as generalized reinforcers (Blackham and Silberman, 1971).

Except for unconditioned stimuli (those that satisfy a physiological need), no stimuli have the innate capacity to reinforce behavior. Stimulus events come to have the capacity to reinforce behavior only through the experience of the organism —hence, their effectiveness is acquired. Therefore, one must be cautious in assuming that a given stimulus is an effective reinforcer for a child's behavior since children differ in terms of their reinforcement histories. The *only* way that a given stimulus can be determined as an effective reinforcer is through functional analysis of behavior, and the assessment of whether the stimulus event increases the strength of the behavior that it follows.

In the development of conditioned reinforcers, the first step exists when the presentation or withdrawal of the stimulus has no effect on the occurrence of the response. However, after the experience of having the initially ineffective reinforcer paired with an effective reinforcer, the former stimulus acquires reinforcing properties by means of association. This is usually a gradual process requiring repeated pairings of stimuli. Once the previously neutral stimulus acquires reinforcing properties it is said to be *based on* the stimulus with which it was associated. In the case of generalized conditioned reinforcers, however, the stimulus (e.g., money) is based on many other stimuli, not just a single stimulus.

The strength of a conditioned reinforcer is inferred from its durability and potency. Durability refers to the total number of responses the individual will emit once the reinforcer on which the conditioned reinforcer is *based* is discontinued. A conditioned reinforcer needs to be followed, at least now and then, by the reinforcer on which it is based; otherwise, it gradually loses its capacity to reinforce behavior. The longer a conditioned reinforcer serves to strengthen behavior in the absence of the reinforcer on which it is based, the more durable it is said to be. In addition, while the reinforcing capacity of a stimulus can diminish in the manner described above, the tendency to respond in the presence of that stimulus also declines—hence its function as a discriminative stimulus diminishes.

The foregoing discussion has focused on positive reinforcement. The same observations apply as well to negative reinforcement. Those stimuli whose removal constitutes reinforcement from birth on are unconditioned, such as is the case with electric shock. Whenever a shock is terminated contingent on a particular response, the probability of the occurrence of that response is increased. However, some aversive stimuli are learned, such as frowning by a parent or a teacher. If a teacher frowns at Dianne when she continues talking with the girl sitting next to her and as soon as she stops talking the teacher stops frowning, one can infer that frowning by the teacher is an aversive if whenever the teacher frowns at her Dianne terminates the behavior. The point to be made is that some aversives, such as frowning, have to be learned; initially, they are not aversive to a child.

WEAKENING OPERANTS

One of the first concerns about behavior expressed by teachers is how to eliminate problem behaviors. It seems to be the acting-out types of behaviors that concern teachers the most, and virtually all of the specific behaviors that constitute "acting out" are operant behaviors. Therefore, in the present section the alternative approaches consistent with the operant conditioning rationale for weakening behaviors will be discussed. When confronted with a problem behavior that you wish to weaken, you can select from three approaches: extinction, satiation, or punishment. It should be kept in mind that certain behaviors are most efficiently weakened by one of the three, and in some instances you may want to combine two of the approaches simultaneously in order to weaken a behavior.

Extinction

The term *extinction* refers to the procedure in which an operant that was previously reinforced is no longer reinforced. The result of no longer reinforcing the response is a gradual decrease of the response. In effect, this breaks the response-reinforcement contingency which supported the behavior and can be represented schematically as follows:

$$\text{Response} \longrightarrow\!\!\!/\longrightarrow S^r \text{ withheld}$$

The line through the arrow indicates that the contingency no longer exists. An analogy might clarify the process of extinction.

Fire requires air in order to keep burning; in a rough sense the air supports the fire. If, therefore, one cuts off the air supply the fire is extinguished. In a similar fashion, if one cuts off the stimulus (S^r) that is supporting a given behavior, the behavior is terminated. As will be shown later, extinction provides a very useful means of terminating undesirable behavior.

One common misconception regarding extinction is that behavior that is extinguished ceases to exist. Bijou and Baer (1961), however, pointed out that behavior that is no longer reinforced weakens until it reaches a strength equal to its strength before it was increased through reinforcement. The strength of the response before it was affected by reinforcement is called its *operant level*. The authors note that a response cannot have an operant level of zero, or it could not have been reinforced.

When one stops reinforcing a response that he has been reinforcing, the response does not atrophy immediately. In fact, at first there may be an increase in response rate before it starts to decline. Keller (1969) and Blackham and Silberman (1971) cited several examples of behaviors that vigorously resist extinction, and warned against impatience on the part of the observer. If the reinforcer is discontinued, the behavior will ultimately extinguish. The sudden increase in behavior that immediately follows the discontinuance of reinforcement is extremely important for purposes of shaping, discussed later in the present chapter. One's behavior in an automobile when he turns on the ignition and the automobile engine does not start but simply grinds away shows this increase in responding when the reinforcer (i.e., the engine starting) is withheld. In such an instance what does he do? Most let the car sit idly for a short time and then begin working on the starter again. This kind of behavior continues frequently until the battery is dead. Even when one knows the car may be flooded, the increase in starting behavior gets quite high. Reynolds (1968) pointed out the changes in topography of a response which occur when extinction procedures are introduced—the form of the behavior becomes more variable and its force increases for a short time.

MODIFICATION OF OPERANT BEHAVIOR

The speed with which a particular response extinguishes following the discontinuance of reinforcement depends on several variables, some operating before extinction procedures are initiated and others after. Taken together they affect the *resistance to extinction* shown by a given individual. According to Reynolds (1968, pp. 33–34), among the variables affecting resistance to extinction are:

1. The *schedule of reinforcement,* or the contingency established which determines which responses will be reinforced. This will be discussed later in this chapter, but in passing it should be mentioned that a *continuous* schedule refers to the practice of reinforcing every response. *Intermittent* schedules, of which there are many kinds, refer to a noncontinuous reinforcement schedule. In general, the latter types are more resistant to extinction. Each type of intermittent schedule results in a definite pattern of responding during extinction. Hence some intermittent schedules are more resistant to extinction than others.
2. The magnitude of the reinforcer and the number of reinforcements prior to extinction affect resistance. In general, the greater the magnitude of the reinforcer and the greater the number of responses reinforced, the greater the resistance to extinction.
3. The number of times a response has been extinguished previously affects its resistance to extinction. The more often a response has been extinguished in the past, the less is its resistance to extinction.
4. The magnitude of the organism's motivation during extinction affects resistance to extinction. In general, the more deprived the organism the more slowly will extinction progress.

Extinction is a procedure that will allow the teacher to weaken operant behavior. However, when he is selecting from the procedures available for weakening behavior, several things should be kept in mind. First, extinction will take time before the behavior will begin to diminish in its frequency; that is to say, the teacher should not expect immediate results. In fact, at first, there probably will be an increase in the maladaptive behavior. In the light of lack of immediacy in the effects of extinction, it should not be used when the behavior endangers the child emitting the behavior, or other children in the class. It is best used with low-frequency behaviors. For example, the generally well-behaved child who swears in class one day, but for whom swearing is a low-frequency behavior, is probably best handled by ignoring the behavior. In most of the educational interventions in which extinction is used, it is used in combination with one of the other techniques for weakening behavior. For example, if the teacher decides to ignore out-of-seat behavior, he will also attempt to reinforce in-seat behavior, which leads to the next procedure for weakening operants.

Counterconditioning

Extinction may take a long time, particularly if the behavior has been reinforced on an intermittent schedule. Counterconditioning, either by itself or in combination with extinction, provides another means to accomplish the same goal, and it too takes time before the behavior diminishes in frequency. In essence, counterconditioning consists of strengthening a more desirable behavior and in doing so, weakening the undesirable behavior. There are two approaches to counterconditioning: (1) providing an alternative behavior to the child which will enable him to obtain the reinforcement he wants, and (2) reinforcing a behavior that is *incompatible* with the behavior one wishes to weaken.

A criticism frequently leveled at punishment can also be applied to extinction; that is, the procedure teaches the child "what you do not want him to do, but does not teach him what you want him to do." Let us assume that the child wants the teacher's attention and that he talks out in class in order to obtain the attention. The counterconditioning approach to weakening the talking-out behavior would consist of finding alternative approaches for the child to obtain the reinforcement (teacher attention) he desires, such as erasing the blackboard, taking messages to the office, or other activities that no longer make it necessary for the child to resort to misbehavior to obtain the reinforcer he wants.

The other approach to counterconditioning is to reinforce a behavior that is physically incompatible with the behavior the teacher is attempting to weaken. By physically incompatible, we mean a behavior that the child cannot be engaged in at the same time as the behavior the teacher is attempting to weaken. For example, if the child is laughing he cannot be crying, if he is in his seat he cannot be out of his seat, if he is walking he cannot be running, and so on. The teacher then makes the reinforcer contingent on the desirable behavior rather than on the undesirable behavior. In essence, the teacher is both reinforcing the adaptive behavior and extinguishing the maladaptive behavior concurrently.

To be used effectively, counterconditioning takes patience and ingenuity. First, the teacher must ascertain what the reinforcer is that the child wants. Second, he must determine behaviors that are incompatible with the one he wishes to weaken. However, the speed with which a behavior will be weakened will be faster if counterconditioning is used in concert with extinction procedures, and in that sense it is worth the additional effort.

Satiation

Laboratory learning research with infrahuman subjects revealed a phenomenon of reinforcement which can be used to weaken certain responses. This research indicated that the strength of a response may decrease as a function of continued reinforcement. In the laboratory situation it has been found that if a behavior is continuously reinforced, that response ultimately will no longer be emitted. This phenomenon has long been understood by fathers as a means for handling youthful experimenting with tobacco. When the father caught his son smoking, he would stock up with an ample supply of cigars or cigarettes and make the child smoke one cigar or cigarette after another until he became nauseated. What occurred in such a situation is that the smoking, while initially reinforcing, ultimately lost its reinforcing value (in effect, the father hoped it acquired aversive properties).

A similar technique was used by Ayllon (1963) in order to control hoarding behavior in psychiatric patients. One woman collected towels and stored them in her room. The daily count revealed that she would have from 19 to 29 towels in her room on any given day. The nurses would take the towels back daily, which compounded the problem of whether the towels were reinforcing or whether the attention the patient received from the nurses as they retrieved the towels was supporting the behavior. A satiation program was initiated in which the nurses would actually give the woman additional towels: 7 towels a day during the first week, and 60 a day during the third week. Finally, after 625 towels had accumulated in her room, the patient began taking them out of her room.

During the past year I have been working with the Multihandicapped Unit at the California School for the Deaf, Riverside, where a problem arose with one young girl; she constantly tore up the clothing of the other children.* This tearing behavior was difficult to cope with because the child whose clothes were torn reacted, and the teacher could not try to extinguish the behavior by ignoring it; hence the teacher attended. Both the child's reactions and the teacher's were possible sources of reinforcement for the tearing behavior. What was finally done was to have the teachers accumulate a large box full of scraps of cloth, being sure to include some "hard-to-tear" pieces. The

* The intervention described here was principally designed by Mrs. Peggy Eaton, a teacher at the Multihandicapped Unit of the California School for the Deaf, Riverside.

next time the girl tore clothing the teacher required her to sit down with the box and for the remainder of the day tear up the cloth in the box into minute pieces. At first, the tearing was a kind of joke; in time, however, the girl's hands began to hurt and the novelty wore off, but the teacher made her continue tearing. That incident took place three months before the end of the school year, and there was no recurrence of tearing behavior by that girl during those three months.

A closely related technique to satiation is called *negative practice*. Blackham and Silberman (1971, p. 46) explain this technique as follows: ". . . the person who exhibits undesirable behavior is encouraged to repeatedly perform the behavior." This technique could be used with stammering, nail-biting, or swearing. Blackham and Silberman (1971) explained the effect of negative practice in the following terms: (1) The response is extinguished since anxiety is no longer associated with it. (2) The fatigue that accumulates by its performance makes the emitting of that response painful and/or aversive. These authors gave the example of a child who frequently made animal sounds in class. The teacher placed the child in an empty room adjacent to the classroom and was instructed to make the imitations for ten minutes. If the child stopped making the imitations, the teacher requested that she please continue. After several of these sessions, the animal imitations ceased.

Some behaviors such as hoarding (pencils, erasers), tearing of clothes, or even swearing might be weakened through satiation approaches. Simply by requiring the individual to "do his thing far beyond the point of enjoyment" can serve to weaken that behavior. The teacher should, however, be certain that there is sufficient time and material to make the activity go beyond the novelty stage. At the same time the teacher should ensure that there is no social approval from teachers or peers during the time the child is engaged in the activity the teacher is trying to satiate. The one advantage of satiation over the practices of extinction or counterconditioning is that its effect is rather immediate (Holz and Azrin, 1963).

Punishment

Finally, let us turn to the most common technique for weakening behavior, which is, at the same time, the most complex and controversial (Reese, 1966). In educational circles, and outside, punishment is probably the most utilized principle in attempting to control behavior. In teachers' rooms newly devised punishments are proudly explained. In society the cry for more severe penalties for lawbreakers is heard. While one might concur that there is a need for some degree of teacher control, and that lawlessness must be curbed, the relative effectiveness of punishment over other procedures seems open to debate.

Hewett (1968) argued that for educational practice, punishment is a dead end since its effects run straight into the teeth of major educational goals. If one gets a child to sit quietly or read because he is afraid not to do so, one is a long way from achieving the oft-stated goals of self-discipline and self-directed learning. In addition to the arguments presented by Hewett (1968), there is a host of ethical arguments against the use of punishment. However, Reese (1966) stated that even when these ethical considerations are put aside in order that objective evidence on the effects of punishment can be studied, scientific opinion differs vastly concerning the efficacy of punishment.

Before one can evaluate the relative merits of punishment, it is necessary to define the procedure. Skinner (1953) differentiated two forms of punishment. First, there is the form in which an aversive, or noxious, stimulus is made contingent on a response, as in the case where a teacher reprimands a child for misbehavior. A second form of punishment consists of the withdrawal of reinforcement contingent on the misbehavior, as when a parent turns off the television when the children are misbehaving. Hence punishment can consist of either the withdrawal of a positive reinforcer or the presentation of an aversive stimulus following the response one wants to weaken.

Reese (1966) explicated the ways in which punishment is a more complex phenomenon than the other procedures for weakening operant behavior. First, punishment can affect emotional respondent behavior as well as the operant behavior on which it is contingent. Second, punishment can affect operants other than the one punished; and third, its effects on the operant being punished are a function of several variables, which will be discussed subsequently.

Many legends persist about the effects of punishment which have no support in the experimental literature (Solomon, 1964). For example, since Skinner's (1938) statements that the effects of punishment are temporary, most research in learning has focused on positive reinforcement, with little being done on punishment because it was considered a poor controller of behavior. Yet, as Solomon (1964) pointed out, even at the time Skinner first drew these conclusions, there was conflicting evidence in the experimental literature pertaining to the short- and long-term effects of punishment. A second legend challenged by Solomon (1964) pertains to the notion that punishment is a technique leading to neuroses, again a conclusion of questionable validity. For a detailed critique of the legends surrounding punishment, the reader is referred to the excellent article by Solomon (1964).

Several variables are associated with the efficacy of punishment in the form of aversive stimuli. For example, the temporary, the long-term, and the permanent effects of punishment depend on the intensity of the aversive stimulus used. The more intense the aversive the longer are its effects. Related to this is the evidence indicating that if the intensity of the aversive is gradually increased, the effects are reduced. This is not presented to endorse harsh and prolonged punishment, but rather to indicate that if a teacher is going to apply an aversive (which may be a reprimand rather than corporal punishment), it should be sufficiently intense to have the desired effect. Furthermore, the teacher should not begin by frowning, then mildly say "please be seated," and then become gradually more forceful. If you decide to use an aversive, make sure it is forceful enough in the first application to terminate the behavior. Another variable associated with possible side effects is the availability of alternative routes to positive reinforcement. As mentioned earlier, one criticism levied at punishment is that it teaches the child what you do not want him to do, but does not teach him what you want him to do—a criticism that can be averted if the teacher provides the child with an alternative behavior that will be approved and reinforced. Third, the relationship between the child and the punishing agent affects the usefulness of punishment. If the child holds the punishing agent in high regard, the aversive stimulus will be effective, whereas if the child does not hold the punishing agent in high regard, the very same aversive may be relatively ineffective (Parke, 1970). Other variables such as age, developmental level, and sex of the child being punished appear to be related to the effectiveness of particular aversive stimuli, but the precise nature of these relationships are unclear (see Parke, 1970; Aronfreed, 1968).

The foregoing is focused on the presentation of an aversive, or noxious, stimulus following operant behavior that one is trying to weaken. The other form of punishment, the withdrawal of a desired stimulus, has been used by teachers historically. For example, "Unless you quiet down you cannot go to recess." In another context, paying your own money for a traffic ticket is based on the same principle for the adult. If used judiciously, this form of punishment would not appear to be as potentially harmful for educational practice. Reese (1966) reported that with response-contingent withdrawal of reinforcement, response strength can be decreased more rapidly than when extinction procedures alone are used.

A variation of this form of punishment, which has been used rather effectively by educators, is labeled *time out*. This practice consists of removing the child from a presumed reinforcing environment to an unstimulating time-out room or box where the child remains for a designated period. For this procedure to be effective two factors must be operating: first, the setting from which the child is removed must be reinforcing to, and desired by, the child; and second, the time-out environment must be neutral in stimulus value, or not desired. Should these conditions not be met, the *time-out* procedure is far less effective.

Summary

In attempting to weaken undesirable behavior, particularly behavior that interferes with the child's learning or that of others in the classroom, the teacher can select from several procedures, depending on whether the behavior should be suppressed immediately, the frequency of its occurrence, and whether it is a behavior that is difficult for the reinforcer to suspend. In order to weaken behavior the teacher can choose from the following procedures:

1. *Extinction*—when the behavior is very infrequent, and when it does not endanger the child or others in the class.
2. *Counterconditioning*—when behavior that is incompatible with the behavior to be weakened is available and easily reinforced.
3. *Satiation or negative practice*—when the reinforcer for the behavior is one that the child will tire of with repeated presentation; or behavior which if repeated excessively will cease to be novel or enjoyable to the child.
4. *Punishment*—when the behavior endangers the child or others in the class and the teacher wants immediate termination of that behavior.

STRENGTHENING OR BUILDING OPERANTS

In the previous section procedures were considered with which a teacher could weaken maladaptive behavior. In so doing, the section addressed itself to the question: "How do I get the child to stop doing something?" While this is of immediate concern to teachers in maintaining discipline in a classroom, most of the teaching process is concerned with teaching children *what to do* instead of *what not to do*. In the present section, attention will be directed to the ways in which operant behaviors that exist, but are not emitted frequently enough, can be strengthened, and how new or more complex behaviors can be developed.

Before discussing various ways of strengthening operant behavior, it may be useful to restate the nature of operant responses. First of all, they are *emitted* and controlled by two sets of stimuli: discriminative stimuli which precede the response and those stimulus events which follow the response (positively reinforcing, negatively reinforcing, punishing, or neutral). In many cases teachers are concerned with increasing the strength of a given response. Clarification is probably needed regarding the meaning of the term *strength* of a response. There are several ways in which the strength of a response can be estimated, and in each case the criteria vary. Bijou and Baer (1961) contended that the most useful criterion measure is *rate of response*, or how often a response is emitted in a given length of time under standard conditions. Teachers ask "How often does John get out of his seat?" or "How frequently does Andrew talk out in class without raising his hand?" Another measure of strength is the *magnitude or amplitude of the response*, or the effort expended in making the response. In verbal behavior, one might measure whether the child whispers or shouts. Finally, the *latency* or promptness with which the response follows a discriminative stimulus; for example, how long does Bruce take to come to the teacher's desk after the teacher asks him to come up to her desk? Which of the foregoing criteria a teacher is concerned with is determined by the nature of the behavior under consideration. In some cases a teacher may want a child to do math problems more rapidly, in other cases to get children to speak up in class, and in yet other cases to get to work more promptly.

Let us now turn to the process of strengthening behaviors that are already a part of the child's response repertoire.

Contingency Management

In many cases a teacher wishes to strengthen a response a child can emit, and has, in the past, emitted, but which the child does not emit frequently enough. For example, the act of raising one's hand before answering in class is one behavior almost all children have performed, but one that some children do not emit often enough in the judgment of their teacher. In cases like this, the approach can be very straightforward and simple. Operant principles indicate that the way to increase the probability of such responses being emitted is to follow their occurrence with a reinforcer. The reinforcer can be either a positive or negative reinforcement, both of which strengthen the behaviors they follow. The fact that bears emphasizing is that such behavior should not be taken for granted, and if it is not reinforced it, like any other behavior, will extinguish.

A slightly different problem exists when the child makes the response quite frequently, but often at the incorrect time. This kind of problem relates to the earlier discussion of discriminative stimuli in that certain behaviors are appropriate only in the presence of certain stimulus conditions. To use the example from the earlier discussion, the teacher does not want the child to jump up and recite the pledge to the flag in the middle of a forest, but rather to learn "when and where" it is appropriate to emit a given response. In such instances the problem is that the response, or behavior, is not under the control of the appropriate discriminative stimuli, and the teacher's task is to assist the child in associating a particular behavior with the discriminative stimuli that should exert control. The way in which this is done is through differential, or selective, reinforcement which, the reader will recall from the discussion earlier in this chapter, consists of reinforcing those responses that occur in the presence of the discriminative stimulus, and failing to reinforce those responses that occur when the discriminative stimulus is absent.

What this boils down to is that the teacher plays the role

of the contingency manager. The teacher, who does control much of the classroom environment, determines when, how, and how frequently rewards will be forthcoming. The recommendation made to the teacher is to be generous in his use of reinforcement for adaptive behavior and not to take any good behavior for granted. Second, he must be sure that he is making the rewards under his control contingent on desired, and not undesired, behavior. For example, he must not get manipulated into attending to misbehavior to any great extent. In summary, increasing the frequency of behaviors that the child already possesses involves the basic principle of reinforcement. A more difficult task confronts the teacher when the behavior is not in the child's response repetoire but, rather, must be developed. The procedures for developing more complex behaviors or new behaviors follow.

Chaining

Most operant behavior encountered in a classroom is more complex than a simple stimulus-response unit, or association. Instead, stimulus-response units get linked together and thereby form more complex behaviors in the forms of verbal sequences or motor patterns. Since there is in essence, as well as in fact, the linking together of stimulus-response units, these more complex behaviors are called *chains*. Many motor response chains are executed on an everyday basis without awareness that one is linking together separate stimulus-response units. For example, buttoning a shirt, tying one's shoes, tying a tie, walking, and shifting gears on an automobile are all examples of chaining, in which separate stimulus-response units are linked together to form these complex behaviors.

Staats and Staats (1963) used the example of teaching a young child how to kick a football in order to clarify the concept of *chaining*. By means of the verbal instructions provided by the instructor, the child comes to self-instruct by talking or thinking through the separate links that must be chained in order to perform the task. These "thinking-produced stimuli" become involved in verbal chains. The child comes to say aloud or covertly: (1) "Hold the ball in front parallel to the ground," (2) drop the football straight down," (3) "swing the right foot up as the ball is dropped" (assuming he is a right-footed kicker), (4) "hit the ball before it hits the ground," (5) "follow through with the right leg."

In the classroom, a child's solving a long division arithmetic problem also exemplifies the chaining process. First, he must learn how to do short division; then he must be able to subtract; then bring down the next number; repeat the division process; and ultimately handle the remainder as a fraction. This is not taught as one process but, rather, as separate processes: the child is taught subtraction separately; short division, separately; and a unit on fractions or decimals, separately. When teaching long division, the teacher puts together each of these skills in a particular sequence in order that the child can perform a task more complex than the child was capable of before.

In some special classes teachers have had difficulty in getting the children to enter the classroom quietly and get started working without incidents. This could be approached by teaching separate units in a sequence that are involved in this chain of behaviors. For example, the teacher might have the class practice (1) lining up outside the classroom door, (2) entering the classroom quietly and proceeding to their desk, (3) sitting down, (4) waiting for the assignment to be given, (5) getting out the necessary materials for the assignment, (6) getting started on the assignment. These units could be worked on separately and then put together into the appropriate sequence once every unit is mastered.

Let us analyze what occurs in chaining. Each link in the chain consists of three elements: a discriminative stimulus, a response, and a reinforcer. However, in all cases except the first and last link, stimuli serve a double function of reinforcer and discriminative stimulus. Hence the links overlap, holding the chain together. In keeping with this overlapping, if there is a break in any of the discriminative stimulus-response-reinforcer units the entire chain breaks. In serving a double function of reinforcer and discriminative stimulus, that particular stimulus first serves as a conditioned reinforcer and as a cue to the individual to make the next response in the chain. Reynolds (1968, p. 53) noted that conditioned reinforcers occur quite frequently within chains of responses and stimuli. To quote:

> A *chain* is composed of a series of responses joined together by stimuli that act both as conditioned reinforcers and as discriminative stimuli. A chain begins with the presentation of a discriminative stimulus. When the organism makes the appropriate response in the presence of this stimulus, a conditioned reinforcer is presented. This conditioned reinforcer is also a discriminative stimulus which occasions the next appropriate response. This response is reinforced with another conditioned reinforcer, which is also a discriminative stimulus for the next response, and so on. The last stimulus in the chain, on at least some occasions, is a primary, or innate, reinforcer.

Once these chains are learned and practiced, they operate so smoothly as to make partitioning of links extremely difficult. Blackham and Silberman (1971) noted the difficulty of performing chained responses in reverse order, such as reciting the alphabet backward. It is equally difficult to begin a sequence in the middle and proceed, like the child playing the piano who must return to the beginning of the musical piece if he makes a mistake.

Gagné (1965) specified five conditions essential for the learning of chains. First, each stimulus-response unit, or link, must be learned separately before the units can be linked together. Second, each link must be executed in the proper sequence, Third, each link must be performed in "close time" succession to ensure linking. If too much time elapses between links, the chain is unlikely to remain intact. Fourth, the sequence must be repeated sufficiently often until the learning has been achieved and the chain becomes somewhat automatic. Finally, reinforcement must be present in the learning of chains, since if the terminal link is extinguished, the chain breaks.

Chaining is an important concept for teachers to understand. First of all, it is important to know whether a child can perform all of the stimulus-response units involved in the chain before frustrating the child and the teacher by trying to put together the units, one or more of which the child cannot perform. By analyzing behavior chains into their component units, the teacher can then test whether a given child possesses the necessary units before proceeding to link them together. Some of the best examples of teaching chained behavior I have observed have taken place on athletic fields in which coaches are involved in teaching blocking or tackling in football. Each complex task is broken down by the coach into units, which are taught individually, then the units are put together into their proper sequence when the athlete attempts to perform the complex behavior in its entirety.

A final reason that chaining warrants the attention of teachers concerns the need for programming units into complex chains. Some teachers operate on the apparent assumption that once a child has mastered the stimulus-response units of a chain, the putting together of these units is an automatic process that requires little effort. Actually, considerable effort must go into sequencing these units properly and executing them repeatedly in sequence until the complex behavior becomes automatic.

Hence chaining provides teachers with a technique whereby more complex behaviors can be developed by combining two or more simple stimulus-response units. In some cases this may involve stimulus-response units the child already has in his response repertoire, whereas in other cases it may involve teaching additional stimulus-response units. Next to be considered are ways of teaching new behaviors, or responses, which the individual does not have in his response repertoire.

Shaping

In certain instances, a particular behavior is not part of a child's response repertoire, making it impossible to reinforce it since it is simply not emitted. How, then, does one go about developing behaviors that are "new" to a given child? One procedure for developing new behaviors is called *shaping*, a procedure that uses positive reinforcement and extinction in combination. Just as the sculptor shapes elaborate figures from a crude piece of clay, so the behavior analyst shapes more complex and new behavior from very crude responses through the combined use of reinforcement and extinction.

By means of shaping techniques, Skinner has taught pigeons to play ping-pong and to play musical tunes on a xylophone (Cohen, 1969)—behaviors that pigeons do not naturally emit but, if systematically developed, are within their capability.

Wenrich (1970, p. 85) defined shaping as "the process in which reinforcement is differentially applied to those responses that constitute closer and closer approximation to the ultimate response one wishes to bring about." In essence, shaping entails reinforcing extremely rough approximations of the ultimate behavior to begin with, and then moving step by step toward that ultimate behavior through reinforcing closer approximations.

For educators, the shaping procedure is critical. Too often teachers assume that their reinforcement should be withheld until the goal behavior is achieved, but learning theory indicates that such a tack is less efficient than moving in smaller steps toward that goal. In short, shaping tells the teacher to "think small," and reiterates the saying that a journey of a thousand miles begins with one step. The class hellion does not become a model student overnight. The child who never remains in his seat more than 2 minutes at a time will not sit quietly for 45 minutes. Instead of expecting such dramatic changes immediately, the teacher must settle for small, and yet significant, improvement in the direction of that ultimate goal. To achieve this goal the teacher should reinforce improvement, and not withhold his reinforcement until the goal behavior is accomplished.

In order to clarify the nature of the shaping process it is necessary to reconsider the effects of positive reinforcement and extinction, since these are the principles of learning used in shaping. It will be recalled that earlier in this chapter it was mentioned that one of the effects of positive reinforcement, in addition to strengthening the behavior it reinforces, is that it also results in a more active organism; that is, the positive reinforcement not only increases the probability of the particular response but also increases many other facets of the individual's behavior. Shaping makes use of this second effect—namely the topography of the response is altered, and closer approximations to the goal behavior are more likely; this is why shaping works. For example, by reinforcing a child's being in the proximity of his desk, the teacher increases the probability that he will sit down in that seat. If he is wandering around the classroom, seldom being near his desk, sitting down at his desk is less likely.

The second learning principle used in shaping is extinction. Again, the reader is referred to the earlier discussion of extinction, in which it was mentioned that when reinforcement is discontinued the topography of the response tends to become more variable and more forceful. Essentially, when the individual no longer gets his payoff for a particular behavior he seems to say to himself, "What happened?" and becomes more frantic in his emitting of the behavior that had previously been reinforced, thus increasing the probability that he will emit a closer approximation to the ultimate goal behavior.

Shaping, then, consists of the use of these two principles, reinforcement and extinction, toward the end of creating new operant behavior. Let us now consider how they are used in combination. The steps the teacher follows would be:

1. Identify an effective reinforcer for the child.
2. Specify the terminal behavior that will be accepted (the goal behavior).
3. Select a response presently emitted by the child which is "somewhat like" the terminal behavior, and reinforce it immediately.
4. Once that response is stable, then no longer reinforce it, and when the behavior becomes more variable, select a

closer approximation, and reinforce it (do not subsequently reinforce the old response).
5. Once stable, extinguish this response and select a closer approximation, and so on, until the goal behavior is achieved.

Note that the teacher reinforces an approximation until it becomes stable, then shifts the criterion for reinforcement to a closer approximation to the goal behavior. Care must be exercised to reinforce the closer approximation *immediately*, since a delay can result in a response different from the one intended. Second, the teacher must be careful about the length of time an approximation is reinforced because if it is reinforced for too long a period it may become too well established, and variations will not occur. On the other hand, if the shaping procedure moves too rapidly, the earlier developed behavior may begin to extinguish (Reese, 1966). Hence the shaping process must be employed with considerable attention to the detail outlined above. Let us now consider this procedure in more technical terms, as described by Reynolds (1968, pp. 28–29):

> This may be done by reinforcing any of its (organism's) responses; however, in order to shorten the shaping procedure, a response somewhat similar to the desired response is chosen for reinforcement. Reinforcement is then withdrawn, and, as discussed above, the variability and force of behavior increase. Before the frequency of the behavior decreases, a response closer to the desired behavior is selected for reinforcement from the more forceful and variable behavior initially produced by extinction. This selective reinforcement increases the frequency of the variation and that is reinforced. After this behavior has been firmly established and is occurring frequently, reinforcement is again discontinued, variation again increases for a short time, and a response still closer to the desired one is selected from the variation and is reinforced.

Teachers can make use of shaping procedures in coping with seat sitting and with attending behavior through gradual increases in the time required for the child to sit or to attend in order to obtain the reinforcer. Such procedures have been used effectively with speech problems, with getting children to do more speaking up and to work faster in class, and with improving handwriting and athletic skills. In most cases involving children in classrooms instruction is used along with the shaping techniques. The teacher can tell the child what degree of improvement is necessary today (the closer approximation) in order for him to obtain the reinforcer.

Modeling

Another technique for teaching new behaviors involves modeling, which was discussed earlier; therefore, a detailed discussion of this technique is not given here. Suffice it to say that teachers can present themselves as models, point out other children in the class as exhibiting the kind of behavior desired, or use films or filmstrips that demonstrate the desired behavior. By so doing they can provide models that children can imitate and thus shortcut the shaping procedure. In general, for promoting new behaviors, modeling is a more efficient technique than shaping because modeling provides prompts for the child and frequently can obtain the target or goal behavior with far fewer steps and in much less time.

Summary

For strengthening behavior or creating new behaviors the teacher can select from several procedures, depending on considerations such as (1) Does the teacher wish to strengthen a behavior emitted by the child? (2) Does the child possess the stimulus-response units that can be linked together to create more complex behavior? (3) Is the behavior a new behavior for that child? (4) Are models available which can be used to demonstrate the behavior desired? After consideration of these variables, the teacher can select from:

1. *Positive reinforcement*—when the behavior is emitted by the child, and the teacher simply wants to increase the strength of that behavior.
2. *Chaining*—when the teacher wishes to develop more complex behavior; this can be done by linking together simpler stimulus-response units which the child can emit, or which can be taught.
3. *Shaping*—when the teacher wishes to develop new behaviors, particularly when there are no prompts by which the teacher can get the target behavior.
4. *Modeling*—when the teacher wishes to develop new behaviors or increase the frequency of behaviors for which there is a model that a child can imitate.

REFERENCES

Aronfreed, J. Aversive control of socialization. *Nebraska Symposium on Motivation.* 1968, pp. 271–318.

Allyon, T. Intensive treatment of psychotic behaviour by stimulus satiation and food reinforcement. *Behav. Res. Ther.,* 1:53–61, 1963.

Bijou, S. W., and Baer, D. M. *Child Development I.* New York: Appleton-Century-Crofts, 1961.

Blackham, G. J., and Silberman, A. *Modification of Child Behavior.* Belmont, Calif.: Wadsworth Publishing Co., Inc., 1971.

Cohen, J. *Operant Behavior and Conditioning.* Chicago: Rand McNally & Co., 1969.

Gagné, R. M. *The Conditions of Learning.* New York: Holt, Rinehart and Winston, Inc., 1965.

Hewett, F. M. *The Emotionally Disturbed Child in the Classroom.* Boston: Allyn & Bacon, Inc., 1968.

Holz, W. C., and Azrin, N. H. A comparison of several procedures for eliminating behavior. *J. Exp. Anal. Behav.,* 6:399–406, 1963.

Keller, F. S. *Learning: Reinforcement Theory.* New York: Random House, Inc., 1969.

Parke, R. D. The role of punishment in the socialization process. In R. A. Hoppe, G. A. Milton, and E. Simmel (eds.) *Early Experiences in the Processes of Socialization.* New York: Academic Press, Inc., 1970, pp. 81–108.

Reese, E. P. *The Analysis of Human Operant Behavior*. Dubuque, Iowa: William C. Brown Company, Publishers, 1966.

Reynolds, G. S. *A Primer of Operant Conditioning*. Glenview, Ill.: Scott, Foresman and Company, 1968.

Skinner, B. F. *Science and Human Behavior*. New York: The Macmillan Company, 1938.

Skinner, B. F. *Science and Human Behavior*. New York: The Macmillan Company, 1953.

Solomon, R. L. Punishment. *Am. Psychol.*, 19:239–53, 1964.

Staats, A. W., and Staats, C. K. *Complex Human Behavior*. New York: Holt, Rinehart and Winston, Inc., 1963.

Travers, R. W. M. *Essentials of Learning*. New York: The Macmillan Company, 1963.

Wenrich, W. W. *A Primer of Behavior Modification*. Belmont, Calif.: Wadsworth Publishing Co., Inc., 1970.

CHAPTER 4

Reinforcement Revisited

SINCE WE, as educators, are primarily concerned with changing or strengthening behavior, it seems natural that much of the discussion about behavior modification is focused on reinforcement. Reinforcement, by definition, refers to any environmental event that increases the probability of a response. In the previous chapters, there has been discussion about positive versus negative reinforcement, unconditioned versus conditioned reinforcers, the function of reinforcement in chaining and shaping, and comparisons of the effects of reinforcement and punishment. One might conclude from this that further discussion is unnecessary; however, there are several dimensions of reinforcement which do need further elaboration: schedules of reinforcement and a continuum of reinforcers.

SCHEDULES OF REINFORCEMENT

Until now the discussion has not considered whether every response must be reinforced in order to increase the probability of occurrence of that response. Obviously not every request for cookies by a child results in his obtaining a cookie, and not every verbal response to the printed symbol in reading is followed by a reinforcer, yet the "begging" and reading are learned. There are two schedules of reinforcement: A schedule by which every response is followed by a reinforcer; such a schedule is called a *continuous schedule of reinforcement*. In most instances, however, a child emits many responses that are not followed by a reinforcer, yet the behavior is strengthened because at least some responses are reinforced. All such schedules, in which some responses are followed by reinforcers and some are not, are called, collectively, *intermittent schedules of reinforcement*. There are infinite combinations of intermittent schedules, some of which depend on the number of responses a child emits (e.g., "When you finish five problems you can go to recess") and others which depend on the passage of a certain amount of time (e.g., "You cannot have lunch yet, it is only eleven o'clock). Those schedules that are based on the number of responses made are called *ratio schedules*, whereas those that depend on the passage of some period of time are called *interval schedules*.

The schedule of reinforcement is one dimension of the contingencies operating between operants and their reinforcers. That is, the schedule determines which responses will be reinforced and which (in the case of intermittent schedules) will pass unreinforced. Hence all schedules except a continuous schedule dictate that some, not all, responses emitted by the individual will be reinforced; these are collectively labeled "intermittent schedules."

As several simple schedules of reinforcement are presented, keep in mind the following effects of schedules of reinforcement. The schedule has a profound effect on the rate of response, the pattern of responses over time, and resistance to extinction. As a result, it is of paramount importance that you ascertain the schedule of reinforcement that is maintaining a behavior you might want to change. Second, in order to stabilize a behavior once developed, you would want to shift from a schedule that is less resistant to extinction to a schedule highly resistant to extinction.

Continuous Reinforcement

The continuous schedule of reinforcement exists when every time the response is emitted it is followed by reinforcement. Bijou and Baer (1961) noted that continuous schedules of reinforcement have two interesting characteristics. First, this schedule produces a regular pattern of responding and, second, responses supported on a continuous schedule of reinforcement extinguish rather rapidly.

In the initial stages of strengthening a response, a continuous schedule of reinforcement is desirable because it is highly efficient. During the acquisition stage, that is, when you are first teaching a behavior to a child and when he is learning the behavior, a continuous schedule of reinforcement is probably better than any of the intermittent schedules because it provides consistent and immediate feedback to the learner. Note how the teaching machine can provide continuous reinforcement to the learner, whereas it is almost impossible for a teacher to do so when working with a large class of children. This probably accounts for the faster acquisition of skills by means of teaching machines. However, in teaching, the continuous schedule of reinforcement is seldom typical of the reinforcement schedule the teacher employs because he cannot notice every correct response made by every child in the class, unless it is a tutorial session or work with a small group. The teacher becomes involved in other activities and with other children, hence several correct responses pass unnoticed and go unreinforced. The teacher should, however, keep in mind that the closer he can approximate a continuous schedule of reinforcement the faster the child will acquire the new behavior.

Figure 4.1 represents the response pattern of behavior supported on a continuous schedule of reinforcement. It should be noted that it applies only to the maintenance (once it has been stabilized) period and the period during extinction. This is because during the acquisition stage the performance is always changing. However, it gradually settles down to a highly pre-

PRINCIPLES OF BEHAVIOR MODIFICATION

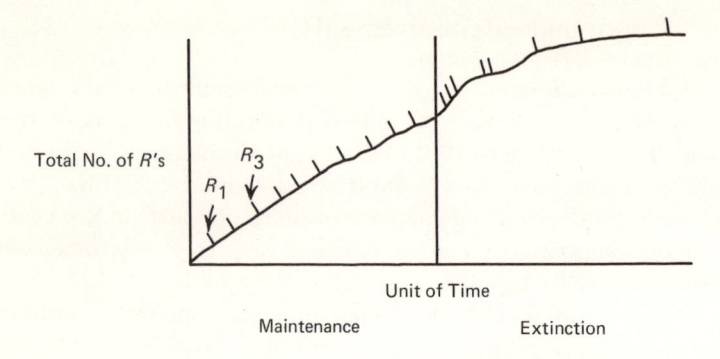

Figure 4.1. *Cumulative record of responding during maintenance and extinction on a continuous schedule of reinforcement.*

dictable maintained performance. Worthy of note regarding the responses during the continuous schedule is the steady rate of response until extinction, then the rapid spurt in response rate, followed by a rapid decrease in response rate to the operant level.

Ratio Schedules

As described earlier, one type of intermittent schedule of reinforcement makes the reinforcement contingent on the number of responses emitted; these are called ratio schedules. Ratio refers to the ratio of the total number of responses to the number of responses reinforced. In a ratio of 10:1, the individual must emit nine unreinforced responses for each reinforced response. The general effect of ratio schedules is the production of rather high rates of responding. This high response rate develops because the speed with which the individual will receive his reinforcement is directly related to how fast he emits the required number of responses. In the classroom, the teacher who tells a child he can go to recess after he completes five more problems, or reads ten more pages, or picks up five more pieces of paper off the floor is employing a ratio schedule. Two basic kinds of ratio schedules—fixed-ratio and variable-ratio schedules—are discussed later in this chapter.

Interval Schedules

A second type of intermittent schedule of reinforcement makes reinforcement contingent on the elapsing of a given interval of time before a response will be reinforced; these are called *interval* schedules. The interval of time that must elapse is commonly measured from the last reinforcement, but could be measured from any event. Whereas ratio schedules place importance on rapid response rates, interval schedules require that only one response be made *as long as* the interval of time has elapsed. Another way of looking at the lower response rates supported by interval schedules is that no matter how rapidly one responds he does not get reinforced until the required time interval has elapsed; hence rapid responding is not differentially reinforced as it is in the case of ratio schedules. One example of an interval schedule in the classroom is when it does a child no good to request lunch at ten o'clock, because the interval of time required for such a request to be granted has not elapsed. Two types of interval schedules will be discussed in this chapter: fixed-interval and variable-interval schedules.

Fixed and Variable Schedules

The two types of schedules described above, ratio and interval schedules, can be divided further into two subclassifications: fixed and variable schedules. The fixed schedules consistently require the same number of responses made or time interval elapsed for every reinforced response. In a fixed-ratio schedule it might require a total of 25 responses for each reinforced response. A fixed-interval schedule would require consistently the elapsing of a time period, say, ten minutes, prior to reinforcing a response.

It is difficult to identify fixed schedules in the classroom context which precisely meet with the specifications outlined. However, it is possible to find several approximations. For example, a six-week grading period is very much like a fixed-interval schedule in that a certain constant period of time must pass before the reinforcement (assuming the child will receive a grade he finds reinforcing) will be given. Another example of a fixed interval would be in classes run on a token economy where tokens are given at certain time intervals (e.g., every 15 minutes). The track coach may require all sprinters to run two laps of the track at the conclusion of each workout before they can shower. This would be an example of a fixed-ratio schedule.

Variable schedules dictate when the number of responses or the time interval vary from one reinforcement to the next in an irregular, but cyclical, fashion. For example, a variable-ratio schedule might reinforce the 5th, then the 25th, then the 10th, then the 120th responses and then recycle to: 5, 25, 10, 120, 5, 25, etc. A variable-interval schedule varies the amount of time that must elapse before a response is reinforced. For example, intervals could be sequenced as follows: 10 minutes, 25 minutes, 15 minutes, 40 minutes, etc.

In the classroom, teachers usually use variable schedules presenting reinforcements after "enough has been done" or "enough time has passed"; however, what constitutes "enough" usually varies from time to time. For example, the child who keeps asking to go to the washroom usually is given permission after he has asked often enough; sometimes that may be five requests, other times ten requests. This would constitute a variable ratio *if* the teacher's decision to let him go to the washroom is based on the number of times he has asked. On the other hand, the teacher may grant permission after, in his judgment, enough time has passed since the last visit to the washroom. In that case, the number of requests is irrelevant, and what counts is the amount of time since the last visit to the washroom. Hence the schedule operating is now a variable interval. In most instances, it is difficult to ascertain whether it is the number of responses or the lapse of a certain amount of time that determines which responses are reinforced and which go unreinforced. The factor that makes the foregoing example a *variable* schedule is that the teacher never requires exactly the same number of requests or the exact same amount of time to elapse before granting the request.

By combining ratio and interval schedules with fixed and variable schedules the four simple schedules of reinforcement emerge: fixed-ratio (FR), fixed-interval (FI), variable-ratio (VR), and variable-interval (VI). These are the schedules to be discussed in this chapter. All known schedules of reinforcement can be reduced to ratio and interval variations. Theoretically, an almost infinite number of schedules could be devised. Should the reader be interested in a more detailed analysis of more complex schedules of reinforcement, he is referred to Reynolds (1968, chap. 7) or Ferster and Skinner (1957).

Fixed-Ratio (FR) Schedules

Piecework in a factory wherein an employee is paid by the units he produces is an example of a fixed-ratio schedule of reinforcement. In the classroom a FR schedule is in effect when the teacher says, "You may go to recess when you finish these five problems." The effect of FR schedules on behavior is the production of a high response rate, which is the intent of the employer or teacher in the foregoing examples. Reynolds (1968) described the performance maintained on a FR schedule as rapid from the first response following reinforcement through the last, and reinforced, response. Following reinforcement, there is typically a pause before responding begins if the ratio is large (200:1 is a larger ratio than 15:1) followed by the transition into the typically high response rate. If, however, the ratio is small, there is no pause whatsoever following the reinforcement.

Figure 4.2 graphically represents the cumulative record of behavior maintained on a FR schedule of reinforcement. Note

PRINCIPLES OF BEHAVIOR MODIFICATION

the absence of a pause following reinforcement on the low-ratio (FR 5) schedule and the presence of the pause on the high-ratio (FR 150) schedule. Using the example of the factory worker being paid on the basis of the number of units he produces, the pauses noted in the chart represent the "breaks" taken after completing, or receiving, the reinforcer.

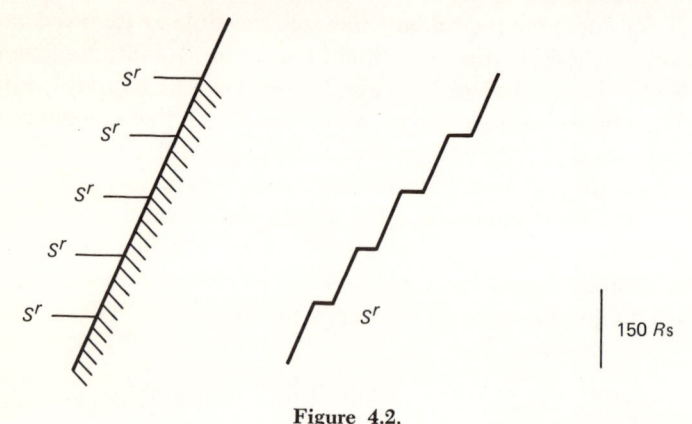

Figure 4.2.

Lundin (1961) noted that with a FR schedule of reinforcement one can begin with a low ratio (e.g., 15:1) and gradually increase the ratio (e.g., to 30:1, 50:1, 75:1, etc.) until extremely high ratios are reached. A word of caution, however, is in order: there is always a danger in beginning with high ratios. In such instances, the response may extinguish before the child receives the first reinforcement. For the teacher, FR schedules could be used to increase the amount of work required in order to obtain reinforcement by gradually increasing the amount of units until high ratios are reached. In addition, teachers should consider FR schedules when attempting to increase the speed of work for a child who does his work accurately but is very slow.

Extinction of behavior supported on a FR schedule is characterized by abrupt pauses, which become progressively longer in duration, followed by another series of responses emitted at about the same rate that prevailed during periods of reinforcement, another pause, more responding, and so on. Figure 4.3 shows graphically the course of the extinction process. Note how the pauses get progressively longer in duration but that the rate of responding, while becoming less frequent, is at the same rapid rate characteristic of the rate during reinforcement when the pauses do occur.

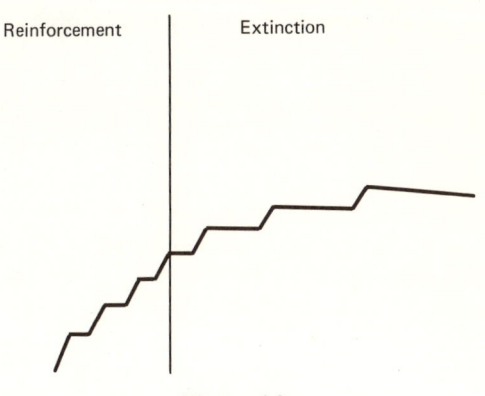

Figure 4.3.

Fixed-Interval (FI) Schedule

Payment of wages at the end of a week is an example of a fixed-interval schedule. In a general sense, the reading of a story by a teacher the last 15 minutes of class contingent on class behavior is another example. The response rate of behavior maintained on a FI schedule might best be described as uneven. The rate of responding just after reinforcement declines to a low response rate, and the rate just prior to the end of the time interval becomes quite high (Lundin, 1961). Reynolds (1968, p. 73) noted that the occurrence of reinforcement becomes a discriminative stimulus signifying a forthcoming period of nonreinforcement. He described how the individual actually forms a discrimination as follows:

> Responding extinguishes in the presence of the stimulus associated with nonreinforcement (the early part of the interval), and the rate of responding increases in the presence of the stimulus associated with reinforcement (the latter part of the interval).

Keller (1969) described the same phenomenon as the organism appearing to "tell time" in that he knows responding immediately after a reinforcement will not be reinforced, but by the time the interval of time has approximately elapsed the required responses are being made.

As mentioned earlier, it is difficult to find examples of FI schedules in the school which precisely adhere to the definition. For instance, the child would be rewarded for the first response *after* the lapse of a certain time period. In most examples for the school, consequences are presented at the end of the time period but not after the child responds. For example, a six-week grading period is somewhat like the FI schedule in that six weeks of time must pass and then the grade (potential reinforcer) is presented and is contingent on the behavior during that six-week period. In Figure 4.4 the behavior maintained on a FI 10-minute schedule is presented to demonstrate the response rate. The pattern of responding is referred to as the "FI scallop," which accurately describes the plotted effect. Note the low response rate immediately after reinforcement and the high rate as the end of the time interval approaches. Think for a moment about the studying behavior of students during the six-week period and note how it fits the scallop effect. After grades come out, the students decide it is a time for a break since grades will not be given for another six weeks, but as the end of the six-week period approaches, there is an increase in response rate, called in educational circles "cramming." If the teacher does not want that kind of scallop effect in studying behavior, he should not use a FI schedule because that is precisely the effect he will get when using that schedule.

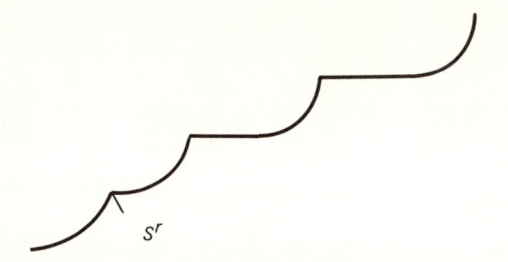

Figure 4.4. *Response pattern on a FI 10-min. schedule.*

When behavior has been supported on a FI schedule and extinction procedures are initiated, the interval following the final reinforcement proceeds normally with a low response rate and then a very rapid rate as the time interval draws to an end. However, as the interval extends beyond that which has been the case, the high terminal response rate continues. After a short time, the responding ceases abruptly. After a period of no responding, suddenly a high response rate is again emitted until it abruptly stops. Gradually the pauses become of greater duration and the periods of responding become shorter until the rate approaches the preoperant level. Figure 4.5 represents schematically the process described above.

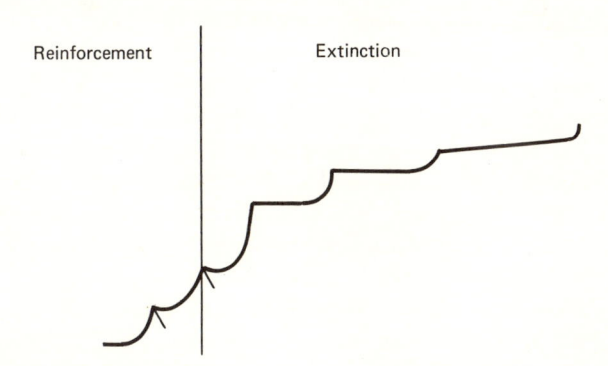

Figure 4.5. *Extinction of behavior maintained on a FI 10-min. schedule.*

Reese (1966) contended that behavior maintained on a FI schedule is quite resistant to extinction. Blackham and Silberman (1971) observed the greater ease with which interval schedules can be administered by teachers than is true for ratio schedules. To count the number of responses emitted by children would require a teacher with superhuman observational skills. Instead, most teachers find it easier to evaluate performance over some period of time. It should be mentioned, however, that such practice does not adhere strictly to what is meant by FI schedules, which dictate that the first response following a time lapse be reinforced.

Variable-Ratio (VR) Schedule

The best example of a VR schedule is the slot machine, or one-armed bandit. The machines pay off "on an average" of every 100 plays, but it is not a constant thing in which every 100th play is rewarded. In some cases, one can go 300 or 400 plays before a payoff; in other cases 2 successive plays pay off. Clearly, if one observes the behavior of the players in Reno or Las Vegas, he gets an indication that a VR schedule maintains a very rapid response rate that is quite resistant to extinction.

VR schedules of reinforcement produce very high rates of responding that are almost constant. These characteristics are understandable since the reinforcement is contingent on the number of responses emitted; hence the faster one responds (regardless of the ratio) the faster one is reinforced. Reynolds (1968) pointed out that constancy of responding becomes a conditioned reinforcer because it is present at the time of reinforcement, so constancy itself becomes reinforcing. Since reinforcement is not predictable (as it is in a FR schedule), the individual tends to anticipate that reinforcement could come at any time.

Plotting of responses emitted on a VR schedule reveals a linear pattern with a rapid rate of responding. Figure 4.6 shows a typical performance generated by a VR schedule of reinforcement. Note the continuous and the constant rate of response and the varying ratios being reinforced.

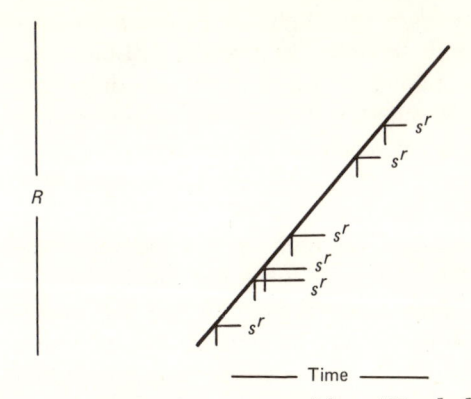

Figure 4.6. *Performance generated by a VR schedule.*

Typically, one specifies the average ratio of a series of variable ratios. For example, if he has a series of ratios such as 5, 30, 15, 45, 10, the average ratio is 21 despite the fact that the number of unreinforced responses between reinforcements is variable.

In attempting to understand children, an understanding of VR schedules is important because there are many situations in which behavior of children is reinforced on a VR basis (Bijou and Baer, 1961). Parents tell children that they can watch TV (presumably reinforcing) when they finish washing the dishes (the number of which vary from evening to evening). Children find that they have to ask whether they can go out to play several times if their father is preoccupied reading the newspaper. Should this happen repeatedly, the child comes to ask repeatedly at a rapid rate.

Anytime a parent or teacher provides the reinforcement after a response has been emitted "enough times," but when the number of responses required varies from reinforcement to reinforcement, he is using a VR schedule of reinforcement. The child continues to respond at a very high rate, anticipating that the reinforcement will be forthcoming "at any time." As a result, the behaviors maintained on a VR schedule are highly persistent.

As mentioned earlier, both FR and VR schedules of rein-

PRINCIPLES OF BEHAVIOR MODIFICATION

forcement generate extremely high rates of responding. Where they differ most dramatically is in the resistance to extinction of behavior maintained by FR and VR schedules. Behavior maintained on a VR schedule is more resistant to extinction than that generated by a FR schedule and far more durable than behavior maintained on a continuous schedule (Bijou and Baer, 1961; Blackham and Silberman, 1971).

A surprisingly high number of responses are emitted by the individual at a high rate following the initiation of extinction procedures. Since reinforcement during the maintenance stage came after ratios varying in number, the individual behaves as though he is thinking that this may simply be a high ratio. After the rather long period of rapid responding, a pause occurs. Gradually, these pauses, during which there is no responding, become longer in duration and the bursts of responding (still at a high rate) become shorter until the response ratio approaches its operant level. Figure 4.7 shows the course of behavior before and after extinction procedures are initiated.

Note the high response rate prior to extinction and after it

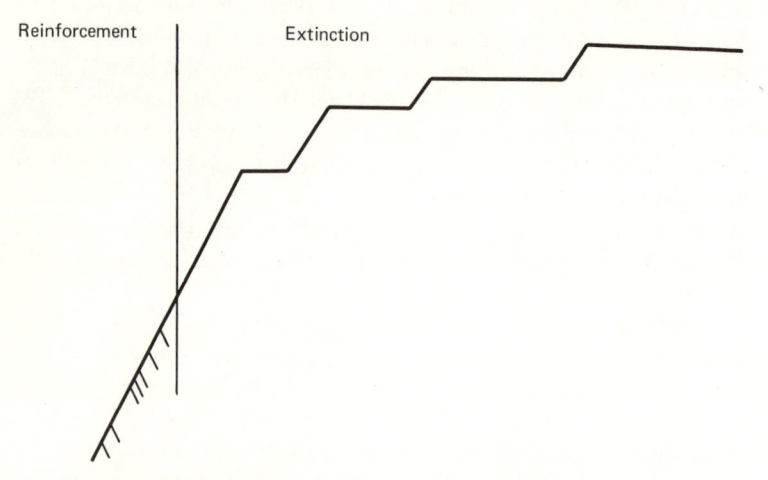

Figure 4.7. *Extinction of behavior maintained on a VR schedule of reinforcement.*

(when the individual is responding). Also characteristic of the VR schedule is the long period of responding following the initiation of extinction procedures, and the pauses of nonresponding, which get longer and longer (Reynolds, 1968; Lundin, 1961).

Variable-Interval (VI) Schedule

A child nags at his mother to give him a cookie, which she refuses to give him until she feels "enough time" has elapsed since the last cookie was given. This is an example of behavior (nagging) being reinforced (with a cookie) on a VI schedule ("enough time" varies). Reynolds (1968) used telephoning a busy number as an example of a VI schedule. The behavior (phoning) is presumably reinforced by hearing the voice of the person at the other end. The schedule of reinforcement varies, depending on the person to whom the person doing the telephoning is speaking. If it was a wrong number it could be a short interval, whereas if a teenage daughter is talking to her boyfriend the interval may seem infinite. Lundin (1961) cited hunting and fishing as examples of behaviors maintained on a VI schedule of reinforcement. The fisherman will fish for extensive periods of time without catching any fish, but during that time he anticipates catching a fish at any moment. Much behavior, often considered offensive by parents and teachers, such as nagging, temper tantrums, and whining is supported by VI schedules quite frequently, since adults give in to the child's wishes after they have listened to the nagging, tantrum, or whining "long enough." As a result, such behaviors are very steady and predictable and extremely difficult to extinguish.

VI schedules are like VR schedules in that they produce almost constant rates of responding; however, the rate is not nearly so rapid as those maintained on ratio schedules. The individual appears to sense that after a slight delay the time interval required is more likely to have passed than would be true if rapid responses were emitted. Hence a slow, even rate of responding is characteristic of VI schedules; however, rate of

PRINCIPLES OF BEHAVIOR MODIFICATION

responding does depend on the length of time interval used—the longer the interval the slower the response rate. Since reinforcement is dispensed contingent on variable time limits and appears to the subject to be dispensed at random, motivation appears to be maintained by the anticipation of reinforcement almost at any time (Blackham and Silberman, 1971). Figure 4.8 shows the behavior of an individual supported by a VI schedule of reinforcement. There are two characteristics worthy of mention regarding the effect of VI schedules on behavior. First, notice the constant rate of response (indicated by the linear relationship between time and responses). Second, the gentle degree of slope reveals the relatively low rate of responding. As in the case of VR schedules, VI schedules tend to develop behavior involved in constant rates of responding and become secondary reinforcers, making constancy itself reinforcing (Reynolds, 1968, p. 69).

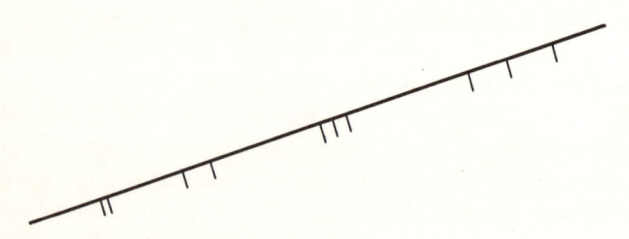

Figure 4.8. *Performance maintained on a schedule of reinforcement.*

The most important feature of VI schedules of reinforcement is that they are highly resistant to extinction—probably the most resistant of any of the four simple schedules of intermittent reinforcement discussed. As a result, behavior strengthened through reinforcement on a VI schedule can, and does, survive for long periods of time without reinforcement or with infrequent reinforcement and irregular occurrences of reinforcement. Obviously, how durable a behavior proves to be depends on the length of intervals used—the longer the intervals the more durable the behavior.

Reynolds (1968) described the process of extinction of behavior on a VI schedule as proceeding in a gradually decreasing rate of responding without abrupt pauses. While there are some irregularities in rate of response during extinction, they are viewed as regular if longer periods of time are considered; hence in plotting the behavior one notes a negatively accelerated curve emerging as shown in Figure 4.9.

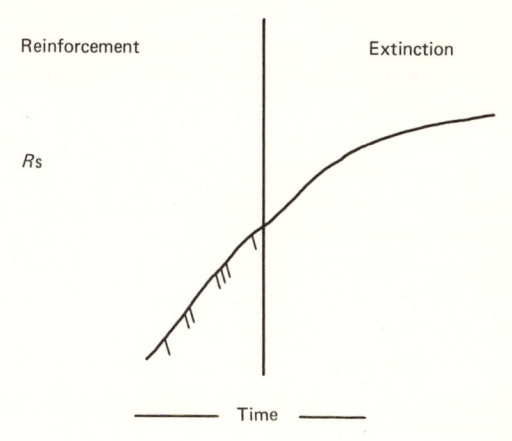

Figure 4.9. *Course of extinction of behavior on a VI schedule of reinforcement.*

In commenting on VI schedules of reinforcement, it is usually noted that such schedules probably account for much persistent behavior in an individual's repertoire—continuance of trying in the face of failure (Lundin, 1961), durability of personality characteristics (Bijou and Baer, 1961), and the extended research of scientists, without reinforcement (Skinner, 1971).

Before we leave schedules of reinforcement, a few comments are in order. Teachers should use various schedules of reinforcement in systematic ways—depending on what they are

PRINCIPLES OF BEHAVIOR MODIFICATION

trying to develop. For example, if a teacher is trying to increase the speed with which a given child completes his math problems, he might use a FR schedule. Where a teacher is trying to strengthen a behavior in the initial stages, he might use a continuous schedule, then later shift to a FR or FI schedule and, later yet, shift to a VI schedule so that the behavior becomes more durable.

For those desiring to alter behavior it probably appears unfortunate that most misbehavior is maintained on VR or VI schedules of reinforcement. As a result, these behaviors resist extinction rather strongly. Hence the teacher should not expect to alter such behavior overnight, because this is simply not going to happen. Another caution was noted by Bijou and Baer (1961): when a parent or teacher ignores certain behavior (to extinguish it) and succeeds in doing so repeatedly, but in a moment of weakness succumbs, the VI reinforcement contributes to the strength and durability of that behavior and prolongs the extinction process considerably.

Hence the schedule of reinforcement is an important variable to consider in attempts to understand (and thus control) the behavior of children. In subsequent chapters we will explore how the teacher can make use of this understanding in school-related situations.

A CONTINUUM OF REINFORCERS

At this time, it seems desirable to consider a basis for the selection of the reinforcers to be used by teachers in modifying the behavior of children. It goes without saying that in order to get a child to be willing to work for an incentive, that incentive *must* be highly desirable to the child (Homme, 1970). Otherwise, it may not serve as a reinforcer (strengthen the behavior) but rather as a neutral stimulus, which does not affect the strength or probability of occurrence of the behavior it follows.

In one sense, behaviors have made a major contribution to

the field of education by questioning certain assumptions underlying educational practice. Educators have long assumed that certain consequences (e.g., letter grades, teacher approval) are universal reinforcers (almost as though they were primary reinforcers). The behaviorists have shown that for certain children the typical incentives do not maintain the desired behavior. Conversely, certain other incentives, often considered unconventional by traditional educators—such as trinkets, money, and free time—have had a marked effect on the behavior of these same children. Homme (1970) noted the concern of some parents and teachers regarding the use of "unconventional" incentives. Some feel that students should be motivated by a desire to succeed rather than by the promise of a reward. Others feel that the whole idea rings of bribery. Still others feel that the child will grow up expecting to be rewarded for every little thing he does. Homme (1970) concluded that, based on experience, these fears are unfounded. MacMillan (1968) suggested that the alternative to altering incentives is to *wait* until the child learns to respond to the common educational incentives (using the verb "learns" quite loosely). Such an attitude results in children stagnating until they reach a certain degree of maturity which would enable them to respond to the common educational incentives.

In yet another way, the contribution of the behaviorists may be frequently misinterpreted and ultimately may have detrimental effects on some children (MacMillan and Forness, 1970). This problem seems to occur when naive practitioners are seduced by the trappings of behavior modification and adopt a program designed for a population which in no way resembles the population they are working with and transfer that program lock, stock, and barrel to their classrooms. By way of example, most of the early clinical and educational programs were used with subjects who deviated markedly from what is considered normal. Ayllon and Haughton (1962) worked with institutionalized psychotic women; Lovaas, Freitag, Gold, and Kassorla (1965) were concerned with autistic children. Even in education, the first classroom based on behavioristic principles (Birnbrauer and

Lawler, 1964) was established for trainable mentally retarded children. Such atypical subjects operated at very immature levels of reinforcement (i.e., responding to only primary rewards or easily established secondary rewards) which, in turn, determined the kinds of incentives used—food, tokens, and check marks. Since these early programs, there has been a proliferation of programs based on M&M's, tokens, and check marks. It is as if M&M's and tokens *are synonymous* with behavior modification.

In the area of mental retardation the early research of Zigler led him to hypothesize a reinforcer hierarchy (summarized in Zigler, 1962) that differs for retarded and nonretarded children. For example, "being right" may not be of as high priority on a given retardate's hierarchy of reinforcers as on that of a nonretarded child. However, since many retarded children do not receive much adult approval, such approval may be higher on the hierarchy of reinforcers for the retarded child than for the nonretarded child.

As early as 1953 Skinner recognized a continuum of reinforcers, and many of the programs for education developed by leading behaviorists (e.g., Hewett, 1968; Whelan and Haring, 1966) either implicitly or explicitly use the notion of a continuum of reinforcement. Little systematic research, however, has been conducted on this topic. It is my belief that those using behavior modification techniques should be sensitive to this problem—far more important than the discussion devoted to it in the literature.

In Hewett's "Hierarchy of Educational Tasks" (1968) he described the three ingredients of the learning triangle: the task, the degree of teacher control, and the reward. This last element, the reward, is relevant to the present discussion. Hewett (1968) related certain categories of rewards to various stages of his "Developmental Sequence of Educational Goals," and in so doing, presented a continuum of reinforcers. Extrapolation from his scheme might result in the following continuum of reinforcers (starting at most immature and moving to the most mature):

1. Tangible rewards—money, food, and trinkets
2. Social attention—attention as a by-product of doing "something"
3. Completion of tasks
4. Multisensory experiences
5. Approval—and avoidance of disapproval
6. Being correct
7. Acquisition of knowledge and skills

The reader is referred to Hewett's discussion of the rewards at each of the seven stages in the rationale, in Part II of his book (1968, pp. 115–236).

MacMillan (1968, p. 71) postulated a tentative continuum, beginning with the least mature:

1. Primary rewards—food and water
2. Toys or trinkets
3. Tokens or checks—with backup reinforcers (toys, food, etc.)
4. Visual evidence of progress—graphs, letter grades
5. Social approval
6. Sense of mastery—"learning for the love of it"

In the light of Zigler's (1962) observation that hierarchies of reinforcement are not universals because the order would differ from one child to another, the foregoing continua are not presented as invariants. Rather, they are presented as points of reference for the following chapters. Sensitivity to the foregoing notions is reflected in the writings of most authorities on behavior modification, yet it has been my experience that it is frequently overlooked by practitioners putting the concepts embodied in these writings into operation. For example, when administering check marks to children it is mentioned, often in passing, that the teacher should praise the child at the same time. Why should this be done? If you will recall the earlier discussion on conditioned reinforcers, it was stated that conditioned reinforcers acquire their reinforcing power by association with either pirmary or effective secondary rewards. Therefore, if the teacher repeatedly pairs praise (initially ineffective as a reinforcer) with check marks (an effective reinforcer), the praise will come to acquire the power to maintain the behavior by itself. Then the check marks can be dropped. You will also note that one uses a more mature reinforcer (praise) in order to move the child to conditions more like the "natural consequences" that must ultimately support the behavior. For this reason the notion of a continuum of reinforcers is singled out for special attention.

In specifying ground rules for behavior modifiers, MacMillan (1970, p. 6) stated the following: "The teacher (clinician) has a responsibility to lead a child along a continuum to more mature levels of performance. That is, the child must not be allowed to stagnate at a reinforcement level on the continuum below the level at which he is capable of functioning." This notion will be discussed at greater length in subsequent chapters.

REFERENCES

Ayllon, T., and Haughton, E. Control of the behavior of schizophrenics by food. *J. Exp. Anal. Behav.* 5:343–52, 1962.
Bijou, S. W., and Baer, D. M. *Child Development, Vol. I.* New York: Appleton-Century-Crofts, 1961.
Birnbrauer, J., and Lawler, J. Token reinforcement for learning. *Ment. Retard.*, 2:275–79, 1964.
Blackham, G. J., and Silberman, A. *Modification of Child Behavior.* Belmont, Calif.: Wadsworth Publishing Co., Inc., 1971.
Ferster, C. B., and Skinner, B. F. *Schedules of Reinforcement.* New York: Appleton-Century-Crofts, 1957.
Hewett, F. M. *The Emotionally Disturbed Child in the Classroom.* Boston: Allyn & Bacon, Inc., 1968.
Homme, L. *How to Use Contingency Contracting in the Classroom.* Champaign, Ill.: Research Press, 1970.

Keller, F. S. *Learning: Reinforcement Theory.* New York: Random House, Inc., 1969.

Lovaas, O. I., Freitag, G., Gold, J. J., and Kassorla, I. C. Experimental studies in childhood schizophrenia: Analysis of self-destructive behavior. *J. Exp. Child Psychol.,* 2:67–84, 1965.

Lundin, R. W. *Personality: An Experimental Approach.* New York: The Macmillan Company, 1961.

MacMillan, D. L. Behavior modification: A teacher strategy to control behavior. *Report of the Proceedings of the Forty-fourth Meeting of the Convention of American Instructors of the Deaf.* Berkeley, Calif.: 1968, pp. 66–76.

MacMillan, D. L. Ground rules for behavior modification. Paper read at the Annual Meeting of the American Association on Mental Deficiency, Washington, D.C., May 7, 1970.

MacMillan, D. L., and Forness, S. R. Behavior modification: Limitations and liabilities. *Except. Child,* 37:291–97, 1970.

Reese, E. P. *The Analysis of Human Operant Behavior.* Dubuque, Iowa: Wm. C. Brown Company, Publishers, 1966.

Reynolds, G. S. *A Primer of Operant Conditioning.* Glenview, Ill.: Scott, Foresman and Company, 1968.

Skinner, B. F. The technology of teaching. In C. E. Pitts (ed.) *Operant Conditioning in the Classroom.* New York: Thomas Y. Crowell Company, 1971.

Whelan, R. J., and Haring, N. G. Modification and maintenance of behavior through application of consequences. *Except. Child.,* 32:281–89, 1966.

Zigler, E. *Rigidity in the Feebleminded.* In E. P. Trapp and P. Himelstein (eds.) *Readings on the Exceptional Child.* New York: Appleton-Century-Crofts, 1962.

PART II
Translating Principles into Practice

CHAPTER 5

Learning Theory and Teaching

For decades now a tremendous gap has existed between the laboratory, in which *learning* was studied and principles verified, and the classroom. Some learning psychologists have been extremely critical of classroom teachers for what they perceived as the teacher's ignorance regarding principles of learning. Conversely, the teacher has been critical of the learning psychologist for dealing with learning at the infrahuman level and in contrived laboratory settings because results were often inapplicable to the relatively uncontrolled classroom (experimentally speaking) with human subjects. Attempts to bridge this gap, such as courses in educational psychology, have been ineffective if one listens to the evaluations of teachers who frequently describe such courses as irrelevant or of little help to them in their teaching.

During the past decade a new breed of learning psychologist has emerged, variously described as applied psychologist, behavioral engineer, or behavior modifier, who attempt to bridge this gap. They use more natural environments as their laboratories (such as classrooms) and have attempted to ascertain which principles uncovered in laboratory settings are applicable to the classroom. Furthermore, they have translated principles of learning into classroom practice. In the process they have relied heavily on laboratory findings and have controlled experimental variables as tightly as possible while being, at the same time, sensitive to the "real world" of the classroom teacher.

As noted by Forness (1970), the behavioristic approach has been most widely applied to exceptional children in special educational settings. Yet behavior problems and inefficient learning are not the exclusive domain of special education—as any regular class teacher can testify. This same observation was made by Fargo *et al.* (1970), who described the early research in dealing with classroom settings and children who were atypical. Classes were usually 6 to 9 children in number—a pupil/teacher ratio which is unheard of in public schools—with consultative services from university personnel and high budgets allowing for extensive equipment and incentives. Hence a far greater degree of control was possible which was unlike the control possible in a public school classroom. In addition, the learning tasks required were usually very simple compared to learning complex abstract material more common in the regular class, making generalizations hazardous. Gradually, the interventions tested by behavioral engineers have been more and more applicable in public schools by teachers without extensive resources.

Part I of this book summarizes the principles of learning judged to be necessarily understood by the teacher desiring to make use of operant techniques. By itself, Part I is not unlike many books of learning read by teachers previously; however, in Part II an attempt is made to show how various individuals have seen fit to translate the principles of Part I into practice in three rather distinct types of classes: special education classes, regular elementary level classes, and secondary level classes. Some techniques or reinforcers may be appropriate across all categories, whereas others will be useful with only one of these groups. Throughout Part II reference will be made to the principle of learning (from Part I) exemplified by a given practice. The reader should keep in mind that what is presented herein is a chronicle of what has been done rather than what can be done. As long as a practice is consistent with the principles of learning it is fair game, and an infinite number of practices presumably could be generated—limited only by the creativity of those involved.

WHAT'S NEW ABOUT BEHAVIOR MODIFICATION?

In describing operant conditioning to teachers and stressing how positive reinforcement, punishment, and sequencing steps to learning operate, one is commonly met with responses like, "What's so new about that?" Hewett (1968, p. 30) told of one teacher's response to such a presentation: "Why, you aren't talking about animal conditioning at all. You're just describing good teaching." Admittedly, the modification of children's behavior did not begin with Skinner, and teachers praised children for desired behavior and punished behavior judged to be inappropriate (see Chapter 1) long before operant conditioning was in the jargon of teachers. Then, what does learning theory have to offer teachers and in what ways can they make use of it?

I see the contributions stemming from behaviorism as several in number and being in several areas. First, it tends to be positive in nature, which seems quite the opposite from the inclination of many, if not most, parents and/or teachers in dealing with children. Desirable behavior emitted by children seems to be viewed by adults as "what comes naturally" and undesirable behavior as what they (adults) have to deal with. Hence, in a class of 30 children, which children get the majority of the teacher's time and attention? The class hellion. In other words, it pays to misbehave and it doesn't pay to "be good," assuming that teacher attention is a positive reinforcer. Learning theory tells us that good behavior too has to be reinforced or it will extinguish. In short, the foregoing can be summarized by the lyrics "accentuate the positive."

Related to the above, the descriptive research on teachers' use of operant principles indicates that teachers do use them, but typically they are used in an unsystematic fashion. Therefore, what is new is the emphasis on being *systematic*. In describing the situation in which teachers use reinforcement unsystematically, Forness (1970, p. 357) wrote: "The misfortune of children and teachers alike is that these reinforcements are seldom used systematically, and their effectiveness is thereby missing or considerably diminished." For example, in some cases it is found that teachers inadvertently are teaching children to misbehave by attending to misbehavior and failing to attend to desired behavior. In this context the behaviorists have sensitized teachers to the need for dispensing positive reinforcement *contingent* on desired behavior.

Third, as a by-product of the many studies conducted in classrooms a wealth of information has accumulated regarding incentives. In some cases, studies have demonstrated that certain reinforcing stimuli (e.g., teacher attention with young children) is a far more potent reinforcer than previously thought, and if used systematically can be a useful incentive. Furthermore, it has been shown that some events, assumed to be punishment, actually serve as positive reinforcers (e.g., "sit down" commands). Finally, research has questioned assumptions underlying the use of universal incentives (e.g., grades) because they are ineffective in certain cases, and at the same time extended the knowledge of other stimuli in the classroom which can serve as reinforcers if used contingent on completion of some specified amount of a task (artwork, free time, interest centers).

Another change that has accompanied the creation of behavioral programs has been the change in emphasis from the collection of classificatory data (IQ, achievement tests, projective tests) that had been used to classify individuals into diagnostic categories to the collection of specific behavioral summaries of strengths and deficits. Collection of the latter type of data is more directly related to the educational needs of a child and precludes the need for a label being attached to the child—teachers can focus on the deficits of a given child rather than the label or category into which a child is placed. Through the contingent use of a variety of reinforcers children heretofore considered unreachables were suddenly learning things thought to be beyond them—particularly in cases of severely retarded children and autistics. Such successes have resulted in reconceptualizing the nature of mental retardation (see Bijou, 1966) and thinking that if children do not learn something it is a teaching failure rather than a child failure. Whereas in the past one could "explain" that lack of learning was due to the child's deficit ("After all he is mentally retarded"), now one can cite Skinner's teaching pigeons to play ping-pong or Ferster's teaching a chimpanzee to do geometry. Now it becomes a problem of sequencing activities in small increments and giving effective reinforcers contingent on successful performance so that the child learns a given task. In other words, an absence of learning is seen as a teaching failure rather than a child failure.

Schwitzgebel (1970) made an interesting distinction between *teaching* and *holding students responsible for learning*. He went on to say that many programs purported to improve instruction are actually devices for holding students responsible for more learning. At the university, we typically hold students responsible for learning twice in an academic quarter. In elementary school, the teacher may give a weekly list of spelling words on which the children are tested on Friday. In essence, we tell students to learn these materials as best they can, but we do not proceed to provide mechanisms for improving instruction. Learning theory, however, has contributed to the field of instruction. As long as 45 years ago Sidney Pressey (1926) reported on the improvement of learning by students when they are informed immediately that their answers are right or wrong. Teaching machines and programmed instruction have incorporated learning principles in a rather pure manner. In a similar vein, Skinner (1971, p. 38) wrote:

The application of operant conditioning to education is simple and direct. Teaching is the arrangement of contingencies of reinforcement under which students learn. They learn without teaching in their natural environments, but teachers arrange special contingencies which expedite learning, hastening the appearance of behavior which would otherwise be acquired slowly or making sure of the appearance of behavior which might otherwise never occur.

A teaching machine, according to Skinner, is simply a device that arranges contingencies of reinforcement. Skinner (1971) specified four cases of arranging contingencies which are applicable to the classroom situation:

1. Shaping, wherein new behavior is developed by reinforcing closer and closer approximations to the goal behavior.
2. Altering temporal or intensive properties of behavior, by programming gradual increments in level of performance.
3. Forming finer discriminations by bringing behavior under control of discriminative stimuli through errorless learning, or prompting.
4. Altering schedules of reinforcement supporting behavior to schedules which are more resistant to extinction (e.g., VR, VI).

Finally, the behavioristic viewpoint provides teachers with a reliable method for analyzing behavior. According to Haring and Lovitt (1967), the teacher's focus is on the child's responses, a specific description of these responses, and the effects of these responses on the child's environment (consequences or reinforcers). In Chapter 1, three frames of reference were described in which teachers might conceptualize behavior judged deviant. Should a given teacher move from one to another in order to analyze the behavior of different children, confusion and inconsistent teacher behavior is likely to result.

THE TEACHER AS A BEHAVIOR ANALYST

Birnbrauer *et al.* (1970; 1971, p. 22) described behavior analysis as consisting of a precise definition of the behavior

LEARNING THEORY AND TEACHING

which is recorded at frequent intervals in a reliable manner. Furthermore, the conditions under which behavior is recorded are standardized and controlled; when changed to bring about changes in the behavior such change is done systematically. These authors characterize this process as being composed of four operations: selection and definition of behavior, measurement of behavior, recording environmental intervention. These operations correspond very closely to the three questions posed by Ullmann and Krasner (1965) for an analyzing behavior judged to be inappropriate (see p. 9 of the present book). By combining elements of behavioral analysis, as described by the foregoing authors and others (e.g., MacMillan, 1970; Lindsley, 1964), the following operations are recommended to the teacher undertaking to analyze behavior:

1. Select the specific behavior to be modified (target behavior).
2. State the goal behavior toward which the target behavior will be modified.
3. Record frequency with which the target behavior occurs.
4. Identify and record antecedent events that may exert stimulus control, as a discriminative stimulus, over the target behavior.
5. Identify and record environmental events following the target behavior that might be reinforcing it.
6. Plan and implement the intervention program,* and record evidence of target behavior during the intervention period.
7. Withdraw intervention procedures or reverse contingencies.

Following is a more detailed discussion of these seven operations.

---

* The interventions possible are numerous and will be described in detail in the following three chapters.

Selection of Target Behavior

In the selection of behavior which you, as a teacher, judge to be inappropriate, ethical questions immediately arise. Behavior modification, as such, provides no guidelines to the teacher in the determination of what constitutes "good" or "bad," "appropriate" or "inappropriate," "adaptive" or "maladaptive" behavior. Hence you must rely on other frames of references for standards against which such judgments can be made. In some cases, the decision is made for you by the larger society (e.g., being able to read is good); however, in other instances (e.g., dialect in speech), there is no definitive guide. For a discussion of ethical considerations, the interested reader is referred to the article by Kelman (1965).

Some direction in selecting target behaviors is provided to the teacher by Birnbrauer *et al.* (1970), who specified the two concerns the behaviorist should have: (1) Will modification of the behavior enable the individual to adapt more effectively to his environment? and (2) How can the occurrence of the behavior be recorded reliably? These concerns are qualified only by the requirement that behavior modification conform to social standards and that it will lead to greater self-sufficiency. An additional caution was noted by MacMillan (1970): specifically, that the teacher be certain that the target behavior is detrimental to the child's learning or well-being, and not simply something that is annoying to the teacher.

In describing the target behavior, the rule of thumb is the more precise and explicit the description, the better. Haring and Lovitt (1967) stated that indirect interpretations of behavior do not suffice for a behavioral program. For example, "hostile," "acting out," "highly anxious," "immature" and "hyperactive," although related to behavior, are not specific enough to enable objective recording of occurrences of the behavior. Rather, descriptions of behavior should be precise enough so that a high degree of agreement (reliability) would be found among several observers of the behavior. Examples of this are "hitting," "out of seat," "talking out of turn," "enters the room after the tardy bell." The specificity desired, and the emphasis on behavior, rather than interpretations of behavior, are very similar to the format for stating behavioral objectives in the curriculum area (Mager, 1962). Buckley and Walker (1970) recommended that teachers, describing *what* the child is doing, avoid implying motives or feelings from behavior, and not try to find causes for the behavior. Instead, the teacher should specify dimensions of a behavioral category specifically enough that when a child emits a behavior the teacher can easily and quickly decide whether it falls within, or outside, that category. Categories, such as those described by Buckley and Walker (1970), enable one to focus on several behaviors that are closely related (e.g., nonattending, being unprepared to work, deliberate disruptive noises).

As a further point regarding the selection of the target behavior, MacMillan (1968) recommended that the teacher focus on the one behavior, or category of behaviors, which is *most* disruptive to the child. Temporarily ignore the child's behaviors that are judged maladaptive, but are less disruptive. Frequently a teacher will describe a particular child as "always misbehaving," and when the teacher tries to consider ten behaviors simultaneously there is not sufficient focus on any one behavior to bring about change. Furthermore, we have found that the reinforcers supporting the target behavior (e.g., teacher attention) may also be supporting several other, less serious, behaviors. As a result, by altering the target behavior through reversing contingencies for teacher attention, the other behaviors supported by the same incentive are modified in the process.

Selection of Goal Behavior

The second step is to describe behaviorally the goal (or nature of the behavior when the child's behavior is adaptive) toward which the teacher is working. Again, the teacher must be careful to describe the goal behavior precisely so that it can be determined easily and reliably when the child has achieved that level. Hence, "well-behaved," "model student," and "unaggressive" are too vague. Instead, goals like "Will wait to speak out until recognized," "Leaves his seat only with teacher permission," or "Is not tardy" enable the teacher to make quick, reliable judgments. When a goal behavior is a long-range one, more immediate subgoals may be necessary; however, the teacher must be careful not to lose sight of the long-range goal behavior in the process of achieving intermediate subgoals.

Allyon and Azrin (1968) provided some direction in the selection of terminal, or goal, behavior that should be helpful to teachers, which the authors term the "relevance of behavior rule." They suggested that one teach only those behaviors that will continue to be reinforced after the intervention program is discontinued; that is, the behaviors taught should be useful or relevant in subsequent activities and supported by natural (as opposed to arbitrary) contingencies. Otherwise, the behavior developed will require a special program to be maintained or it will extinguish. These authors concluded that unless this rule is followed, generalization and transfer will not occur. Lack of transfer has been a major source of discouragement for teachers, and it may well be that much of what is taught in contrived settings has little relevance for more natural settings.

Birnbrauer *et al.* (1970) extended the "relevance of behavior rule" to suggest that one teach behaviors that increase the child's opportunities to learn more. For example, it is probably more useful to the child to have an increased sight vocabulary initially than to memorize transformational rules of grammar. These same authors offered two steps in selecting goals: (1) Study the environments for which the children are being prepared, and (2) observe current behavior to determine the individual's strengths and deficits in the light of those environments. For the elementary teacher the subsequent environment might be upper grades or junior high; for the special class teacher it might be the regular elementary class; and for the secondary teacher it might be a particular occupational setting or college.

Recording Target Behavior

The third step in behavior analysis is to determine the frequency with which the target behavior occurs. Buckley and Walker (1970, p. 71) stated that, "Before we can ask *why* a child is behaving as he is, we need to ask *what* he is doing and *how often* the behavior occurs." In the interests of precision, a statement like "He was out of his seat without permission six times in a 60-minute period" is far more precise than "He gets out of his seat frequently."

The need for frequency counts cannot be overemphasized. Scientists have found that one's estimates of the frequency of occurrence of behavior are very poor. Without assessment of behavior before, during, and after a particular intervention one cannot assess the effects of the intervention. To quote Birnbrauer *et al.* (1970, p. 31), "How else can nonfunctional and harmful teaching and therapeutic practices be discarded and replaced by more effective ones? It is not progress to use new techniques without evaluating them." It should be added that teachers themselves need reinforcement (in addition to their salaries), and one kind of reinforcement important to most teachers is evidence that their attempts to teach something are resulting in changes in behavior. However, in a situation where a child's out-of-seat behavior reduces from 20 times in 60 minutes to 16 times in the same time, and the teacher relies on subjective impressions of whether improvement has occurred, she is likely to "sense" no progress and her own behavior might extinguish. Conversely, with a frequency count, she can see some progress or improvement which would go undetected without the precision.

Forness (1970) contended that "charting" of behavioral data is of particular value to teachers and psychologists, in which one records the frequency of the occurrence of particular data in a given period of time to establish an estimate of their frequency. Charting requires only clerical skills on the part of the teacher or observer, particularly when the target behavior is clearly defined. The teacher simply records whenever the child exhibits the target behavior such as completes his homework, brings pencil and paper to class, speaks out of turn, hits other children, throws a temper tantrum, completes an assignment. Always, this should be done in terms of some unit of time such as a 20-minute period, an hour, or the school day. Variations have been devised in which the child himself records the time unit, records his own behavior, or that of another child, thus reducing the time required of the teacher. For a more detailed description of charting and quantification, the interested reader is referred to Schaefer and Martin (1969) or Bijou, Peterson, and Ault (1968).

A common response from teachers when they hear about recording of behavior goes something like this, "Sure it would be great, but I've got 35 children to teach and I can't spend that much time recording behavior of one child." One solution to the foregoing problem is to secure the help of an observer. Certain personnel in the school would be ideal, but in most cases too involved, such as school psychologists, counselors, and supervisory personnel. In other instances, PTA volunteers, with some pretraining, could serve in this capacity, as could college and high school students or teacher's aides. Buckley and Walker (1970) suggested that, in such instances, the teacher herself can keep track of behaviors occurring fewer than 20 times a day on a *continuous* basis, and where the frequency is much higher (say, 150 times a day) resort to *time sampling*. Time sampling refers to recording behavior at certain times in the day (e.g., 10:00 to 10:30 A.M.) rather than continuously. The unit of time required would vary, depending on the specific behavior.

The most common unit recorded is *rate* (number of occurrences/time). However, certain behaviors, such as being out of his seat, independent reading, attending to assignments, or being tardy, do not lend themselves to a rate count. In these cases,

LEARNING THEORY AND TEACHING

duration or length of time the child is engaged in the behavior is a more useful unit of measurement. The duration is the period of time during which each separate instance of the particular behavior occurs.

Transferring the raw data (recordings of rate or duration) to graph form facilitates reading. The two most common graphs used for this purpose are the histogram (bar graph) and the polygon (line graph). Typically, the vertical axis represents the rate or duration of the behavior, and the horizontal axis represents the observation periods. Figure 5.1 shows a histogram representation of fictitious data on out-of-seat behavior of one child for one week. Figure 5.2 shows the same set of data on a polygon graph.

The recording of behavior prior to the implementation of the intervention constitutes what is called *baseline* data. These data will serve as the standard against which the effectiveness of the intervention can be determined. Recording and charting continue, however, through the intervention program period and then to the reversal period, which will be discussed later in this chapter.

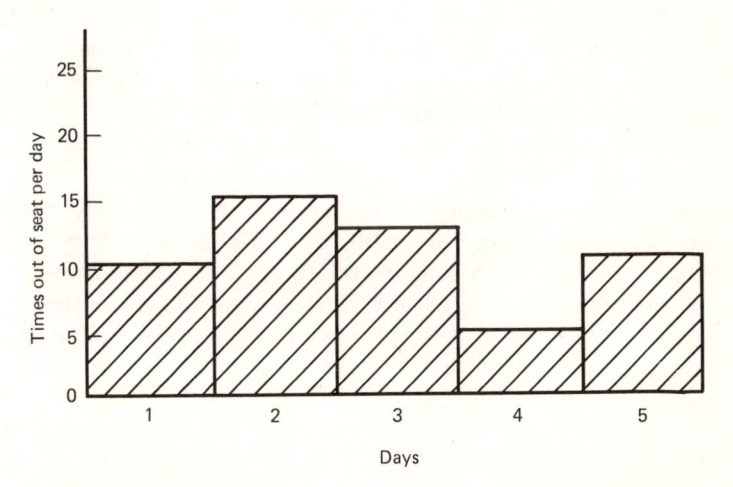

Figure 5.1. *Charting of out-of-seat behavior over a five-day period as a histogram.*

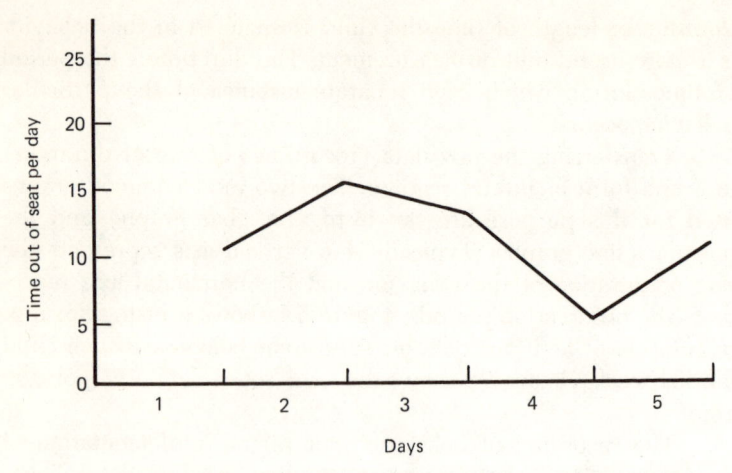

[Figure: line graph showing time out of seat per day (y-axis, 0-25) over Days 1-5 (x-axis), with values approximately 11, 15, 13, 6, 11]

Figure 5.2. *Charting of out-of-seat behavior over a five-day period as a polygon graph.*

Identification and Recording of Antecedents

In certain cases one finds various examples of misbehavior occurring at rather high rates under certain situations, while being virtually nonexistent at all other times. For example, some children begin to "fall apart" just before recess, lunch, or the end of the school day; others seem to have trouble settling down after recess, PE, or lunch when they have been physically active. In other cases, maladaptive behavior occurs only during certain subject matter periods. In such a case, a child who is poor in math begins talking out loud or hitting other children and as a result gets sent to the office and thereby avoids demonstrating his inability in math (misbehavior is negatively reinforced). Others may misbehave when competition is brought into activities (MacMillan, 1968).

Forness (1970) noted that after it is determined *how often* a behavior is emitted, it becomes helpful to know *when*, or under what circumstances, the target behavior increases in probability. Does it occur when a particular girl is likely to notice him, or when the teacher is close or far away from him? If the teacher can note such things anecdotally it may provide clues to when interventions are needed. Furthermore, Forness (1970) suggested a means of accounting for this in the charting process. The chart could be divided into squares representing activities in the day, or 15- or 30-minute time segments. By seeing when the behavior occurs most frequently the teacher can be attentive to various antecedents that might exert stimulus control over the behavior in the form of a discriminative stimulus. By piecing together charts of several days, certain trends may emerge which enable the teacher to focus his efforts, since the target behaviors become limited to certain parameters.

Identification and Recording of Consequences

As was noted repeatedly throughout Part I of this book, behavior that is persistent is being supported by some payoff in the environment. In more technical terms, for any persistent behavior there is a positive or negative reinforcer that is maintaining it. It is worth reiterating here that most behavior in the natural setting is reinforced on some intermittent schedule of reinforcement, rather than on a continuous schedule. This has two side effects, both of which make the teacher's task more difficult. First, the behavior will be more resistant to extinction than would be true if it were reinforced on a continuous schedule. Second, it means that the teacher, by observing what happens after each occurrence of the target behavior, may not see the reinforcing stimulus being presented (or the aversive stimulus being terminated if negative reinforcement is operating).

At this point in the process, one can only make an educated guess about the consequence supporting the behavior based on observation and recording. However, several common sources of "payoffs" for maladaptive behavior in classrooms have cropped up so frequently in the literature that they might be good points for beginning. For openers there is *teacher attention,* which is often given contingent on misbehavior. Think for a moment about the children in your present, or past, class whom you spent most of your time talking to or waiting for. It is usually the children who are moderate to severe behavior problems. The child is told to be quiet, to get to work, to please sit down, etc. As the teacher you *assume* you are punishing him, but in fact you are positively reinforcing him, or teaching him to misbehave. Another common source for reinforcement of misbehavior is peer attention and approval. When classmates laugh at a child's antics it makes any mild punishment worthwhile. A third one is the avoidance of having to perform tasks which, for some reason, are seen as aversive. Hence when the child is sent to the office just before an exam for which he is unprepared or an oral book report which he dreads giving, the teacher is doing exactly what he wants. The list of possible payoffs would be of infinite length, but these three types of payoffs reoccur so often in the literature that they warrant particular attention.

In identifying what appears to be the reinforcement for misbehavior, the teacher is in the position of testing an hypothesis—which is all it is at this time. During the subsequent intervention period the teacher will be careful to alter the contingencies between the target behavior and the hypothesized reinforcer (e.g., when the child emits the target behavior the teacher now ignores it). The acid test comes when the teacher observes the decrease in target behavior which indicates support for the hypothesis. Conversely, if there is no change in the rate of target behavior, the teacher has apparently hypothesized incorrectly and begins again looking for other possible payoffs.

Intervention Program

Once the teacher has specified the target behavior, goal behavior, taken a baseline count of the target behavoir, and noted antecedent and consequent events which might affect the target behavior, he is ready to initiate the intervention program. Such a program is designed to modify maladaptive behavior (either increase or decrease) toward the goal behavior specified. The only limitation placed on the nature of this program is that it be consistent with principles of learning outlined in Part I of this book. The translations of these principles into practice are limited only by the ingenuity of those making these translations.

In the following three chapters a detailed account will be given of how various individuals have seen fit to design interventions consistent with operant principles of learning, so no detailed recommendations will be presented at this time. Some of the principles used rather frequently to guide interventions are listed below:

1. To weaken behavior
   a. Extinction (sometimes combined with countercondiing)
   b. Punishment—in the form of removal of positive reinforcer
   c. Satiation
   d. Counterconditioning incompatible behavior
   e. Desensitization
2. To strengthen behavior
   a. Positive reinforcement—tokens, tangible social reinforcement, activities
   b. Negative reinforcement
3. To develop new behavior
   a. Shaping
   b. Prompting and fading
   c. Modeling

The manner in which these principles have been used will be discussed in detail in the following three chapters.

As noted before, throughout the intervention period, the recording and charting of target behavior continue. Do not look for an immediate turn about in the behavior. It took the class hellion years to learn to behave in this manner and it is going to take some time for him to unlearn it or to learn an incompatible behavior—*so do not discard the intervention after one or two days*. Furthermore, follow the planned intervention to the letter, since a few breakdowns on your part may provide intermittent reinforcement for the behavior (if teacher attention is the positive reinforcer) making the behavior even more resistant to extinction.

Reversal of Contingencies

Finally, the teacher may observe some decline in the incidence of target behavior and nevertheless not be convinced that the technique chosen to decrease the behavior is functionally related to the behavioral change. That is to say, other things are happening to the child outside the school setting which may be what accounts for the changes observed (Haring and Lovitt, 1967; Buckley and Walker, 1970). If the change was due to the contingencies operative during the intervention, the target behavior should return to its baseline level when the contingencies are reversed. For example, assume that it was thought that teacher attention was the reinforcement for out-of-seat behavior. A baseline was collected and the intervention called for the teacher to ignore out-of-seat behavior. After a week the out-of-seat behavior declined markedly, so the teacher reversed the contingencies in order to determine whether the relationship between teacher attention and out-of-seat behavior was a causal one (that is, she attended to out-of-seat and ignored in-seat behavior). If the relationship was a causal one the polygon graph in Figure 5.3 might be what the plotting would look like. Had a causal relationship not existed between teacher attention and out-of-seat behavior the line would not have progressed upward during the reversal period. Sometimes, even when a causal relationship might have existed, a marked change does not occur during reversal—possibly because other reinforcers (peer ap-

LEARNING THEORY AND TEACHING

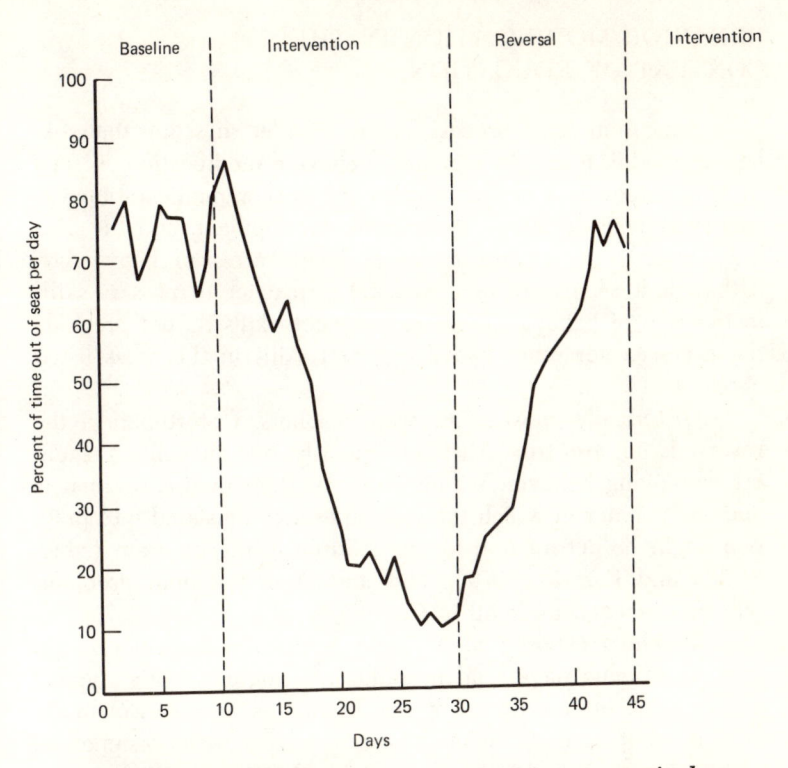

Figure 5.3. *Out-of-seat behavior of one child during an entire behavior modification program.*

proval, obtaining better grades) are dispensed for other behavior accompanying the staying in seat behavior.

At first one may feel overwhelmed by the detail and work that go into the process of behavior analysis. However, those teachers trained in operant conditioning and who have employed it in their classrooms are pleased with the results. As Birnbrauer et al. (1970) suggested, the best way to learn how to perform the analysis of behavior is to perform one with a child in your class exhibiting behavior that is interfering with his academic or social growth.

BEHAVIOR MODIFICATION IN THE CONTEXT OF EDUCATION

Education, as a process, is far broader in scope than behavior modification. As a result, behavior modification is seen by this author as a useful *supplement* to therapeutic rationales, curricular considerations, theories of development, and the like; but certainly not a *substitution* for these areas of knowledge. Although it seems advantageous for a teacher to possess skills in the area of behavior modification, such skills do not preclude the necessity for other knowledge and skills in the areas listed above.

Historically, most saints were teachers. Unfortunately, the reverse is not also true. All too frequently, one encounters teachers employing behavior modification for their own convenience, and the manner in which the principles are translated into practice might be detrimental to the children in the program (MacMillan and Forness, 1970). This and other potential problems will be discussed in detail in Chapter 8.

Teachers exposed to a single lecture on behavior modification, or who have read accounts of programs with atypical children, are often seduced by the "trappings" of behavior modification; that is, early behavioristic programs were designed to effect change in subjects who deviated quite markedly from what might be considered normal, which, in turn, necessitated the use of low-level incentives such as food, tokens, and check marks. Although these incentives were necessary to reach the children in the early programs (e.g., trainable mentally retarded in the Birnbrauer and Lawler, 1964, study), they are not recommended for average achieving sixth-grade classes. Yet one can find cases where a program like the Hewett (1968) engineered classroom is adopted lock, stock, and barrel for a class of children who are not in need of the kind of help that is needed by emotionally disturbed and learning disabled children, for whom the rationale was developed. The point that needs emphasis is that the nature of the program, and the practices derived from principles of learning, must be consistent with the characteristics of the children who will be affected by it. Hence chronological age, motivational characteristics, sex, mental age, and socialization patterns are all critical parameters in determining the appropriateness of a given practice.

Another explanation for the uncritical acceptance of "packaged programs" may lie in confusing a research design with recommended practice (MacMillan and Forness, in press). In many of the behavior modification programs reported in the literature, the experimental treatments often consisted of *all* children getting tokens or check marks at given intervals. What seems to be ignored or misinterpreted by those reading these accounts is that the tokens or check marks serve as a data collection device or a system of accountability. The authors are not recommending that, in practice, every child be put on a token economy. This type of confusion was vividly shown me in a course I teach on behavior modification for teachers. On the last day of class one woman stated: "I can see no way in which I can use the principles of learning in my class, since token economy is beneath my students." To her a token economy and principles of learning were synonymous—and I failed in teaching.

For the teacher mentioned above, and for that matter any teacher or parent, the choice is not between using and not using principles of learning when dealing with other human beings. The choice is between using the principles systematically or unsystematically. As noted in the introduction to this chapter, teachers and parents have used rewards and punishments since time immemorial—what is new is the *emphasis on contingency management*. More specifically, one should be more sensitive to the relationship between the consequences (rewards and punishments) and the behavior they follow. For years we have given rewards (attention, presents, food, activities) to children but usually on an unsystematic basis. We give presents to children (at birthdays and Christmas) when the calendar indicates the time is right, regardless of the behavior of the child; we give food when the clock (mealtime) indicates the time is right. While this writer does not wish to abolish gift giving or feeding, the relationship between these positive consequences and behavior is unsystematic. In everyday interactions with other adults, we constantly shape behavior. For example, we each have acquaintances with whom we do not discuss certain topics (e.g., religion and politics) because attempts to do so in the past have resulted in no response (they are trying to extinguish your registration and voting behavior) or a punishment (they question your intellect for voting for a particular candidate or party). Since we have no choice but to use principles of learning, it is advantageous to use them systematically.

The key to the systematic use of these principles is contingency management. Homme (1970) described this relationship as following Grandma's Law, "First clean up your plate, then you may have your dessert." Becker, Engelmann, and Thomas (1971, p. 28) extended Grandma's Law to state that "You do what I want you to do, before you get to do what you want to do." The point is that the reinforcer (be it candy, tokens, a desired activity, teacher attention) is contingent on the desired behavior. The specifications of the contingency determine when, and only when, the reinforcer will be forthcoming. If the child performs the desired behavior, he gets paid off; if he does not perform there is no payoff. Here is where behavior modification differs from bribery. When a bribe is given, the payoff is given first and then you pray the child will live up to his part of the bargain—the child is in control. An example of bribery would be when a teacher tells the class, "You may continue your art activities if you promise to work hard on math, which will follow." In behavior modification, the child must finish what you want done, and then he is permitted to perform the desired activity—the teacher is in control. For example, the teacher might schedule math before art and tell the class, "If you finish your math assignments early you can spend the time saved on your art activities."

One source of problem behavior in classrooms may lie in

the failure on the teacher's part to specify the contingencies operating. This writer observed in a fourth-grade class wherein two boys were sitting side by side right in front of the teacher's desk. When they came in from recess and were seated, the first boy proceeded to punch the second boy on the arm. The teacher gave him a kind of sickly grin which did not communicate anything clearly. It might have been interpreted as "Stop that, I won't permit it," or it could have meant, "Why don't you hit him harder, he's been a problem right along." So the first child looked at the teacher and again hit the second boy, and got the same sickly grin. This again happened, and the teacher sent the first boy to the office. Had the teacher immediately specified the rules of the game, the hitting behavior might have stopped there.

Hewett (1968) described the contingencies operating in classroom assignments as: *what, when, where, how, how much,* and *how well*. Therefore, when a teacher says "John come read to me," there are implicit parameters such as (1) he will read, (2) he will read in a minute or so, not after lunch, (3) he will read at the teacher's desk, (4) he will read aloud, and (5) he will read one paragraph with fewer than two unrecognized words or with 80 percent comprehension or better on a series of questions pertaining to the passage read. In making assignments, the clearer the contingencies are the less likely one will encounter maladaptive behavior resulting from confusion or misunderstanding of the rules of the game. One study illustrated this point graphically with regard to school regulations. Lahaderne (1971) found that the most common manner in which children learn the school regulations is by coming in conflict with them; that is, a child learns he cannot go down a particular stairway when he is "caught" going down it. Had teachers explained the rules beforehand, the child could avoid sanctions stemming from his "rule breaking" by following the rules, whereas when rules are not clarified, he unwittingly comes into conflict with them.

One final point regarding the role of behavior modification in education relates to the search by some teachers for a panacea that will solve all teaching problems once and for all. In so doing, they ask for a system which can be employed in their classroom of 12 to 35 children and which works for them all. If they are asking for one reward, one task, and one contingency, the problem cannot be solved by behaviorists. The essence of behaviorism is that what reinforces one child may not work for another, what is an appropriate task for one child is inappropriate for another—in other words, *individuality*. MacMillan (1970) noted that in the earlier works of applying principles of learning by clinical psychologists, nurses, psychiatrists, and educators the researchers contacted subjects on a one-to-one basis. In the process, the appropriate task, contingency, and reinforcer were determined on an individual basis. Conversely, the classroom teacher must abstract principles found useful on the one-to-one basis and apply them in the context of the classroom. The principles will apply across all children; however, the number of math problems, the difficulty level of the math problems, and the reinforcer to strengthen the behavior must vary from child to child. In conclusion, the axiom that "all behavior is learned" must not be interpreted to mean that "all children learn alike."

REFERENCES

Ayllou, T., and Azrin, N. H. *The Token Economy: A Motivational System for Therapy and Rehabilitation.* New York: Appleton-Century-Crofts, 1968.

Becker, W. C., Engelmann, S., and Thomas, D. R. *Teaching: A Course in Applied Psychology.* Chicago: Science Research Associates, Inc., 1971.

Bijou, S. W. A functional analysis of retarded development. In Ellis, N. R. (ed.) *International Review of Research in Mental Retardation*, Vol. I. New York: Academic Press, Inc., 1966.

──── Peterson, R. F., and Ault, M. H. A method to integrate descriptive and experimental field studies at the level of data and empirical concepts. *J. Appl. Behav. Anal.*, 1:1975–91, 1968.

Birnbrauer, J. S., Burchard, J. D., and Burchard, S. N. Wanted: Behavior analysts. In R. H. Bradfield (ed.) *Behavior Modification.* San Rafael, Calif.: Dimensions Publishing Co., 1971.

Buckley, N. D., and Walker, H. M. *Modifying Classroom Behavior.* Champaign, Ill.: Research Press Co., 1970.

Fargo, G. A., Behrns, C., and Nolan, P. (eds.) *Behavior Modification in the Classroom.* Belmont, Calif.: Wadsworth Publishing Co., Inc., 1970.

Forness, S. R. Behavioristic approach to classroom management and motivation. *Psychol. Schools,* 7:356–63, 1970.

Haring, N. G., and Lovitt, T. C. Operant methodology and educational technology in special education. In N. G. Haring and R. L. Schiefelbusch (eds.) *Methods in Special Education.* New York: McGraw-Hill Book Company, 1967.

Hewett, F. M. *The Emotionally Disturbed Child in the Classroom.* Boston: Allyn & Bacon, Inc., 1968.

Homme, L. *How to Use Contingency Contracting in the Classroom.* Champaign, Ill.: Research Press Co., 1970.

Kelman, H. C. Manipulation of human behavior: An ethical dilemma for the social scientist. *J. Soc. Issues,* 21:31–46, 1965.

Lahaderne, H. M. School conduct: An exploration of the way rules and regulations operate in elementary schools. Unpublished paper. Los Angeles, Calif.: Institute for the Development of Educational Activities, Inc., 1971.

Lindsley, O. R. Direct measurement and prosthesis of retarded behavior. *J. Educ.,* 147:62–81, 1964.

MacMillan, D. L. Behavior modification: A teacher strategy to control behavior. *In Report of the Proceedings of the Forty-fourth Meeting of the Convention of American Instructors of the Deaf.* Berkeley, Calif.: 1968.

MacMillan, D. L. Ground rules for behavior modification. Paper read at the Annual Meeting of the American Association on Mental Deficiency, Washington, D.C., May 7, 1970.

MacMillan, D. L., and Forness, S. R. Behavior modification: Limitations and liabilities. *Except. Child.,* 1970, 37, 291–297.

MacMillan, D. L., and Forness, S. R. Behavior modification: Savior or savant? In R. K. Eyman and C. E. Meyers (eds.). In press.

Mager, R. F. *Preparing Instructional Objectives.* Palo Alto, Calif.: Fearon Publishers, 1962.

Pressey, S. J. A simple apparatus which gives tests and scores—and teaches. *School Soc.,* 23:373–76, 1926.

Schaefer, P., and Martin, P. (eds.) *Behavior Theory.* New York: McGraw-Hill Book Company, 1969.

Schwitzgebel, R. Behavior modification: Past, present and future. In

R. H. Bradfield (ed.) *Behavior Modification*. San Rafael, Calif.: Dimensions Publishing Co., 1970.

Skinner, B. F. The technology of teaching. In C. E. Pitts (ed.) *Operant Conditioning in the Classroom*. New York: Thomas Y. Crowell Company, 1971.

Ullmann, L. P., and Krasner, L. *Case Studies in Behavior Modification*. New York: Holt, Rinehart and Winston, Inc., 1965.

CHAPTER 6

Behavior Modification in the Special Class: A Token Economy

THE EARLIEST, and by far the most frequent, application of learning principles to education occurred in special self-contained classes for exceptional children such as the mentally retarded and emotionally disturbed. Traditional special educational approaches have assigned children to diagnostic categories (e.g., educable mentally retarded [EMR], trainable mentally retarded [TMR], emotionally disturbed), labeled the children, and utilized techniques considered appropriate for the group of children variously labeled. Recently, concern has been expressed that labels and categories serve as self-fulfilling prophecies and that children given deficit labels behave differently as a result of being labeled, and are treated differently by those coming into contact with them once they are labeled. Furthermore, others fear that deficit labels enable teachers to "explain" a lack of progress in terms of the label—"After all, he is mentally retarded." The behaviorists have argued that the reasons for learning failures are far more complex than the categorical labels imply (Fargo *et al.*, 1970). Rather than a "defective child" approach, behaviorists look to the child as being a casualty of an environment that was not adequately arranged to enable the child to learn, that is to say, the rewards offered were not meaningful to the child, the tasks were not appropriate, or the contingencies were not appropriately arranged. Therefore, Lindsley (1964) and others have called for a "prosthetic environment" adapted to the learning needs of particular children.

The behavioristic orientation plays down categorical affiliation (e.g., EMR), since such affiliations are based on diagnostic data such as IQ, projective test performance, and psychological indices of "neurological impairment." Instead, emphasis is placed on precise descriptions of behavior that can be observed and measured. Therefore, while article titles may imply a program or technique for use with EMR or emotionally disturbed children, the focus of the program is on the alteration of specific behaviors manifested by the children in that class rather than on a categorical affiliation of children. It would be consistent with this approach to group children, for educational purposes, on the basis of the behaviors they need modified (or treatment) rather than on the basis, currently operative, of presumed *cause*. The present grouping procedure is analogous to grouping cases of broken legs in wards according to how the leg was broken—in Ward A are those who broke their legs skiing, in Ward B are those who broke their legs falling off barstools, etc. A test for mixing diagnostic categories in schools is presently being run by Hewett (1970) in the "Madison Plan" wherein EMR, learning disability, emotionally disturbed, deaf, and blind children are all in a single engineered classroom. The preliminary results of this venture look promising.

The literature abounds with investigations which alter the behavior of one child in a classroom (see Ullmann and Krasner, 1965; Krasner and Ullmann, 1965; *Journal of Applied Behavior Analysis*). To a limited extent, the way in which these children were approached will be discussed in the context of the regular elementary classroom (Chapter 7). In the present chapter the emphasis will be on situations in which the entire class is organized according to a behavior modification rationale. In most cases this has taken the form of a token economy. Almost all such programs are modeled after the pioneering work done at the Rainier School in Buckley, Washington (Birnbrauer and Lawler, 1964; Birnbrauer, Bijou, Wolf, and Kidder, 1965; Bijou, 1966). As a general rule these programs have been instituted to modify inappropriate behavior and replace it with appropriate behavior of a level prerequisite to functioning in a regular classroom. In Hewett's (1968) words the focus in special classes is on "spoonfuls" of learning as contrasted to the "bucketfuls" of learning desired in a regular classroom. In general, readiness activities such as paying attention, following directions, following rules, and acquisition of basic tool subjects are the target behaviors.

Population

In Chapter 5 a point was made that the manner in which one translated principles of learning into practice was determined, in part, by the characteristics of the population with which one was dealing. Keeping the children enrolled in classes for the TMR, ERM, emotionally disturbed, or learning disabled are atypical in several dimensions. The degree of their deviancy on any one parameter (e.g., IQ) varies, as do the dimensions on which they vary. For example, a TMR child typically demonstrates a greater deficiency in school learning (grade level/chronological age) than does an EMR child, whereas a learning disabled child may have learning problems on behavior problems similar to those of an EMR child but does not show the global deficit in IQ that is more characteristic of the EMR child.

The children for whom token economies have been devised most commonly, however, share several common characteristics worth noting. First of all, the overwhelming majority of these children have had academic careers best described as a *history of failure*. Regardless of the reasons, these children have simply failed too often, and in some cases have associated books, teachers, classrooms, or certain subject matter areas with the aversiveness associated with failure. The common by-product of this association is that the child becomes "turned off" to education, and the stimuli listed above (teachers, books, and so forth) become discriminative stimuli to exhibit escape behaviors.

A second common characteristic is that the incentives offered in the traditional classroom (e.g., letter grades) have been ineffective as reinforcers for these children. Either the incentives were not worth the effort required to obtain them—for the particular child secondary reinforcers such as praise or approval had never been developed—or because an adult's unfortunate learning praise was an aversive rather than positive stimulus. Again, the common characteristic is that for many, if not most, of the children traditional incentives are ineffective.

Third, when a token economy with backup reinforcers is instituted, it is done with children who are either young, chronologically, or immature to the point where the backup reinforcers (trinkets, candy) are not perceived as childish. Beyond elementary age, token economies may be seen as too infantile unless masked in such a way as to avoid such perceptions. Obviously, a TMR in adolescence may function at a mid-elementary level, and has interests and tastes in keeping with that level, in which case no problem would occur. However, for a high school child of average ability (IQ), but a reading problem, working for tokens to exchange for candy or models just is not being "cool." Since the children with whom the token economy is employed are young, it is usually the case that the teacher's attention and approval are potent positive reinforcers, if used systematically. In the light of Zigler's (1966) research on motivation with subjects with histories of failure, this seems a viable hypothesis (see MacMillan, 1970), except with certain of the emotionally disturbed who, it has been found, prefer food to social rewards (Levin and Simmons, 1962).

Although not a characteristic of the child, a characteristic of the setting should be noted. Typically in the token economy classrooms, the teacher/pupil ratio has been far lower in a regular elementary class. Ratios in the order of 6:1 to 15:1 are common, and in some cases a teacher aide or assistant is also employed. Therefore, the feasibility of employing a token economy in any elaborate form will, in part, be determined by the teacher/pupil ratio in the classroom under consideration. Furthermore, most such classes to date have had rather substantial budgets with which to purchase backup reinforcers. If one must have tangible backup reinforcers, finances are a definite consideration.

Environment to Which Children Will Move

In the selection of task objectives for children, Birnbrauer (1970) recommended a study of the environments for which the subjects are being prepared. At the elementary level, in the case of most emotionally disturbed and learning disabled children that environment is the regular classroom. This being the case, a token economy must ultimately evolve into a program which, in terms of tasks, reinforcers, and contingencies, approximates the regular classroom.

In the case of the TMR classroom, return to a regular class is unlikely for virtually all of the children. The environment for which these children must be ultimately prepared is the home and some form of employment. As the child enters the final stages of his school career, the transition to this subsequent environment must be programmed carefully so that he can perform the tasks required, respond to the natural reinforcers that will be operative, and be sensitive to the contingencies in existence.

For the EMR child, the environment for which these children are being prepared varies. MacMillan (in press) has argued that two, apparently competitive, objectives are often cited for EMR children. One objective is to return the children to the regular class, as is the case for emotionally disturbed and learning disabled children. The second objective is to make the individual a productive member of society by means of a work-experience curriculum, which is not academically oriented and hence does not develop tool subjects that would enable the child to move into a regular class. Therefore, the environment for EMR children varies, depending on the perceived prognosis for a given child.

THE TOKEN ECONOMY

If employers had to identify individual incentives for each of their employees in order to get them to perform their various jobs, you can imagine the problem that would confront a corporation like General Motors. Instead, a type of token economy exists for our society, and money is the token. One must learn the value of money and know the difference between a dime and a dollar. But why does money serve as a reinforcer for almost everyone? As a child he learns that money can buy gum, candy, bicycles, or admission to the movies. Therefore, while money per se does not satisfy any basic needs, one learns that it can be exchanged for objects he either needs or wants. Unlike some conditioned reinforcers, money is *based* on many unconditioned and/or conditioned reinforcers—hence it is a generalized conditioned reinforcer.

In much the same way, a teacher confronted simultaneously with ten or more children who differ in terms of what is reinforcing to them finds himself in a situation similar to that of General Motors—granted it is on a slightly different scale. In order to cope with such differences in incentive effectiveness, numerous behaviorists have turned to a token economy in the classroom. The token is simply a stimulus like a plastic chip, a check mark, stars, or a numerical rating, which has some value and can be exchanged for any number of desired objects or activities. The objects and activities for which the tokens can be exchanged are called backup reinforcers. If money could not be exchanged for things one wanted or needed, money would lose its reinforcing properties. In the same vein, one attempts to select a wide enough variety of backup reinforcers so that presumably every child can find something he desires.

O'Leary and Drabman (1971) listed three ingredients of a token reinforcement program: (1) a set of instructions to the class regarding the behaviors that will be reinforced (a prompt or prompts), (2) a means of making the token contingent on behavior (contingencies), and (3) rules governing the exchange of tokens for backup reinforcers. With most children the teacher can simply discuss the nature of the token economy with the children prior to initiation. However, with some young children, or older children whose behavior is typical of younger children, it may be necessary to establish the reinforcement value of the token. This can be done by giving a token and displaying the backup reinforcers and asking the child what he wants to buy. Or, you can give the child a token and then present an object that is probably desired (candy). As the child reaches for the candy, remove the token from his hand, then hold the candy in front of him with the token, then give him the candy.

Birnbrauer *et al.* (1970, p. 42) listed as some advantages of token systems the following:

a. It permits immediate reinforcement for all members of a group by means of a common object.
b. Tokens are not consumed by the children, so there is no post reinforcement pause.
c. Since tokens are like money, the behaviors can gradually be brought under the control of a powerful natural reinforcer.
d. Since tokens have a variety of back-up reinforcers they are not likely to lose their reinforcing power (through satiation).

Although there are definite advantages of token economies over individual reinforcers, the reader must not infer that this should be undertaken as a first step with all children. This is a type of "last resort" when the entire class needs such a high degree of structure, and the entire class is functioning at, or below, this reinforcement level (see the section "A Continuum of Reinforcers" in Chapter 4). As a general rule, social reinforcers should be considered prepotent until proved otherwise. Only at this point, should the token system be instituted. To some, as described in Chapter 7, token economy and behavior modification are synonymous. The position taken here is that a token economy is a rather drastic intervention to be undertaken only after the more natural reinforcements have been ineffective. Becker *et al.* (1971, pp. 55–56) recommended a token system in cases where schoolwork means failure and punishment, and where there is a need for strong, obvious, and immediate reinforcement. As for rules for establishing such a program, they wrote:

   a. Start with tokens that can be quickly and easily given.
   b. Tokens are learned reinforcers that can be traded for other reinforcers. Use a variety of payoffs to increase the chance that you have an effective reinforcer for most children.
   c. Reinforce often in the beginning and gradually reinforce less (intermittently) as the behavior improves.
   d. To get off the system, so you won't need it forever, tokens should be paired with praise and affection so that these social reinforcers will gain reinforcing power.

Selection of Tokens and Backup Reinforcers

As noted by O'Leary and Drabman (1971, p. 389), the particular type of tokens and backup reinforcers used have varied considerably from program to program but have received scant attention regarding the relative merits of each for a particular population. These authors recommended that tokens have the following properties:

   a. Their value should be readily understood.
   b. They should be easy to dispense.
   c. They should be easily transportable from the place of dispensing to the area of exchange.
   d. They should be identifiable as the property of a particular child.
   e. They should require minimal bookkeeping duties for the teacher.
   f. They should be dispensable in a manner which will divert as little attention as possible from academic matters.
   g. They should have some relevance to real currency if one's

desire is to teach mathematical or economic skills which will be functional outside the classroom.
h. They should be dispensable frequently enough to insure proper shaping of desired behavior.

In keeping with these suggestions, the teacher must consider the children for whom the program is designed. For some children, such as the retarded, the more concrete the token the more meaning it may have for them. Hence plastic chips might be more appropriate than ratings given in notebook because the chips can be carried, touched, and serve as a reminder. However, for a child functioning at a more mature level, the rating may be more appropriate. When there is stealing of chips, or throwing them, or when ratings are being torn up, then keeping the ratings at the teacher's desk or displaying them in front of the classroom may prove to be superior. When behaviors are easily divided into units (e.g., number of problems done correctly, pages read), then check marks would be ideal; however, ratings may be preferable when behaviors are not so easily divided (e.g., behavior on the playground). Among the types of tokens used in various programs are plastic chips, check marks, numerical ratings, tags, rings, stars, tickets, and play money. The advantages of any one of these would depend on the considerations discussed above.

The selection of specific backup reinforcers for which tokens can be exchanged is important, since the reinforcement value of the tokens is dependent on them. The selection obviously depends, in part, on the developmental level of the children. With young children candy, toys, trinkets, activities, and events are commonly used backup reinforcers. Homme *et al.* (1963) used some rather unusual activities as backup reinforcers for preschool children such as pushing an adult around in a swivel chair, kicking a wastebasket, or throwing paper cups across the room. Blackham and Silberman (1971) provided a list of potential backup reinforcers which are broken down by grade level, sex, objects, and activities.

In residential programs it is possible to program the entire environment, and use meals, social activities, recreational activities, dormitory rooms, and even the type of bed (cot versus springs and mattress) as things that must be purchased with tokens. As a general rule the backup reinforcers should represent a wide variety of objects and activities, and should be changed frequently. A final guide to the selection is offered by O'Leary and Drabmann (1971), who suggested that one simply ask the children what they will work for.

A slightly different posture on the backup reinforcer issue was assumed by Hewett (1968). He contended that the value and nature of the exchange items are unimportant. What is important is that the item was "earned" in school. Hewett went on to explain that some children come to school with enough money in their pocket to buy out the "store," and yet are delighted with earning a five-cent item with their check marks. The essence of the token system, according to Hewett (1968), is that the child's accomplishments are being recognized in a systematic way, and in the process the child learns that his own behavior determines certain consequences. Hence there is disagreement on the relative importance of backup reinforcers, and empirical evidence to resolve the issue is not available.

IMPLEMENTING A TOKEN SYSTEM IN A CLASSROOM

In proceeding through a step-by-step discussion of how to go about introducing a token system, an attempt will be made to note specific principles of learning exemplified by a practice. Again, let it be emphasized that this represents *only one way* in which principles have been applied in the context of education. While a token system may be appropriate for certain children, it is totally inappropriate for certain other children.

Introduction of System to the Class and Establishment of Token Value

It is advisable to introduce the token system at a natural break in the school calendar; that is, do not introduce it in midweek of a six-week period, but rather at the beginning of the school year or after Thanksgiving or Christmas vacation.

Such programs have been introduced to the class in several ways. O'Leary and Drabman (1971) suggested that in discussing the program the target behaviors (academic, behavioral) be specified. In so doing, the teacher *prompts* the class on what behaviors are to be reinforced. Hewett (1968) had the children met by the teacher at the classroom door and given a check mark card. All that was said was that this classroom was unlike any other they had been in. The children were instructed to go inside and find the desk with their name on it. Immediately, they were given ten checks for (1) finding their desk, and (2) being ready to work, which was explained to them by the teacher. At the same time, a piece of candy was placed on top of each check in order to establish the value of the checks. For two days, the candy was given with each check in addition to the exchange value of the checks at the end of each day (Hewett, 1968, pp. 252-53).

Of principal importance is that the teacher very quickly specify the target behaviors and clarify the contingencies. In the Hewett (1968) project, check marks are given for (1) starting work (2 checks); (2) working and following through on assignment (3 checks); and (3) "being a student" (5 checks). The 5 checks refer to how the child respects limits of time, space, and the working rights of others. Obviously the target behaviors might be any number of things like study behavior, increases in academic achievement, following class rules. Keep in mind the usefulness of check marks and ratings as tokens for the target behavior. The main point is do not play games with the students and make them figure out what specific behavior you want. Spell it out for them in very precise terms. Kuypers, Becker, and O'Leary (1968) had the teacher of a class going on a token program follow these guides in introducing the system:

1. A list of the rules was written on the blackboard—such as "stay in seats," "raise hand," "quiet," "face front," etc.
2. Since a numerical rating was to be used, the teacher told the children that they would be rated on how well they

followed the rules, and the rating (1 to 10) would be placed in spiral notebooks attached to their desks.
3. The teacher explained that by earning points the children win prizes, and then showed various prizes and how many points were needed for each.

This, then, along with several other instructions which dealt strictly with that program, was how they introduced a token program to third- and fourth-grade children.

Immediately establish the value of the tokens. Hewett's (1968) technique is described above. Earlier, the manner of associating tokens with their purchasing power was discussed for children functioning at low levels. One way of doing this with most groups of children is to allow them to exchange their tokens more frequently, to begin with. You might have an exchange period just before lunch and another at the end of the day until the children understand the token system. Such a practice if used initially should not be continued for more than two or three days. Quickly get on the planned schedule of biweekly or weekly exchange periods.

One last point on this topic. In specifying the target behavior be positive whenever possible. For example, instead of "You cannot leave your seat without permission," use something like "You must have permission before leaving your seat." Stress the DOs instead of the DO NOTs.

Acquisition Stage

Once the program has been introduced and the medium of exchange is understood, the first concern becomes the acquisition of new behaviors (academic or social) or the reduction of inappropriate behaviors. While teachers employing a token economy can, and do, use principles other than positive reinforcement, the major thrust is toward the acquisition of new behavior, rather than toward simply weakening an inappropriate behavior. Therefore, while ignoring misbehavior with the intent of extinguishing it would be used, the token economy would lend itself more readily to counterconditioning—for example, when one rule in the class is that children can speak out only when given permission, and a child yells out at will. At the time, the teacher would ignore the yelling out (unless it disrupts others), but when it comes time for dispensing tokens that child would not get the full complement. He would be told why not and what he could do to ensure getting the full complement in the next period. Hence, the teacher is paying off on behavior (being quiet) which is incompatible with the misbehavior that child exhibited (yelling out). If he learns what the teacher wants, he cannot exhibit the inappropriate behavior.

Throughout the program's existence, recording of target behavior continues which provides feedback to the teacher on the effect the tokens have with given children. In one way, the tokens earned by a child can serve as data from which the teacher can infer the effectiveness, as long as he can ascertain what behaviors correspond to which tokens. Otherwise, one of the procedures outlined in Chapter 7 should be followed in order that reliable data on the target behaviors (which presumably are the behaviors for which tokens are given) can be collected.

Kuypers *et al.* (1968) suggested that during the acquisition stage, before beginning the day, or rating period, the teacher go over the rules with the children as a reminder and point out that they can earn prizes. If, for any reason there needs to be a modification of the rules, the teacher should be sure to notify the class, and if rules are written on the board, the change(s) should be put on the board. Except when prizes are being shown to the class or when tokens are being exchanged, backup reinforcers should be kept in a place where children cannot get them. Throughout the program the teacher should remain sensitive to other backup reinforcers, and if children mention things they would like to work for, he should note them for later use.

A decision must be made on when and how often tokens will be given. In deciding, the teacher should keep in mind the evidence on the effects of various schedules of reinforcement. For example, if speed is what the teacher is trying to improve (i.e., the child works too slowly), then a FR schedule is dictated. FR schedules were employed by Quay *et al.* (1966) and by Birnbrauer *et al.* (1965) in their programs for emotionally disturbed and mentally retarded children, respectively. These two projects would be useful to obtain ideas for the reader interested in adopting an FR schedule in his classroom. One way of using a FR schedule and not having to count responses is to have the child come to the teacher's desk when he completes a certain amount of work (has solved five math problems; has read three pages). Generally, since ratio schedules require that responses be counted they become unwieldy for an entire class. Therefore, the majority of classes on token economies are on bastardized interval schedules, since this requires only timekeeping. The description of these schedules as bastardized is used advisedly (O'Leary and Drabman 1971, p. 393) since the contingencies in the classroom do not meet classic scheduling definitions. For example, a fixed-interval schedule dictates that the first response following the time interval will be reinforced; however, in most classrooms, teachers dispense tokens after the time interval elapses regardless of whether the children exhibit the target behavior. Hence one cannot extrapolate too casually from the effects of FI schedules in laboratories to the classroom.

Several programs provide examples of dispensing tokens after the passage of a given time period, and the interested reader should consult more detailed accounts of these procedures. Hewett (1968) had teachers give check marks after every 15-minute period. Therefore, each hour period was divided into three 15-minute work periods, each followed by a five-minute period for dispensing check marks. O'Leary and Becker (1967) had teachers give ratings (1 to 10) in notebooks every 20 minutes. During the early phase, these investigators had the children exchange ratings for backup reinforcers at the end of each day for the first 3 days, every other day for the following 2 days, then every 3 days for the next 15 days, and finally, every 4th day.

Regardless of whether a ratio or interval basis is adopted in a given class, the rule of thumb to be followed during the acquisition stage is to give the tokens frequently. The behaviors the teacher is trying to shape are, at first, extremely fragile, and the more immediately the reinforcement follows the behavior the greater the impact. Therefore, if the number of problems solved (a ratio) is the contingency, then the numbers should be small at first—that is, 5 problems rather than 25. If a time interval is used, then it should be short—probably no longer than 20 or 30 minutes.

Another point that must not be overlooked by the teacher when employing a token economy is that it is a "temporary" stage. Hewett (1968) stated that the token stage is necessary for a short period of time. From its inception, the giving of tokens is a means by which the teacher develops other secondary reinforcers which will be operative in the regular class, in order that the tokens can be dropped and the behavior maintained. In Part I, conditioned or secondary reinforcers were discussed; these principles are translated into practice as follows: every time the tokens are dispensed the teacher praises the child for those tokens earned. In this fashion, praise (initially possessing no reinforcing properties) comes to be associated with the tokens (effective reinforcers), and ultimately through this association become conditioned reinforcers. Therefore, it is crucial that the teacher be aware of the dynamics of the token dispensing, and not treat it lightly.

Kuypers *et al.* (1968) suggested that when giving tokens the teacher review the rules related to the target behaviors by pointing out to the child specific behaviors he performed in order to receive the tokens he earned. For example, "You earned six tokens because you _____." They further recommended that the teacher indicate the behaviors that need improvement in order that the child can receive his full complement of tokens.

Some teachers express distaste for the token economy; they see it as mechanistic and impersonal and hence it detracts from the interpersonal relationship of teacher and pupil. In some cases, this is because they ignore the process of developing conditioned reinforcers and are blinded by the "trappings" of some programs (e.g., checks, tokens). Another response to this concern is provided by Hewett (1968), who argued that teachers in his program must interact with *every* student at least once every 15 minutes—something that does not happen in many "humanistic" classes. When Hewett's (1968, p. 252) teachers moved the class off the check mark system to no checkmarks, the children's social and academic behavior did not change noticeably, which led him to conclude that they "apparently had become far more than purveyors of checkmarks and had acquired secondary reward value of their own through association with the primary checkmark reward system."

The acquisition stage, as used here, refers to that initial phase of the token program during which the target behaviors are beginning to be modified and when the token program is being introduced. The major points to keep in mind are:

1. Be certain that the children know exactly what behavior you want.
2. Be certain that the exchange value of tokens is understood.
3. Select a token that is appropriate for the children and the behavior.
4. Continue recording target behavior.
5. Use a schedule of reinforcement that is appropriate for target behaviors, and keep the ratio small and the interval short.
6. Pair dispensing of tokens with social approval.
7. Be positive and reinforce as frequently and immediately as possible.

Maintenance Stage

Lindsley (1964, p. 65) stated, "There is a great tendency today to confuse the acquisition of behavior with its maintenance." In line with this notion, the maintenance stage of the token program refers to that time when the target behavior is either a part of the individual's response repertoire or it is occurring at a rate that is judged appropriate. Then, unlike what was recommended during the acquisition stage, no longer must it be reinforced as immediately or as frequently. In fact, it is undesirable to reinforce the target behavior continuously. The reader will recall the discussion in Part I concerning the effects of schedules of reinforcement on extinction. The point was made that behavior maintenance on continuous schedules of reinforcement extinguish very rapidly, and that longer ratios and intervals resulted in behavior more resistant to extinction than behavior maintained on small ratios and intervals. Therefore, once the target behavior is emitted frequently, the next task is to solidify it—to make it resistant to extinction, or to strengthen appropriate behavior that has been acquired (Whelan and Haring, 1966). In this context, it becomes important to study the environment for which the child is being prepared. For example, what kind of schedule of reinforcement do regular class teachers employ for giving praise or feedback? The child must be able to emit the target behaviors and have them maintained on an intermittent schedule if the behavior is to generalize to the regular class.

Second, the class should be moved from the tokens with backup reinforcers to consequences that are both social in nature and intrinsic to the successful completion of tasks. That is to say, they should be "weaned" from the extrinsic tangible reinforcers as soon as the transition to natural consequences is feasible. MacMillan and Forness (1970) took the position that the use of extrinsic reinforcers is legitimate as a means to an end, but such reinforcers must not be allowed to become an end in and of themselves. Here is where some teachers balk at "fiddling" with something that is working and keeping their class under control (i.e., the token economy). Yet to allow children to remain at this relatively low level on a continuum of reinforcers is indefensible. The children must be moved to respond to reinforcements that are existent in the natural environment (Ferster, 1967).

The acid test for any given program is not the extent to

which the maladaptive behavior can be modified in a contrived environment but, rather, the extent to which the adaptive behavior developed in that contrived environment generalizes to natural settings. MacMillan and Forness (in press) describe several approaches that have been tried in order to get the desired generalization:

1. *The Do Nothing Approach.* In this approach the implied reasoning (or rationalizing) goes as follows: Once a behavior-shaping program has brought about the adaptive behavior with whatever reward that worked, the natural environment will dispense natural rewards which will support the new behavior. Implicit in this approach is that the natural environment would have maintained the behavior initially except that the child did not emit the adaptive behavior.
2. *Development of Conditioned Reinforcers.* This approach dictates that the teacher systematically pair potent lower-level reinforcers with higher-level rewards which will operate in the natural environment to which the child will be returned. By means of pairing initially ineffective stimuli with effective reinforcers the teacher moves the child along the continuum of reinforcers.
3. *Manipulation of Schedules of Reinforcement.* This approach would be employed in combination with number 2 above, in that one would extend the length of time or the number of responses necessary prior to reinforcement. Ultimately, the reinforcement schedule would approximate the six-week grading period with intermediate grades of assignments, tests, etc., and social praise.

Baer *et al.* (1968) contended that if generalization is desired, one must program rather than simply expecting it to occur. Therefore, teachers must not just hope that generalization will occur, but they must systematically program so that the newly learned behavior transfers from the special class to the regular class. Several suggestions that follow might be considered in this programming for transfer.

In order to begin the weaning process, one of the first steps would be simply to inflate the economy. If, for example, a model plane kit "costs" 100 points or 6 completed check mark cards, the teacher announces that the same kit will now cost 200 points or 12 check mark cards. As a result, the child must emit more appropriate behavior (or wait longer) in order to obtain the backup reinforcer he wants (Kuypers *et al.*, 1968). Throughout, the teacher continues to give social approval when dispensing tokens, but the child is now required to delay gratification.

One might use a technique used by Hewett (1968) which involves replacing backup reinforcers with graphing of behavior. In this case, a teacher might continue giving check marks or points, but instead of exchanging them for backup reinforcers which are tangible, the teacher has a histogram on each child's desk which the child fills in at the end of each day so that he can see a visual record of improvement or lack thereof. Again, the teacher should praise each child when his graph indicates progress. This graphing can then be modified from once a day to once a week, then to every two weeks, and gradually approximate the six-week grading period.

Another alternative is to extend gradually the ratio or interval in operation. Once the child solves 5 problems easily (ratio), then require 10, later yet 15 until the assignment is comparable in number of problems or pages to assignments in the regular class for the same level of student. If the teacher is on a 15-minute interval, he should gradually extend it to 20 minutes, then 30 minutes, and so on. The teacher should always keep in mind, and work toward, the conditions (contingencies and rewards) that the child will have in the environment to which he will return. Whelan and Haring (1966, p. 284) gave the following advice to the teacher:

> When the behavior needs to be maintained, then it is no longer necessary to provide accelerating consequences to each behavioral response. Maintaining behavior requires that the teacher reduce considerably the number of accelerating consequences provided; indeed, it is a necessity if a child is to develop independent learning skills and self-control. It is during this maintenance process that appropriate behavior is accelerated by

consequences which are intrinsic to completion of tasks, social approval, feelings of self-worth, and the satisfaction of assuming self-responsibility. Therefore, dependence on numerous teacher-applied consequences gradually loses significance to a child.

Although some of the reinforcers mentioned in the foregoing passage (e.g., feelings of self-worth) defy objective measurement, one would expect the process to go as follows: tokens are associated with praise; later, praise is associated with being correct; being correct is associated with a sense of competence or feeling of self-worth. Therefore, though in the initial stages of a program a child may perform academic tasks simply to obtain tangible reinforcers, he later finds that he can perform successfully and at that point the tangible backup reinforcers are no longer necessary.

In order to have the behavior generalize, O'Leary and Drabman (1971) offered several suggestions, which they admit have not been systematically evaluated. First, they suggested that the teacher, in the context of a token economy, offer a good academic program because when the child returns to the regular class he is less likely to be disruptive if he has the skills required. Second, they recommended that the teacher provide the expectation that the child is capable of doing well—the expectation that he can succeed if he works hard, and the expectation that he will be able to work without a token program. Gradually the teacher should involve the child in the selection of his own behaviors that should be reinforced. Fourth, as the program progresses, the child should be taught to evaluate his own behavior. Fifth, the teacher should involve the parents because too frequently the child learns to discriminate between the classroom (discriminative stimulus) and all other settings when parents attend to misbehavior the teacher is ignoring. In such a case, the teacher and parent are working in opposition. Another suggestion is to reinforce children in a variety of situations and reduce the discrimination between situations which lead to reinforcement or nonreinforcement (O'Leary and Drabman, 1971, pp. 395–96).

One additional suggestion for programming entails the involvement of the regular class teacher to whose class the child will be returned. The more sensitive that teacher is to the principles upon which the token economy was based, the more likely the teacher can provide praise and privileges contingent on desired behavior. Without much adjustment in the class routine, interest centers can be used as reinforcers when the child behaves or completes assignments. Obviously the more behaviorist-oriented the receiving teacher is the greater the similarity between the special and regular class. The discussion in Chapter 7 might prove helpful to receiving teachers.

The last thing to be covered on the programming for generalization will be discussed in Chapter 7 regarding Homme's (1970) recommendations for involving the student in the specification of tasks and rewards.

INDIVIDUALIZATION

To some the notion of a class of children on a token economy rings of regimentation and uniformity. Admittedly, in the hands of some teachers regimentation and uniformity are the result, yet this need not be the case. While the tokens and the exchange value of the tokens may be uniform for all members of the class, the contingency between academic tasks and number of tokens can be individualized for each child. For example, in the same class there might be two 8-year-old-boys, one of whom is achieving in arithmetic at third-grade level and the other, at first-grade level. For the 15-minute interval 10 tokens are possible. What it takes for these two boys to earn the maximum number of tokens would differ in possibly the level and number of problems required. Thus, you individualize the task requirements, not the number of tokens possible, because you wish to minimize competition between children.

In Hewett's engineered classroom, 10 check marks are the maximum in the 15-minute work period: 2 for starting, 3 for following through on the assignment, and 5 for "being a student." It is with these last 5 check marks that the teacher can individualize the program. For example, one child is given all 5 for attempting the task, because for him even trying is difficult. To another child, the 5 check marks are given for working without bothering other children, because for him the principal problems are in the social realm. And to another child the check marks are given on the basis of how rapidly he worked, because he is inclined to waste time and get distracted.

Individualization requires the teacher to assess the present functional level of every child and then select tasks that are appropriate for each. It means a separate assignment for each child in the class. Obviously this places the teacher in a different role from the dispenser of wisdom from a lecture format. Particularly in a special class, the range of abilities is so vast that to have an assignment in an academic area is to invite trouble. The teacher, in keeping with the foregoing discussion, would assume the role of task selector, contingency arranger, and reinforcement dispenser.

SOME ADDITIONAL CONSIDERATIONS

Variations off the basic theme are possible, and yet to date there is simply not enough evidence bearing on some of these variations to take any definitive stands on their advisability. For example, O'Leary and Drabman (1971) discussed group versus individual contingencies. The foregoing discussion of O'Leary and Drabman's work dealt exclusively with individual contingencies. A group contingency would be one in which the reward is made contingent on the collective behavior of the group, and all class members get the same consequence. For example, teachers use group contingencies when they tell a class, "If you all work quietly for the rest of the morning, I'll read a story to the class for the last half-hour." In shaping specific behaviors, individual contingencies would seem preferable to group contingencies. However, when peer influence is a powerful reinforcer, the group contingencies do serve to direct peer approval, or disapproval, toward the behavior of individuals within the group.

O'Leary and Drabman (1971) cautioned the teacher who would use group contingencies, because several negative results can occur. First, the possibility that one member of the group may not be able to perform the required behavior can result in a degree of unfairness to the remainder of the group who perform adequately. A lack of reinforcement for them may lead to the deterioration of the target behavior. In addition, that child who cannot perform the requisite behavior may become a scapegoat and may suffer undue pressure exerted by his peers. Finally, one or two children may find it enjoyable to undermine the system. This can be particularly true in the case of the "toughest" boy in the class, who does not have to fear reprisal, who gains satisfaction and a sense of power in being able to "wreck it" for everyone else.

Another of these variations involves loss of tokens or fines as a form of punishment (removal of a positive reinforcer). As noted by O'Leary and Drabman (1971) comparisons of cost procedures and positive reinforcement have not been conducted. In a residential setting Phillips (1968) found the loss of tokens to be effective in reducing aggressive verbal behavior and a lack of punctuality. In a recent case with a multihandicapped child [*] (deaf-retarded) for whom positive reinforcement alone did not seem to result in any substantial improvement on a simple discrimination task, it was hypothesized that, by chance, this girl could get 50 percent reinforcement, and she was willing to settle for this even though her tutor was not. Therefore, cost procedures were instituted in which case she received one unit of reinforcement for every correct choice, and lost one for every incorrect choice. This did result in a significant improvement during that session. Again, however, side effects of such procedures have not

---

[*] This was a tutorial project by Mrs. Peggy Eaton conducted under the direction of the author and Mr. Robert Lennan, Director of Multihandicapped Unit, California School for the Deaf, Riverside.

been studied. Does the teacher come to focus on the maladaptive behavior rather than the adaptive, or do we fall back on the punitive emphasis which has been so typical in education? These aspects need further investigation before recommendations can be made.

An area that has received very little attention in token economies concerns the effectiveness of various forms of intervention when things are not going well. Hewett (1968) specified interventions, but they are tied intimately to his engineered classroom and its developmental sequence of educational tasks. The interventions are used to reduce expectations for the child when he has difficulty coping, and throughout the first seven steps are positive in that the student continues to earn tokens. Enumerated below are the interventions described by Hewett:

1. Send child to a study booth or office with the same assigned task. This breaks any boredom and serves to cut down on distractions.
2. Modify the task in terms of making it easier, different, or more difficult. This could be used in combination with sending child to study booth.
3. Verbal restructuring of what the child is to do by the teacher, and use of social approval and disapproval. This does not mean to spend an inordinate amount of time with the child, since the teacher attention could be the reinforcer for not working.

The subsequent four interventions correspond to levels on the hierarchy of educational tasks by progressing from more mature to less mature levels. The child could be sent to activity areas in the classroom and engage in the tasks located at the (4) exploratory center—science, art, and communication tasks; (5) order center—direction following activities; (6) response task—any activity agreed upon by child and teachers; and (7) attention task—one-to-one tutoring which may include an increase in the number of tokens that can be earned. Only at this time, if the foregoing interventions are ineffective does the child cease to earn tokens and is removed from the room. For a detailed discussion of Hewett's interventions the reader is referred to his text (1968, pp. 259–67). This is the only reference to planned interventions encountered, and even Hewett's ideas need systematic evaluation.

CRITIQUE OF TOKEN ECONOMIES

That token economies have proved effective is beyond debate. However, what must be considered is their effectiveness with what kind of children and with what kinds of behavior. First of all, they have been most effective with children who deviate quite markedly from what is considered "normal" (e.g., TMR, severely emotionally disturbed) (Baumeister, 1969). Second, and quite closely related to the first point, token programs appear to be more successful in changing behaviors such as getting out of one's seat, talking out of turn, and failure to follow directions than in altering academic behaviors (O'Leary and Drabman, 1971). Thus it would appear that behaviors that consist of well-defined response topographies lend themselves nicely to token programs, and with the atypical child these are precisely the kinds of behaviors in need of shaping. Baumeister (1969) argued that there is little convincing evidence that the behavior modification techniques can be applied in the development of complex phenomena which do not lend themselves to a step-by-step program, such as issues of cognition, socialization, and acculturation. In a slightly different vein, O'Leary and Drabman (1971) contended that children are likely to have social behaviors in their response repertoire, thereby making the incentive program simply increase the frequency with which these behaviors are emitted; however, the academic skills are not in the child's response repertoire, necessitating the development of new behaviors—a more difficult task for the teacher.

Another issue that underlies token economies is to ascertain *what* specifically accounts for the changes in behavior observed. That is to say, what subcomponents (e.g., tokens) are responsible for the changes in behavior which occur. One impression that seems prevalent among teachers recently exposed to token classes is that the critical aspects in the program are the tokens and backup reinforcers—the trappings. Yet several alternative explanations exist which have not been tested—for example, the desensitization phenomenon described by Hewett (1968). Many children with histories of failure are so "turned off" on school and other things associated with it (e.g., teachers, books, rules) that these stimuli become discriminative stimuli. When these children encounter these stimuli they try to escape or attack. Yet classrooms with token economies are frequently unlike any classroom these children have encountered—physically, they are arranged differently, assignments are "packaged" so as not to resemble textbooks, and tangible incentives are used instead of symbolic grades. As a result, the children might give it a chance, perform well, and succeed academically before they realize that they are, in fact, in school and learning.

Another possible explanation is as follows: The tokens are worthless and what is really important is that the child has social contact and gets feedback every 15 or 20 minutes. Therefore, if a teacher were to circulate among all class members every 15 minutes and comment on the child's performance, he might be able to eliminate the tokens entirely and still get the same behavioral changes. In reviewing the literature, I have not encountered any study concerned with the relative importance of the tokens per se.

Yet another explanation may be the effect that the giving of tokens has on the teacher's behavior. It may be that the value of token economies lies in the requirements that the teacher specify the desired behavior, spell it out for the students, focus on the positive, and acknowledge performance. One might argue, then, that token economies are useful for shaping the behavior of teachers, and the changes in child behavior come in response to more systematic teacher behavior.

One finding in the Santa Monica Project (Hewett, 1968) could be interpreted to support this last argument. One of the experimental classes in the project was on a token economy system during the first semester and then went off the system the second semester. There was no decrement in behavior or achievement when token economy was dropped. Could this be due to the fact that the teacher's behavior had been shaped sufficiently during the first semester that she was more systematic and positive than she had been the preceding year? Obviously one could argue that the children's behavior had been shaped and brought under control of social reinforcers and no longer needed the token economy. Again, no evidence is available on this issue.

While the issues raised above may not be of as much interest to the classroom teacher as to the researcher, answers to some of these questions would allow for greater efficiency in the classroom. For example, if the tokens themselves are of no benefit they could be eliminated in practice, and make the teacher's job that much easier. Part of the problem stems from apparent confusion of research design with recommended practice (MacMillan and Forness, in press). In some of the projects, which were research projects, tokens were used as a data collection device or a system of accountability. Furthermore, in such projects a given "treatment" group necessitated that the entire class be put on a token economy so that the token economy could be evaluated against a control (no tokens) treatment. That does not mean that the authors are recommending that an entire class of children should be put on a token system. In fact, one might argue that to do so regresses some children to a reinforcement level below that at which they are capable of functioning (MacMillan and Forness, 1970). Others might argue that they are trying to use desensitization and want the class to be totally unlike those classrooms which the child associates with failure, and the tokens are one means of achieving that end. Evidence is lacking on the merits of either position.

In any token program to date, variables other than those mentioned in this chapter are operating and influence the overall effectiveness of the program. Most of these variables will be discussed in the next chapter; for the classroom teacher with a token economy these procedures should be used in conjunction with the token economy. Among such variables mentioned by O'Leary and Drabman (1971) are teacher use of praise and ignoring, teacher expectations of success for the program, the extent of the teacher's training in behavior modification, the number of children in the class, and characteristics of the children in the program such as age, IQ, and diagnosis.

What can be said with a considerable degree of certainty is that, regardless of what subcomponents might be responsible for the changes in behavior, the entire package has been effective, at least on a short-term basis. Only recently have investigators begun to study the long-range effectiveness of such programs. It would seem that the dispensing of tokens provides a clear form of communication or feedback by which a teacher tells the child that he has done well. The providing of a very structured environment may well make "school" a predictable place, and the outer predictability could lead to an inner security.

REFERENCES

Baer, D. M., Wolf, M. M., and Risley, T. Some current dimensions of applied behavior analysis. *J. Appl. Behav. Anal.*, 1:91–97, 1968.
Baumeister, A. A., More ado about operant conditioning—or nothing? *Ment. Retard.*, 7:49–51, 1969.
Becker, W. C. Engelmann, S., and Thomas, D. R. *Teaching: A Course in Applied Psychology*. Chicago: Science Research Associates, Inc., 1971.
Bijou, S. Application of experimental analysis of behavior principles in teaching academic tool subjects to retarded children. In N. Haring and R. Whelan (eds.) *The Learning Environment: Relationship to Behavior Modification and Implications for Special Education*. Lawrence, Kans.: University of Kansas Press, 1966.
Birnbrauer, J., Bijou, S., Wolf, M., and Kidder, J. Programmed instruction in the classroom. In L. Ullmann and L. Krasner (eds.) *Case Studies in Behavior Modification*, New York: Holt, Rinehart and Winston, Inc., 1965.

Birnbrauer, J. S., Burchard, J. D., and Burchard, S. N. Wanted: Behavior analysts. In R. H. Bradfield (ed.) *Behavior Modification: The Human Effort.* San Raphael, Calif.: Dimensions Publishing Co., 1970.

Birnbrauer, J., and Lawler, J. Token reinforcement for learning. *Ment. Retard.,* 2:275–79, 1964.

Blackham, G. J., and Silberman, A. *Modification of Child Behavior.* Belmont, Calif.: Wadsworth Publishing Co., Inc., 1971.

Fargo, G. A., Behrns, C., and Nolen, P. (eds.) *Behavior Modification in the Classroom.* Belmont, Calif.: Wadsworth Publishing Co., Inc., 1970.

Ferster, C. B. Arbitrary and natural reinforcement. *Psychol. Rec.,* 17:341–47, 1967.

Hewett, F. M. *The Emotionally Disturbed Child in the Classroom.* Boston: Allyn & Bacon, Inc., 1968.

Hewett, F. M., Taylor, F., and Artuso, A. A. The Madison plan really swings. *Today's Educ.,* 59:15–17, 1970.

Homme, L. E., deBaca, P. C., Devine, J. V., Steinhurst, R., and Rickert, E. J. Use of Premack principle in controlling the behavior of nursery school children. *J. Exp. Anal. Behav.* 6:544, 1963.

Journal of Applied Behavior Analysis. Ann Arbor, Mich.: Society for the Experimental Analysis of Behavior, Inc., 1968.

Krasner, L., and Ullmann, L. *Research in Behavior Modification.* New York: Holt, Rinehart and Winston, Inc., 1965.

Kuypers, D. S., Becker, W. C., and O'Leary, K. D. How to make a token system fail. *Except. Child.,* 35:101–108, 1968.

Levin, G., and Simmons, J. Response to praise by emotionally disturbed boys. *Psychol. Rep.,* 11:10, 1962.

Lindsley, O. R. Direct measurement and prothesis of retarded behavior. *J. Educ.,* 147:62–81, 1964.

MacMillan, D. L. The problem of motivation in the education of the mentally retarded. *Except. Child.,* 37:579–586, 1971.

MacMillan, D. L. Motivational style: An important consideration in programs for EMR-labeled children. *J. School Psychol.,* in press.

MacMillan, D. L., and Forness, S. R. Behavior modification: Limitations and liabilities. *Except. Child.,* 1970, 37, 291–297.

MacMillan, D. L., and Forness, S. R. Behavior modification: Savior or savant? *Am. J. Ment. Defic.,* in press.

O'Leary, K. D., and Becker, W. D. Behavior modification of an adjustment class: A token reinforcement program. *Except. Child.,* 33:637–42, 1967.

O'Leary, K. D., and Drabman, R. Token reinforcement programs in the classroom: A review. *Psychol. Bull.,* 75:379–98, 1971.

Phillips, E. L. Achievement place: Token reinforcement procedures in a home-style rehabilitation setting for "predelinquent" boys. *J. Appl. Behav. Anal.*, 1:213–23, 1968.

Quay, H. C., Werry, J. S., McQueen, M., and Sprague, R. L. Remediation of the conduct problem child in the special class setting. *Except. Child.*, 32:509–15, 1966.

Ullmann, L., and Krasner, L. *Case Studies in Behavior Modification.* New York: Holt, Rinehart and Winston, Inc., 1965.

Whelan, R. J., and Haring, H. G. Modification and maintenance of behavior through systematic application of consequences. *Except. Child.*, 32:281–89, 1966.

Zigler, E. Research on personality structure in the retardate. In N. R. Ellis (ed.) *International Review of Research in Mental Retardation,* Vol. I. New York: Academic Press, Inc., 1966.

CHAPTER 7

Behavior Modification in the Regular Class

IN THE elementary classroom, there appear to be two ways in which use can be made of applied behavior analysis. First, behavioral research conducted to date has provided insights into the effectiveness and ineffectiveness of certain teaching techniques which apply to virtually all elementary classrooms in a very general sense. Second, techniques have been evaluated which are useful to the elementary teacher in cases of one or two behavior problem children in a class of thirty children. Therefore, for organizational purposes this chapter will be divided into two major sections: one dealing with what behavior modification has to contribute to the elementary classroom, in general; and a second section on approaches useful with individual children who are problems in the class.

Forness (1970) suggested that although the impact of applied behavior analysis has been greatest in special education, there are techniques which have been developed in this context which are applicable in the regular classroom as well. In fact, with greater specificity in communicating expectancies, more systematic use of contingencies, and greater flexibility in the rewards used in regular classes it is reasonable to hypothesize that placement of many children in special classes for the mentally retarded, learning disabled, or emotionally disturbed might be forestalled, or even prevented. That is to say that some children who are placed in special classes are casualties of a classroom that was not adapted to their learning needs. Altman and Linton (1971) contended that the behaviors of many such children can be shaped to respond to the reinforcers and contingencies operating in a regular class.

A greater sensitivity on the part of teachers toward the variety of potential reinforcers and how they are being dispensed and on what basis would indeed be helpful in the prevention of behavior problems. In the case of social reinforcement, for example, one finds that often reinforcers are used arbitrarily and with the intent to control rather than motivate (Jackson, 1968). For the below average child, his efforts go unrewarded since they fail to reach a standard deemed worthy of praise by his teacher. The result of this dose of nonreinforcement is that the child becomes more and more discouraged because he cannot obtain the praise and recognition he desires. Sometimes he resorts to other means of getting the teacher's attention—misbehavior. After all, at least the teacher notices him, and Becker *et al.* (1967) showed that some children preferred negative attention, such as reprimands, to being ignored.

Even in the case of average and above average children, greater effectiveness and efficiency can be achieved when the teacher uses principles of learning systematically. Application of such principles might take the form of programmed instruction or teaching machines, or the principles might be used for purposes of behavior control; but regardless of this, in the following discussion, ways in which these principles can be and have been translated into practice with beneficial results will be discussed.

Since a major goal of education is the modification of behavior (both academic and social), the role of the teacher as a contingency manager is consistent with that goal. Most teachers develop over time techniques which are effective for them in controlling classroom behavior. Altman and Linton (1971) pointed out that this is usually done by trial and error, which is inefficient, unnecessary, and frequently unsuccessful. Since teachers possess almost absolute control over the classroom and its students, it is possible for them to control environmental variables to the extent that it is necessary to employ behavior modification techniques. In this chapter, ways in which principles of learning can be translated into practice will be discussed when such is possible in the context of a class of approximately 30 children with one teacher. It should be noted, however, that far less systematic work has been done in this setting as compared to that done in special classes with far lower teacher/pupil ratios. Nevertheless, that which has been done will be discussed, and extrapolations made from work done in alternate settings which seem generalizable.

Population

The children for whom the following suggestions are applicable are those children typically found in regular elementary classes. In other words, they range in chronological age from approximately 5 to 12, and though a considerable range is to be found in abilities, they are of average or above average intellect. Furthermore, it is assumed that no serious behavioral problems have existed for the children, except in that section of the chapter dealing with specific behavior problems.

Considering the span of ages subsumed under the elementary school, variability exists on such variables as maturity, what constitutes appropriate social behavior, and the reward value of peers and/or teachers. Developmentally, one observes a gradual decrement in the reward value of teachers and a corresponding increase in the reward value of peers. As a result, while most first-grade children are most sensitive to the approval and disapproval of the teacher, by sixth grade these same children are more concerned with what their peers approve or disapprove of. Thus teacher approval is generally a powerful reinforcer with first-grade children, but not nearly so potent with sixth-grade children.

The shift in the relative potency of adult approval to peer approval is of considerable significance in teacher behavior. With increased age the child becomes gradually more and more peer oriented, and comes to look to the peer group for approval. In time, should the peer group reward behavior that is incompatible with the behavior approved by the adult, the behavior rewarded by the peer group is more likely to be emitted. Therefore, while the primary teacher's systematic use of his attention and approval might prove to be effective, the same technique used by the sixth-grade teacher would probably prove less effective.

Considering the fact that the population of children enrolled in regular classrooms, in general, do respond to attention and approval, and do work for letter grades, for being correct, and for status, the translation of principles of learning into practice in the form of a token economy is inappropriate. These children are functioning at a reinforcement level more mature than a token economy, and to put such children on tokens would be to regress them to a level of reinforcement below that at which they are capable of functioning. This, however, does not mean that the principles of learning are not applicable in the regular classroom; in fact, quite to the contrary, they are most appropriate. The difference lies in the manner in which they are translated into practice.

The reticence on the part of a sizable portion of regular classroom teachers may stem from the confusion in the minds of some that a token economy *is* behavior modification. Obviously this is not the case, and in this chapter ways in which the principles of learning relate to the regular classroom will be explored. Basically, the elements of specified rules, positive reinforcement, and extinction are in common with the token economies.

GENERAL CLASSROOM PROCEDURES

The role of the regular classroom teacher as a contingency manager requires considerable preplanning. Becker *et al.* (1971)

recommended that the teacher plan ahead of time such things as What rules will be employed? What available reinforcers will I use? What forms of punishment will I use if they are necessary? In other words, the teacher tries to organize and structure the classroom, the daily activities, her own behavior, and the behavior of the children in a manner consistent with behavioristic principles.

Madsen, Becker, and Thomas (1968) listed the following as crucial elements of classroom control: *Rules, Praise,* and *Ignoring*. The significance of rules, which was discussed with regard to the token economies, applies equally to the regular classroom. Do not assume that the children know what they are to do, or what you wish. Rather, make sure they know. One example given by Becker *et al.* (1971) described what one teacher did in introducing her class to the rules. She displayed a list of the rules in the front of the class on the first day, where they remained. Each day the children were reminded of the rules by having them read the rules, and when their behavior was in keeping with one of the rules, she made praising comments. For example, if raising one's hand before talking was a rule, the teacher might say, "I like the way John raised his hand, and that's why I called on him." In this way, one might avoid the problem described earlier—the problem of children learning the rules by coming into conflict with them.

The second element, praise, goes hand in hand with specifying the rules. Becker *et al.* (1971) noted that rules become important when following them is reinforced. This relates back to the point made earlier—do not take good behavior for granted, but reward it. Rather than simply punishing children when they break a rule, reward them for following it. Praise is but one of many secondary reinforcers that are social in nature. Others include physical contact, compliments, smiles, nods, winks, and verbal approval, virtually all of which are effective social reinforcers for children in regular classes. Whereas the children for whom a token economy was recommended in Chapter 6 did not respond to social reinforcers, the vast majority of children in the regular classrooms do. Therefore, the teacher must be sensitive about the contingencies relating his social reinforcement to behavior of his children. Be generous in the use of praise for desired behavior, and withhold all forms of attention for undesirable behavior.

This brings us to the last element, ignoring. When children break a rule or exhibit disruptive behavior, our first inclination as teachers is to tell the child to stop it. In one study (Becker *et al.*, 1967) it was shown that for some children the only teacher attention they had received followed misbehavior and thereby the teacher unknowingly maintained the misbehavior. Instead, learning principles tell us that when a response is followed by a neutral stimulus the response will weaken and, if repeated, extinguish. Therefore, the recommendation to teachers is to ignore inappropriate behavior whenever a child, or his classmates, are not in danger of being hurt. The teacher should focus time and attention on the behaving children.

The role of planning cannot be overemphasized, because good organization can prevent problems. Several general rules for planning were suggested by Becker *et al.* (1971, pp. 176–80). Included are using *cushion activities* which children who finish early can engage in while others complete the task, consistently following a routine in the day so that it is not necessary to explain what comes next, and providing a change of pace, with sedentary activities following physical activities and games following serious work.

Strengthening Behavior

In most cases the classroom behavior you desire is part of the behavioral repertoire of the children. You will recall that in Part I it was noted that when you wish to increase the frequency of a behavior, you simply follow its occurrence with a positive reinforcer. With increased studies conducted in the context of education we are becoming far more sensitive to a number of events that are reinforcing to children. This has been important in two ways: first, teachers can be more sensitive to withholding these events following undesirable behavior and thereby not support it; and second, teachers are aware of more events that can be applied to strengthen desired behavior. Following is a discussion of three types of rewards that one might find useful in the regular classroom: *social reinforcers, activity reinforcers,* and *symbolic reinforcers.*

SOCIAL REINFORCERS. Social reinforcers are conditioned, or secondary, reinforcers, so-called because they are learned. The newborn child does not respond to praise, compliments, or smiles. However, he soon learns to respond to social stimuli since they are repeatedly paired with primary or unconditioned stimuli. The mother smiles at the child while she feeds him, or talks to him while she changes his diaper and removes a source of discomfort. Conversely, some children have not experienced being held, talked to, smiled at, or praised sufficiently often to make these social stimuli effective reinforcers. For these children the token economy described in the previous chapter may be useful in teaching the child to respond to these stimuli.

Becker *et al.* (1971) divided social reinforcers into four subcategories: praising words, facial expressions, nearness, and physical contact. Let us look briefly at the last three. Teachers can use and have used smiling, winking, laughing, and nodding when children are behaving in an appropriate way. Nearness, or proximity, can be used by joining a group of children or standing by a child. Physical contact such as putting your arm around the child, hugging him, holding him on your lap is a potential positive reinforcer. Teachers should practice using a wide variety of these techniques and become comfortable with them. They all constitute forms of attention, and as will be discussed later, attention is probably a far more potent reinforcer than we ever dreamed possible.

Praise cannot be overused in the elementary classroom. Children of this age group never seem to get too much complimenting or praising. Short words or phrases of praise such as "Good," "Good work," "Nice going," "I like the way you're working" are all useful. Becker *et al.* (1971) distinguished between *descriptive praise* and *evaluative praise,* and such a distinction is in order. To say to a child who has been in trouble for misbehavior for years, "You're an angel" is not likely to be believed by that child. However, to tell him that for the last half hour he has paid close attention is believable. Giving a detailed description communicates that you, the teacher, have taken the time to notice what he is doing. As a general rule, then, be descriptive, not judgmental in your praise. Becker *et al.* (1971) recommended that you describe the behavior and indicate that you appreciate it. This has considerable merit in that you not only compliment the child but you carefully point out precisely what he has done to warrant the praise—hence it is educational.

To show the importance of teacher praise, a study by Becker *et al.* (1967) investigated the behavior of children in five different classrooms. For five weeks baseline data were recorded, and then the teachers were told to give the children rules of good classroom behavior, give praise and smiles for desired behavior, and ignore misbehavior. During the baseline period the percentage of misbehavior was 62.13 percent and after the intervention 29.19 percent, a significant decrease. In a follow-up study (Madsen *et al.*, 1968a) the investigators were able to determine the relative importance of the three crucial elements: rules, praise, and ignoring. Rules and ignoring had no appreciable effects on the misbehavior, but when praise for appropriate behavior was added, the inappropriate behavior decreased significantly.

Particularly in the lower elementary grades, teacher attention is a powerful reinforcer and should be used judiciously. A widely quoted study (Zimmerman and Zimmerman, 1962) demonstrated the powerful effect of teacher attention on student behavior. In that study, one boy was having difficulty with spelling, and whenever he was called on he would have to be urged by the teacher. The teacher, in prodding the child to "spell correctly," was attending (and thus reinforcing) the misspelling of the boy, and the investigators hypothesized that he continued to misspell in order to maintain the teacher's attention. Therefore, they instructed the teacher to ignore the boy when he misspelled and to give him attention when he spelled correctly. The teacher would then send the boy to the board with a word to spell, whereupon he spelled it incorrectly and looked at the teacher (presumably waiting for her to correct him), but now she just kept working at her desk (ignoring the misspelling). After several other incorrect spellings, he spelled the word correctly and the teacher gave him encouragement. Note the change in contingencies. At first, teacher attention was contingent on incorrect spelling, and incorrect spelling was maintained. However, when the teacher began making her attention contingent on correct spelling and withholding her attention after mispelling, the frequency of the maladaptive behavior (incorrect spelling) decreased markedly. The point to be emphasized is that teachers often inadvertently can be reinforcing the behavior they are trying to extinguish.

Similar studies have been reviewed by Altman and Linton (1971) ranging from work with preschool-age children (Baer and Wolf, 1968), to special classes, to regular elementary classrooms. The Becker *et al.* (1967) and Madsen *et al.* (1968b) studies have been discussed previously. Hall *et al.* (1968a) demonstrated the same phenomenon when study behavior, rather than classroom behavior, was the target behavior. In that study, when teachers attended to study behavior there was a marked increase in study behavior, and when a reversal procedure was implemented (teacher attended to nonstudy behaviors) there was a marked decrease in study behavior. Hence the attention contingent on desired behavior, coupled with ignoring the behavior not desired, seems to be an effective technique in classroom control.

Another outcome of the classroom research on behavior analysis is the finding that consequences assumed to be aversive or punishing may, in fact, be positive reinforcers for the behaviors they were meant to punish (Holmes, 1966; Madsen *et al.*, 1968b). With some mothers, feeding or changing diapers was accompanied with scolds or reprimands, frowns, etc., and as in the case where such a primary reinforcer (food, removal of a wet diaper) for most children is paired with smiles and compliments, these children learn to respond to scowls and reprimands. Hence when the teacher says "Stop that," or "Be quiet," or "Sit down," some children take these commands as punishment; however, to others these words are reinforcing. The investigations by Thomas *et al.* (1968) and Madsen *et al.* (1968a) clearly demonstrated that reprimands serve as positive reinforcers for some children. The more the teacher tells them to stop doing something the more they do it; the more they are told to sit down the more they stand up. Koser (1971) likened this to "lollypopping" children; that is, the best way to quiet down a group of crying and yelling children is to go around and stick lollypops in their mouths. This stops the noise immediately, but as soon as the lollypops are eaten—look out! because the children know how to get them. The same goes for reprimands and attention; the children learn that they can get them by misbehaving. As a result, the teacher should be sensitive to the precise behavior for which she gives attention.

By way of example of the destructive function of reprimands, let us take a closer look at the study of Madsen *et al.* (1968b). The investigators had the teachers record the frequency of out-of-seat behavior in their classes as well as the number of "sit down" commands, and the frequency of praise for appropriate behavior during the baseline period. After baseline, the teachers were told to use "sit down" commands three times as often as they had during the baseline period. Whenever the frequency of "sit down" commands was increased, out-of-seat behavior increased. Conversely, when teachers praised in-seat behavior and ignored out-of-seat behavior, the out-of-seat behavior decreased. Therefore, this study points out that what might be thought to be a punisher (in this case, the "sit down" reprimand) can instead serve as a positive reinforcer.

Another source of attention which can support maladaptive behavior emanates from the peer group. Therefore, in some cases a teacher may systematically control her own behavior (praise good behavior and ignore inappropriate behavior) only to find no decrease in the target behavior. In some cases, the explanation may lie in the fact that the peer group approves of the behavior the teacher is ignoring through laughs or giggles, smiles, or in some cases even negative attention (which the target child finds reinforcing). These cases are more prominent in the upper elementary grades and beyond where peer attention supersedes adult attention. In comparing results of two studies that attempted to control the behavior of hyperactive children, Patterson (1965) attributed the more substantial success of one program to the greater involvement of the peer group.

When the peer group influence is considerable the teacher must attempt to get the peer group to reinforce appropriate behavior. Several techniques have been used by teachers to bring about such behavior—for example, when the teacher says, "The entire class can go to recess when everyone is quiet." This presumably gets the peer group to pressure individual member's behavior, since the group reward (going to recess) is contingent on group rather than on individual behavior. Little research has been conducted on the effect of peer attention (Altman and Linton, 1971). There are potential dangers in the use of group contingencies, which were discussed in Chapter 6. These should be reviewed by the teacher prior to initiating such practices.

ACTIVITY REINFORCERS. The use of an activity to strengthen a behavior uses the Premack principle mentioned in Chapter 6. Premack (1959) indicated that if arranged on a contingent basis, a more desired activity can be used as a reinforcer for a less enjoyable activity. Essentially, the Premack principle states that any high-probability behavior, if made contingent on a low-probability behavior, will increase the frequency of the low-probability behavior. Homme (1970) coined the term "Grandma's Law": "First you clean your plate, and then you get dessert." Becker *et al.* (1971) interpreted it in a variety of ways, such as "You do what I want you to do, before you get to do what you want to do." In other words, the child gets to engage in the activity he desires (the high-probability behavior) when, and only when, he has completed the task the teacher wants him to do (the low-probability behavior).

In employing activity reinforcers in a classroom the teacher should identify for the class in general, and for specific children in particular, activities they select to engage in when given a free choice. As a beginning, one can consult the list of activities given by Becker *et al.* (1971, p. 134), which includes privileges (collecting papers, leading the flag salute, choosing a game at recess), free time (for reading, listening to music, additional recess), and status activities (assisting classmates or younger children, being team captain). The teacher is advised to point out *why* the child is permitted to engage in the activity, such as "Since Andrew completed his arithmetic first, he can collect the papers." This points out to Andrew what he has done, and also provides the model to the rest of the class for the behavior that will result in activity reinforcers.

The classroom contains a number of activities that are potentially reinforcing, yet in many classes these activities are not contingent on any behavior. For example, art, music, recess, plus any number of privileges, are activities children enjoy and could be used as activity reinformers. Yet in most classes the children are allowed to engage in these activities *because* it is time for art or music. The behavioristic approach would suggest making participation *contingent on* behavior. One form of using activity reinforcers is that described by Addison and Homme (1966), in which for a specified amount of a task, a low probability behavior (LPB), the child selects from the reinforcing event menu an activity he would enjoy engaging in for a specified length of time. Even though some of the items on their menu are unique, most are available in a traditional classroom. Another way of making use of these activities entails scheduling activities in the day so that high probability behavior (HPB) and LPB are alternated. For example, the day might begin with the social studies period (here assumed to be a LPB) followed by music, followed by math, followed by recess, etc. Then, in order to participate in music (HPB), the child must complete his social studies assignment. Here, the HPB is contingent on academic work. The teacher could, however, make the HPB contingent on behavior—getting started quickly, working quietly in his seat, etc.

Becker *et al.* (1971) suggested that after the child has learned to work for a variety of reinforcers, the teacher can begin treating activities as if they would be as enjoyable as the activities he has been obtaining. By saying, "When you finish your math you can read your geography book for the time remaining in the period." In this way the teacher emulates Tom Sawyer's means of convincing his friends that whitewashing a fence was a very enjoyable activity.

SYMBOLIC REINFORCERS. As noted in Chapter 6, the use of tokens should be practiced only after reinforcers higher on the continuum of reinforcers have proven ineffective. Furthermore, a token economy for an entire class of children without serious learning or behavior problems seems difficult, if not impossible to justify. However, in certain instances a given child may require a token economy, in which case all of the parameters discussed in Chapter 6 apply. In addition, the teacher should be careful to make the token system as unobtrusive as possible so that the child is not singled out as being "different." To prevent this, particular care should be taken in the selection of the type of tokens adopted.

Assume for a moment that a teacher placed one child in a regular classroom on a token economy in the form of points recorded in a notebook at 30-minute intervals. One approach that has worked rather well is for the teacher to keep the notebook at his desk, then ask the child to come to his desk at the 30-minute interval when points earned are given, and tell the child why he has received the points he has earned.

Hall *et al.* (1968b) studied a token economy in the form of a point system. Each time a child was disruptive for 5 seconds, a mark was placed on the board which reduced the 5-minute break between periods by 10 seconds (24 such incidences eliminated the break entirely). Study behavior (the target behavior) increased from 47 percent during baseline to 76 percent when this token system was used to supplement teacher attention for appropriate behavior. Note, however, in this case how tokens were contingent on misbehavior (nonstudy behavior) and tokens led to punishment in that they reduced break time. When the token system was dropped, study behavior decreased by 16 percent. Altman and Linton (1971) reported another study by Schroer and Johnson in which a token system was employed in a regular classroom of sixth-graders. In that study, children were given ten arithmetic problems to solve in 10 minutes. For each correct problem 5 minutes of lunchtime was granted. Quantity of problems solved increased with no sacrifice in quality of performance.

In addition to tokens, a number of symbolic rewards, including letter grades, are used in the classroom. For those children with aspirations along academic lines, grades serve as powerful incentives for which these children work very hard. In using grades as reinforcers the teacher is advised to be sensitive to the precise behavior he is trying to strengthen. For example, high grades are commonly given contingent on *products*, such as term papers, exam papers, science projects, etc. Yet most teachers contend that they are trying to develop *processes*. In such a case, the child who has his father write a paper and his mother type it receives an A grade while the child who writes his own paper in longhand receives a C for his efforts. In the case of the A student, the teacher has taught him that when he has a paper to do, he asks his father and mother to collaborate on his behalf. It is difficult to determine the effect of a C grade, but for the college-oriented student it would probably be taken as a neutral or aversive consequence. As teachers we should think about the ways in which we use grades—as positive incentives in some cases (the promise of an A or B) or as the threat of punishment (the threat of a D or F) in others. I recall one of my teachers who gave every student 100 points at the beginning of a grading period and then students *lost* points for errors. To begin with, the entire approach was negative, but, in addition, after losing enough points to put one in the F category, he thought, "Well if I'm going to fail I might as well have a good time doing it." Some had F's after 1½ weeks, and from that time on were completely out of control. This is reminiscent of the case where a student approached the instructor and asked, "Why did I get an F?" The teacher replied, "Because I can't give anything lower." Once one has earned an F he knows that the teacher could give him no less.

Again with grades, sensitizing the teacher to *what* he is rewarding is a valuable contribution of the behavioristic orientation. If one wishes to reinforce *processes* as opposed to *products*, then praise and compliments may be used to strengthen appropriate process behaviors such as attending, persistence, attempting difficult problems, working to completion of a task.

Hence a variety of reinforcers are available for teachers to employ. The key to the entire sensitization issue is that teachers *be aware of what they are rewarding*, and not inadvertently reinforce behavior that is inappropriate. One point bears reemphasis: social reinforcers should be considered prepotent until proved otherwise. Teachers must not quickly resort to tokens when dealing with children in regular classes because to do so means regressing the child to reinforcement levels below those at which the child is capable of functioning. It is like taking a sixth-grade child who is having a slight reading problem and putting him in a preprimer. It is reinforcement overkill.

Developing New Behaviors

When you, as a teacher, want to increase behaviors in frequency, you employ an effective reinforcer after occurrences of the desired behavior. What can you do, however, when you want to develop new behaviors the child does not emit at present? You are referred to the discussion in Chapter 3 which indicated that two techniques are available for this purpose: shaping and modeling. These two techniques provide a means for teachers to develop in children new behaviors.

SHAPING. Teachers, in general, reserve their rewards (social and symbolic) for the few excellent papers or the several insightful answers given in class. The same phenomenon can be observed for student behavior—the child must exhibit a bit of extraordinary behavior before the teacher praises him. For those children who never or rarely write the excellent paper or exhibit the extraordinary behavior, the teacher must begin by reinforcing smaller bits of behavior that are prerequisite to the goal behavior. Koser (1971) summarized this as *think small*. For example, if a child is rarely in his seat when he is supposed to be, the teacher might begin by reinforcing his being in close proximity to his seat. Once that bit of behavior comes under control, the teacher starts reinforcing the child whenever he is in his seat, regardless of the length of time he is there. Subsequently, the teacher can reinforce him for being in his seat for 5 minutes, then 10 minutes, and so on until the child remains in his seat for the length of time originally specified. In cases where the child is not completing assignments, it may be necessary that the teacher reinforce his coming to class with the necessary materials (e.g., pencil and paper), putting marks on the paper, attempting the task, persisting, and other such process behaviors. Later, the teacher might reinforce completing the assignment on time, and later yet finishing on time with a certain degree of accuracy. The teacher should try to catch students getting better or improving on their past behavior, whether it is academic or social.

Becker *et al.* (1971) listed the following as behaviors best improved through shaping: working longer, working faster, staying in one's seat, participating in class discussion, and improving athletic skills. To increase the efficiency of such a program, the teacher could use verbal prompts to tell the child what he is expected to do—for example, "I want you to remain in your seat working on this assignment until you complete it. When you finish you can go to any of the interest centers."

In the process of reinforcing approximations to the desired behavior, the teacher can employ social, activity, or symbolic reinforcers. However, in the context of the regular classroom, praise and compliments are the most readily available and the easiest to dispense. Teachers, in some instances, seem reluctant to overuse praise; this reluctance finds no support in the research literature, for elementary age children do not seem to tire of compliments. Koser (1971) suggested that 20 or 30 compliments per hour should be the bare minimum, and rates as high as 50 to 70 per hour do not result in satiation. When the teacher sees something that is appropriate, such as getting started on an assignment, he should tell the child that he likes the way the child got started. The teacher does not take appropriate behavior for granted—he reinforces it, no matter how small it is.

MODELING. Another technique for developing new behaviors in modeling (see Chapter 3). Again, this is related, in practice, to the use of positive reinforcement. The teacher is a model for the children, and in addition, points out certain children in the class for the others to model.

Becker *et al.* (1971) related the case of a teacher who herself, through imitation, was teaching children in her class to exhibit the precise behavior she was trying to control. She talked a great deal, yelled at children, and hurried around the class. In order to provide a calmer model, she began moving around the class more slowly, spoke more softly and slowly, and quit yelling at children. She reported that the modification in her own behavior had a dramatic calming effect on the behavior of the children in her class. This example should sensitize teachers to the fact that their behavior and attitudes are copied by children, and teachers should periodically look at what they are doing. Are you calm? Are you aggressive? Do you convey the impression that learning is fun? This is reminiscent of the parent who observes his oldest son hitting his younger brother, and proceeds to spank the older child while saying, "I'll teach you to hit your brother!" In fact, he is teaching him, through modeling, how to hit his brother harder.

As mentioned above, the teacher also points out the models in the classroom. When the teacher says, "Arline, sit down," or "Barbara, be quiet," or "Walter, get started working," she is in effect establishing misbehaving children as models for the other class members. The reprimands say that if the rest of you want my attention, then start behaving like the children I have just attended to. Reverse the contingencies and establish well-behaved children as the models. If John is sitting quietly and ready to work while Andrew is out of his seat talking, say something like "I like the way John is ready to get started," and ignore Andrew's behavior. The McAllister *et al.* (1969) study demonstrated that what the teacher does in the first 2½ minutes determines the number of discipline problems for the remainder of the period. If the teacher compliments groups of students for desired behavior at the rate of once every 15 seconds for the first 2½ minutes, problem behavior will be held to a minimum. In cases where one child is exhibiting some inappropriate behavior, rather than reprimanding him, try to find another child near him who is doing what you want the first child to do, and praise him. The strengthening of behavior which occurs as a function of observing others who are reinforced for emitting that behavior is far from thoroughly understood (Altman and Linton, 1971). It would appear that such behavior is weak and relatively short lived unless additional steps are taken to strengthen it further. Altman and Linton (1971) concluded that the probable dynamics of this technique are that praising Bruce serves as a discriminative stimulus for Kelly to behave similarly. However, unless Kelly's behavior is reinforced, it is unlikely that it will persist or be maintained. It is interesting to note a possible "spillover" effect of praise by teachers. McManis (1967) reported that children sitting next to a partner who was praised by an experimenter increased in task performance despite the fact that they themselves were not praised.

The use of modeling techniques appears to hold promise for working with children who exhibit low self-evaluations and/or highly dependent behavior (Blackham and Silberman, 1971). Such characteristics are frequently found in EMR, learning disabled, and other children who have experienced substantial amounts of failure. When the model behavior may be too difficult for the subject-observer initially, it may be necessary to reinforce each element of behavior like that exhibited by the model. In a sense, this practice is like shaping in that the teacher tries to strengthen bits of behavior approximating the behavior ultimately desired.

Weakening or Eliminating Behaviors

In some cases, teachers attempt to develop positively desired behaviors, but in spite of their systematic use of the foregoing practices a given child's behavior continues to be inappropriate. What other steps can be taken? Several techniques were discussed in Chapter 3 for weakening behavior: counterconditioning, extinction, and punishment. In practice, counterconditioning uses positive reinforcement to increase behaviors that are incompatible with the behavior the teacher is trying to eliminate. For example, if the teacher can increase the amount of time a child sits in his seat, the out-of-seat behavior *must* decrease; if study behavior is increased, then nonstudy behavior has to decrease. This is accomplished by making reinforcement, be it social activity or symbolic in nature, contingent on the desirable behavior, while extinguishing undesirable behavior through ignoring it.

EXTINCTION. Withholding reinforcement following inappropriate behavior (ignoring) will result in a weakening of the inappropriate behavior. The speed with which the behavior extinguishes depends on many variables (discussed in Chapter 3) with the most influential being the schedule of reinforcement which maintained the behavior. Unfortunately, most misbehavior is maintained on some type of intermittent schedule, and therefore is more resistant to extinction than would be true if it were maintained on a continuous schedule.

Behaviors that do not endanger the child or his classmates and are not detrimental to the learning of others should be ignored by the teacher. This is difficult for some teachers because they are oriented to searching out the "bad" and "punishing it." However, as was mentioned in a preceding section of this chapter, reprimands assumed by teachers to be punishments can actually serve as positive reinforcers. The result is that the behavior the teacher is attempting to decrease is actually increased.

The potency of extinction procedures, if used alone, seems questionable (Koser, 1971). In order to make it effective the teacher must be sure to reinforce the desired behavior generously. What all of this seems to say to the classroom teacher is to ignore minor infractions and catch the children doing something right and then reinforce it. In some instances, however, the behavior is dangerous to the child or his classmates, or is so disruptive that others cannot work. In these cases, ignoring is not appropriate and the teacher must resort to punishment, preferably of a mild sort which is not self-defeating.

PUNISHMENT. Reese (1966) noted that while punishment is probably the most common technique of behavior control, it is also the most complex and controversial. Scientific opinion regarding the effectiveness of punishment varies considerably, even when ethical considerations are put aside. Two forms of punishment will be discussed: (1) withdrawal of a positive reinforcer, and (2) presentation of a noxious, or aversive, stimulus. Both forms are contingent on behavior, and in this way differ from extinction that is noncontingent.

Withdrawal of reinforcement contingent on behavior suppresses behavior more rapidly than does extinction (Reese, 1966). The reinforcer may be taken away (such as paying for a traffic ticket), or the opportunity to procure reinforcement may be withheld (such as having one's allowance docked for breaking a window). Teachers have frequently made the class come in from recess when children misbehave on the playground. Parents turn off the TV when their children argue. By taking away recess and TV watching, the tendency to misbehave is reduced.

As mentioned earlier (Chapter 3), one variation of the withdrawal of reinforcement that has been found to be effective is the procedure called *Time out*. This procedure involves removing a misbehaving child from a presumed reinforcing environment (e.g., the classroom) to an area of isolation for a specified period of time—usually quite short, such as 2, 5, or 10 minutes, and should not exceed 15 minutes. A study by Tyler (1965) demonstrated this procedure very well. Several delinquent boys in a treatment center repeatedly exhibited undesirable behavior around the pool table. They bounced the balls on the floor, wrestled, threw the balls, and so forth. The first step was to confine the boys in a time-out room for 15 minutes whenever the target behavior was shown. This was the "automatic" consequence. It resulted in a marked reduction in such instances. In the second phase, the use of time out was discontinued and warnings and threats were tried. This resulted in a rapid increase in the misbehavior. In the third phase, time out was again used, and the misbehavior decreased.

For this procedure to be effective, one must be able to assume that the classroom is more rewarding than sitting in a stimulation-free, time-out area. If this is not a valid assumption, the teacher of that class is in trouble and had better set about remedying the situation. Many teachers have employed techniques that are somewhat like time out, but differ in several important ways. For example, teachers send a child to sit in the principal's office, or to stand out in the hall. In most instances these are highly rewarding situations. In the school office the child can talk to the secretary (all secretaries in elementary schools are extroverts), watch new machines be demonstrated by salesmen, see other children come in with skinned knees or a bloody nose, or find out what new school rule will go into effect the next day. The principal's office is hardly a nonstimulating environment. If the hall door to the classroom has a window, the hall can be an even more stimulating environment than the office. When the teacher has his back to the door, the child can squash his nose against the glass, make faces, and when others in class laugh they get in trouble all because of him. I recall a situation from my elementary school days in Ohio where cloakrooms were the "time-out" rooms for teachers, who assumed that a room in which odors from snow melting off coats and boots and from a variety of lunches would be repelling to the child, was even worse than a neutral situation. On one occasion a child was sent to the cloakroom, where he proceeded to go through every other child's lunch and take one bite out of everyone's sandwich. This type of setting obviously allows children to get attention (favorable or unfavorable) which can reinforce the behavior the teacher is trying to weaken.

Becker *et al.* (1971) made the point that time out and isolation are not one and the same thing. Time out is the removal of a child from positive reinforcement. Hence putting a withdrawn child in isolation may not be considered punishment by the child, and thus isolating him would be a positive reinforcement. Likewise, if the classroom is not reinforcing then removal of a child from the classroom cannot serve as a punishment.

Koser (1971) described time out as a mild symbolic form of punishment used to suppress inappropriate classroom behavior. In establishing a time-out place in the classroom several things should be kept in mind. First, the teacher must be sure it is isolated from interesting things to look at or play with. The more free of stimulation it is, the more likely it will serve effectively. Some teachers have turned a file cabinet around and placed a chair between the file and a wall (without a window). In other cases, a setting such as above is a first step, and if the child refuses it or fools around while he is in it he is sent to the school office where a time-out room is constructed. The other school personnel should be informed not to interact socially with the child but to direct him quickly to the time-out area.

Some teachers have discussed the procedure with the class and told them that one, and only one, warning will be given, and when the misbehavior occurs a second time the child goes into the time-out setting. This practice avoids the problems inherent in differential treatment of different children, or when the nature or severity of a punishment becomes a function of the teacher's mood when the misbehavior occurs. If the child refuses to take the mild form of punishment, the time he must spend in time out is automatically doubled. The teacher must refrain from talking or discussing the behavior before or after time out and should not allow the child to take along any materials to the time-out area.

The length of time might be minimal (e.g., 5 minutes) for first offenses, and then increased for subsequent violations, or the time in time out is increased for any giggling, moving the chair, or noise making. Refusal by a child to accept a time-out punishment should not be debated. If refused in the classroom, he should be sent immediately to the office. If he refuses the office time out he should be suspended or the parents should be contacted. Koser (1971) reported that while parents might not cooperate in cases of suspension for misbehaviors (like talking too much, baiting the teacher), when the parents are told that their child refused to accept a very mild form of punishment, their cooperation is easily obtained.

When a child returns to the class after he has spent time in time out the teacher must not "hold a grudge" or ignore the child. In fact, the opposite should be the case. As soon as the teacher notices some good behavior, he should praise the child for improvement. Unless the teacher capitalizes on the improvement immediately following the punishment, no constructive purpose is served.

A further word of caution. In some cases, the teacher should be careful in removing children from class since it serves as a negative reinforcement if by being removed the child escapes some anxiety-producing situation—for example, if the child is not prepared for giving a book report, so just before it is his turn he misbehaves and the teacher sends him to the time-out area, which enables the child to avoid exposing his lack of preparedness. The next time he is not prepared one might expect him to misbehave again. Checks can be kept if the teacher is using the recording procedures suggested earlier, in that one may identify trends such as the misbehavior of a child just prior to the arithmetic lesson from which he wishes to escape. The recording of antecedents and consequences is essential if such trends are to be found.

Another form of punishment is the presentation of an aversive, or noxious, stimulus following the behavior. This is by far the most common form of behavior control used by parents and teachers (Blackham and Silberman, 1971; Reese, 1966). The reason punishment is used so frequently is well explained by Reese (1966), who contended that punishment negatively reinforces the punisher. That is, when a mother slaps her child for whining (aversive to the mother) the whining stops, and as a result the mother's slapping behavior is negatively reinforced. In the context of the classroom, Buckley and Walker (1970, p. 44) cited a teacher's lament, "I must tell Brian five times a day to stay in his seat, yet the minute my back is turned helping another child he is out of his seat again." Brian returns to this seat when instructed to do so, and the teacher's behavior (telling him to return to his seat) is strengthened since it terminates his out-of-seat behavior. This is unfortunate, however, because the precise behavior being strengthened in the teacher may be the attention that is supporting Brian's getting out of his seat.

Early generalizations about the effects of punishment indicated that it was useless because its effects were only temporary. More recently, however, Azrin and Holz (1966), after reviewing the literature pertaining to punishment, concluded that punishment has the exact opposite effect on behavior from reinforcement. That is, to argue that the effects of punishment are temporary is like arguing that if you reinforce a behavior once, the strengthening of that behavior is temporary. In summary, the effect of an aversive stimulus consequent on behavior depends on the intensity and quantity of the aversive stimulus, as well as the schedule which determined those responses that are punished.

There are several reasons, however, which counsel caution in the use of aversive stimulation. First, punishment may lead to aggressive behavior on the part of the child being punished—either by striking back at the punishing agent or at an irrelevant object (a desk, a door). Second, one is never sure what stimuli may be associated with the punishment, and hence become a discriminative stimulus which warns the child to *escape* or *avoid* the situation. For example, when a teacher ridicules a child during an arithmetic period, the child may associate the punishment with that teacher (or all teachers), arithmetic, the classroom, etc. In the future, when confronted with some of these stimuli (teachers, arithmetic) he seeks to escape. Third, punishment tends to be inconsistent, often dependent on the mood of the teacher, and can lead to confusion on the part of the child. When one punishes a behavior, other undesirable behaviors can be strengthened—for example, a child lies in order to avoid punishment for being tardy; he cheats on an examination in order to avoid receiving a low grade. Finally, for educational purposes punishment is inconsistent with a major educational goal—learning should be enjoyable and self-directed. To get a child to read, or to sit in his seat, or to manifest any other desirable behavior *because* he is afraid not to would seem incompatible with the goal of self-direction.

When teachers resort to punishment there are guides to its application which should be heeded. Becker *et al.* (1971, p. 157) suggested that it should be immediate, carried out in a calm manner, paired with reinforcement of incompatible behavior, and be consistent; and the teacher should be careful that the behavior punished does not receive reinforcement. Buckley and Walker (1970) also recommended that the teacher refrain from warnings and threats but instead punish the first occurrence, and every one thereafter.

The earlier discussion on reinforcement included mention of the frequent reinforcing function of a consequence the teacher assumes to be a punishment, such as reprimands. As a result, the teacher must not assume that a particular consequence is a punishment. The acid test comes when one determines the effect on the behavior—if it strengthens or weakens the behavior. To reemphasize the point, both reinforcement and punishment are defined solely by their effect on behavior. In fact, there is evidence that the same consequence can have *either* reinforcing or punishing effects which depend on the manner in which the punishment is given. Thomas, Becker, and Armstrong (1968) demonstrated that when frequent reprimands were used, and were audible to at least several other children, there was an increase in the disruptive behaviors. O'Leary and Becker (1968) concluded that low rates of disapproval, soft reprimands (so other children cannot hear them), and high rates of praise would be the most effective in changing behavior in the classroom.

In focusing on the regular classroom, an attempt was made to show how principles of learning have been, and can be, translated into practice with the population of children served. As a result, the translations tend to be "more natural" than was the case in a token economy class. Yet, the same principles apply in trying to strengthen behaviors, develop new behaviors, or weaken behaviors in the regular class—only the manner in which they are put into practice differs.

To ensure that there is not any misunderstanding, these procedures discussed in this chapter should be used in conjunction with the data collection techniques which we presented in Chapter 5. Remember, the only way to determine whether a consequence is serving as a reinforcer, punisher, or neutral stimulus is to see its effect on the behavior it follows. The only way to measure its effect is by keeping records of the incidence of the behavior, which must be done systematically.

CONTRACTING

One means of translating principles of learning into practice is by use of *contracts* between student and teacher (and possibly others such as parents or school administrators)—a technique that might be used in a special or regular class. The use of contracting is probably best exemplified by Homme's (1970) recent programmed book. Contracting incorporates the elements of learning theory with its major focus on the explication of the contingencies. By involving the student in "negotiating" the contract, one ensures that what he (the student) must do is clearly understood, and what reinforcement he can expect when he completes his part of the contract. The form of the contract can range from a verbal agreement to a written contract actually signed by the parties involved. Furthermore, the contract can be established with an individual student, a small group of students, or an entire class.

In establishing contracts two elements must be established: (1) the *task* which the student is expected to perform, and (2) the *reinforcer* which the student gets when he completes the task in the manner agreed upon. The nature of the *task* might vary from academics to classroom deportment. At the same time, the reinforcers might include any of those mentioned previously—tokens, tangibles, or activities (recreational or preferred academics). In summary, the contract consists of two parts, the task and the reinforcer. The wording of the contract follows Grandma's Law: "First you clean your plate, and then you get dessert." Or, in other words, "When you finish A, then you may do B." One minor point bears mention regarding the wording of the contract. Should the teacher say, "If you do A, then you may do B" the student can come back with, "And if I don't?" However, "When you do A" makes it less challenging and implies, "When and only when you complete the *task* can you get the reinforcer." Another guide to the wording of the contract, which was pointed out by Homme (1970, p. 20), is consistent with the previous discussion of classroom rules—they should be *positive*. The teacher should avoid negative contracts in which he specifies what punishment will be forthcoming when the child misbehaves. Instead, the teacher should specify the task he wishes the student to perform and then identify a positive reinforcer for that student or group of students.

Homme (1970, pp. 18–21) listed ten rules of contracting, many of which are reminiscent of the discussion in Chapter 6 and the first part of this chapter. One rule, however, warrants some elaboration. Rule #7, according to Homme (1970, p. 20) states, "The terms of the contract must be clear." This means that both the task and reinforcer sides of the agreement must be made explicit. For example, a poor contract might be "Do some reading and then you can do something you enjoy." Far more explicit would be, "Read Chapter 6 in your social studies text and answer the questions at the end and you can listen to music for ten minutes." The need for clarity strikes this author as relating closely with Hewett's (1968) admonition to specify *what, when, where, how, how much,* and *how well.*

Negotiation of contracts can obviously entail either party exerting varying degrees of control over the contract negotiated —that is, the teacher can determine both the task and the reinforcer; the student can determine both; or there can be mutual participation with teacher determining one part (task or reinforcer) and the student the other. Homme (1970) argued that the ultimate goal is to achieve self-contracting by the student—a step toward self-management. Toward that end Homme recommended successive approximations (closely related to the weaning process discussed in Chapter 6). For purposes of clarity, let us use *teacher* and *student* as the two parties engaged in the establishment of the contract. However, one can substitute parent for teacher, counselor for teacher, or any number of other terms and maintain the same procedures.

Homme (1970) identified three kinds of contracts: *teacher-controlled, student-controlled,* and *transitional.* In the teacher-controlled, it is the teacher alone who determines the amount of the task and the amount of the reward. In moving from this stage to student-controlled contracts (wherein the student determines the amount of the task and the amount of the reward), Homme (1970, pp. 45–49) suggested five transitional stages of contracting.

STAGE I—TEACHER-CONTROLLED. At this stage the teacher determines both the amount of the task and the amount of reinforcement, and then presents the contract to the student. The student accepts the terms and performs the task, whereupon the teacher presents the reward called for in the contract.

STAGE II—FIRST TRANSITION. At this stage, the student is given partial control over *either* the amount of the task *or* the reinforcer, but the teacher retains complete control over whichever aspect is not being jointly determined. For example, if student and teacher jointly decide the amount of reinforcement, then the teacher alone decides on the amount of the task. It should be noted, that prior to moving to Stage III, the student should practice determining the amount of the task as well, and the teacher then controls the amount of reinforcement.

STAGE III—SECOND TRANSITION. Equal control is exerted by teacher and student over both task and reward. Homme (1970, pp. 47–48) specified three substages. Form A involves teacher and student sharing in the determination of *both* task and reward. In Form B, the student has complete control over the amount of reinforcement and the teacher has control of the amount of task. Form C reverses Form B, with the student assuming control over task requirements and the teacher in control of the reinforcement. All three forms should be practiced prior to moving on to Stage IV.

STAGE IV—THIRD TRANSITION. Here one sees the teacher gradually phasing out in terms of control. At Stage IV, the student has complete control over the amount of reinforcement but shares control with the teacher in determining the amount of the task (Form A). In Form B, the student determines the amount of the task and shares control with the teacher in deciding the amount of reinforcement. Both forms should be practiced prior to moving to Stage V.

STAGE V—STUDENT-CONTROLLED. At this stage the student exerts complete control in determining the amounts of task and reinforcement, and one finds the student is far more self-directed than at the beginning of the program. The reader is encouraged to consult Homme's (1970, pp. 43–50) account of self-contracting in its original form.

Contracting can be, and has been, used in regular and special classes alike. It incorporates many of the principles of learning in a very explicit manner and with results that support the optimism of its advocates. The teacher contemplating its use must consider whether his class would need written or oral contracts, and must identify appropriate tasks and effective reinforcers. Unless these elements are appropriate, the contracting approach is unlikely to succeed.

REFERENCES

Addison, R. M., and Homme, L. E. The reinforcing event (RE) menu. *National Society for Programmed Instruction Journal*, **5**:8–9, 1966.

Azrin, N. H., and Holz, W. C. Punishment. In W. K. Honig (ed.) *Operant Behavior: Areas of Research and Application*. New York: Appleton-Century-Crofts, 1966.

Altman, K. I., and Linton, T. E. Operant conditioning in the classroom setting: A review of research. *J. Educ. Res.*, **64**:277–86, 1971.

Baer, D. M., and Wolf, M. M. The reinforcement contingency in preschool and remedial education. In R. D. Hess and R. M. Baer (eds.) *Early Education*. Chicago: Aldine Publishing Company, 1968.

Becker, W. C., Engelmann, S., and Thomas, D. R. *Teaching: A Course in Applied Psychology*. Chicago: Science Research Associates, 1971.

Becker, W. C., Madsen, C., Arnold, C., and Thomas, D. The contingent use of teacher attention and praise in reducing classroom behavior problems. *J. Spec. Educ.*, **1**:287–307, 1967.

Blackham, G. J., and Silberman, A. *Modification of Child Behavior*. Belmont, California: Wadsworth Publishing Co., Inc., 1971.

Buckley, N. K., and Walker, H. M. *Modifying Classroom Behavior*. Champaign, Ill.: Research Press, 1970.

Forness, S. R. Behavioristic approach to classroom management and motivation. *Psychol. Schools*, **7**:356–63, 1970.

Hall, R. V., Lund, D., and Jackson, D. Effects of teacher attention on study behavior. *J. Appl. Behav. Anal.*, **1**:1–12, 1968(a).

Hall, R. V., Panyan, M., Rabon, D., and Broden, M. Teacher applied contingencies and appropriate classroom behavior. Paper read at the American Psychological Association, San Francisco, September, 1968(b).

Hewett, F. M. *The Emotionally Disturbed Child in the Classroom*. Boston: Allyn and Bacon, Inc., 1968.

Holmes, D. S. The application of learning theory to the treatment of a school behavior problem: A case study. *Psychol. Schools*, **3**:355–59, 1966.

Homme, L. *How to Use Contingency Contracting in the Classroom.* Champaign, Ill.: Research Press, 1970.

Jackson, P. W. *Life in Classrooms.* New York: Holt, Rinehart and Winston, Inc., 1968.

Koser, K. P. Behavior modification lecture to teachers. Unpublished paper. Madison, Wisconsin, 1971.

McAllister, L. W., Stachowiak, J. G., Baer, D. M., and Conderman, L. The application of operant conditioning techniques in a secondary classroom. *J. Appl. Behav. Anal.,* **2**:277–85, 1969.

McManis, D. Marble-sorting persistence in mixed verbal incentive and performance level pairings. *Am. J. Ment. Defic.,* **71**:811–17, 1967.

Madsen, C. H., Becker, W. C., and Thomas, D. R. Rules, praise, and ignoring: Elements of elementary classroom control. *J. Appl. Behav. Anal.,* **1**:139–50, 1968(a).

Madsen, C. H., Becker, W. C., Thomas, D. R., Koser, L., and Plager, E. An analysis of the reinforcing function of "sit down" commands. In R. K. Parker (ed.) *Readings in Educational Psychology.* Boston: Allyn & Bacon, Inc., 1968(b).

O'Leary, K. D., and Becker, W. C. The effects of the intensity of a teacher's reprimands on children's behavior. *J. School Psychol.,* **7**:8–11, 1968.

Patterson, G. An application of conditioning techniques to the control of a hyperactive child. *Behav. Res. Ther.* **2**:217–26, 1965.

Premack, D. Toward empirical behavior laws: I. Positive reinforcement. *Psychol. Rev.,* **66**:219–33, 1959.

Reese, E. P. *The Analysis of Human Operant Behavior.* Dubuque, Iowa: William C. Brown Company, Publishers, 1966.

Thomas, D. R., Becker, W. C., and Armstrong, M. Production and elimination of disruptive classroom behavior by systematically varying teachers' behavior. *J. Appl. Behav. Anal.,* **1**:33–45, 1968.

Tyler, V. O., Jr. Exploring the use of operant techniques in the rehabilitation of delinquent boys. Paper read at the American Psychological Association, Chicago, September, 1965.

Zimmerman, E., and Zimmerman, J. The alteration of behavior in a special classroom setting. *J. Exp. Anal. Behav.,* **5**:59–60, 1962.

CHAPTER 8

Controversies Surrounding Behavior Modification

LIKE ANY OTHER technique, behavior modification would appear to have its strengths and weaknesses. However, unlike some of the alternatives, behavior modification appears to have proponents and opponents making extreme statements regarding its usefulness. To some, a teacher familiar with behavior modification techniques need know nothing else, whereas others would argue that there is no place in education for behavior modification. The truth, if it exists, probably lies somewhere between these two positions. One positive statement, however, can be made about behavior modification—it is controversial. A second point regarding behavior modification is that it has been effective (Forness and MacMillan, 1970) in select instances.

In the present chapter, the intent is to explore areas of controversy. In so doing, it is hoped that the reader will keep in mind a subtle distinction regarding the controversies; namely that one can criticize the theoretical framework upon which practice rests, or one can criticize practices commonly used as being inconsistent with the theoretical framework upon which they presumably rest. In exploring areas of controversy, my intent is to show what I see as the point where behavior modification now is insofar as the contributions it could make to education—to ascertain where, how, and with what children behavior modification can be a useful supplement for educators. I hasten to say that I do not believe it can be, or should be, a substitute for knowledge about child development, curriculum, or any other subfields within education.

Popularity

For the past few years nothing else has caught the imagination of educators as has behavior modification, which has been enthusiastically received by many in the field. MacMillan and Forness (1970) accounted for this popularity as stemming from the reported successes of this approach with children heretofore considered unreachable (i.e., custodial retardates, autistic children, brain injured) coupled with teachers' desperate need for something that works. Finally an approach was offered which said more than the old adages like "be fair and be consistent" with regard to discipline, and was successful.

Baumeister (1969) accounted for the popularity in terms of several considerations in a somewhat tongue-in-cheek article. First, he contends that the positivistic outlook of behavior modifiers is contagious. It is next to impossible to find a pessimistic behavior modifier. The fact that behavior modifiers eschew labels, etiology, and other nonobservable information as irrelevant fits with the rhetoric of relevance so popular today. Baumeister went on to explain that such optimism may reflect the faith in the power of operant techniques to alter behavior. In fact, among behaviorists there is little concern expressed over the limits of possible behavioral change possible for an individual child. The only limits are those imposed by the limitations of the behavior modifier—not those possessed by the individual whose behavior is being modified.

Another feature that attracts some followers is its precise and distinctive language. Baumeister (1969, p. 50) described this language as being comprehensible to only other behavior modifiers, and made the whole approach seem so very scientific. He gave an example:

> Thus, we have FRs, FIs, VRs, and VIs, mands and tacts, S^ds, and $S^\triangle$s, and schedules that are tandem and chained. To cite a more concrete illustration, it may be possible to reinforce IRTs. in an MR by employing a chained FR-1 dro scheduled.

MacMillan and Forness (in press) detected a polarization between those *for* and those *against* behavior modification. Should this develop to a substantial degree, the results would be drastic. Behavior modification may fall subject to its own publicity in that those who promise everything to everybody may oversell the approach. Once limitations appear, the entire approach may be discarded as "useless" when, in fact, the approach may have a great deal to contribute.

LIMITATIONS OF THE MODEL

Criticisms of the operant conditioning model as a guide to behavior modification programs have been limited in number. Most have focused on the directive to be objective and use observable and measurable units, as opposed to hypothetical constructs inferred from behavior. That is, the emphasis on observable and measurable behaviors and environmental events would appear to be a step toward the scientific method; however, at the same time, one risks ignoring important bits of data.

The emphasis on precision, according to Maehr (1968), precludes the possibility of uncovering general principles that enable one to predict behavior across divergent situations. For example, one concludes that a specific environmental event served as a reinforcer on a *post hoc* basis—if the probability of the behavior it followed is increased, then it was a reinforcer. In solving math problems one might find that, for Barbara, knowledge of being correct is a reinforcer. However, what is the nature of "being correct" in other activities such as playing the piano, swimming, or sewing? Maehr (1968) opted for a broader (and admittedly less precise) definition of being correct, as having one's expectancies confirmed, fulfilled, or surpassed. Thus, a broader definition sacrifices some precision and objectivity but enables one to predict what will be reinforcing in a wider variety of situations.

MacMillan and Forness (1970, in press) argued for the need to place behavior modification within the context of education, and identify things it *cannot do* as well as extolling what it can do. Toward that end, they discussed several theoretical constructs which they feel learning theory treats in a reductionistic manner: human learning, motivation, and reinforcement.

Human Learning

As one surveys the literature on operant conditioning he is struck by two features: the populations most frequently used, and the nature of the behaviors being modified. First, the majority of studies deal with subjects who are functioning at rather immature levels—preschool children, mental retardates, emotionally disturbed children, or those in regular elementary classes. Investigators have been less willing to work with adolescents or those whose behaviors are more complex. Second, as noted by Baumeister (1969), the preponderance of published work on behavior modification has dealt with behaviors consisting of well-defined response topographies—toileting, seat sitting, hand raising, and talking out in class. As important as these behaviors may be, Baumeister (1969) contended that the ultimate criterion hinges on the more complicated behaviors of cognition, socialization, and acculturation. In these areas there has been little convincing work by the behavior modifiers. The question must be asked whether only behaviors that lend themselves to a sequential step-by-step programming are the ones amenable to the behavioristic approaches. To date, these are the kinds of behaviors altered reliably by behavior modification techniques.

As noted in Chapter 1, the verb "to learn" encompasses a multitude of different kinds of learning, and the foregoing discussion indicates that some kinds of learning are more adequately explained by the behavioristic paradigms than others. MacMillan and Forness (1970) stated that the usual learning situation for human subjects is far more complex than is suggested by the behavioristic paradigm. The complexity is even more pronounced in the learning of symbolic material, wherein the inherent logic in the material to be learned is thought by some to be extremely important. For example, Piagetians (Flavell, 1963) contended that schemata (organized information) result from two complementary processes—assimilation and accommodation. If new material to be learned is presented in a manner that enables an existing schema to be broadened in order to incorporate it (accommodation) or so that it fits an existing schema (assimilation), learning can be facilitated. Robert Gagné (1962), operating outside the Piagetian framework, contended that the nature and structure of the task to be learned is vastly more important than the behavioristic principles of learning, such as practice and reinforcement.

Maehr (1968) took issue with the notion of intermittent reinforcement as being more effective than continuous reinforcement for promoting memory. The animal research supports this contention, but when one looks to the literature on linear type programs with human subjects, the applicability of this principle is questionable. Rotter (1955) showed that intermittent reinforcement is more effective if, and only if, the child perceives the reinforcement as unrelated to his own efforts. That is, if the child perceives reinforcement as resulting from chance factors, then partial reinforcement has a greater effect in avoiding extinction. However, if the child perceives reinforcement as being a consequence of his skill or ability, then 100 percent reinforcement is actually more effective.

Much of programmed instruction and teaching machines

falls subject to the same criticisms (Stafford and Combs, 1967). Certain abstractions may not be as thoroughly taught through means consistent with behavioristic principles as through less structured means. At this point, inadequate evidence prevents one from knowing which tasks might be best taught through which methodology.

Motivation

Coleman (1969) distinguished between "push" and "pull" conceptualizations of motivation. In the "push" approaches, the drive that activates the organism is seen to be within the individual. Conversely, the "pull" approaches consider motivation to arise out of the desire of the individual to obtain a consequence that is external to the self. Obviously, behavior modification represents the "pull" approaches to motivation. MacMillan and Forness (in press) contended that ignoring or discounting potential ways of motivating children ("push" sources) on the grounds that such sources cannot be observed or measured but rather must be inferred from behavior seems to limit the teacher. Furthermore, sound empirical evidence exists in support of "push" sources of motivation which cannot be adequately incorporated into the behavioristic paradigm.

From within the behavioristic framework, behavior analysts attempt to get children to read, sit quietly, dress themselves, attend, and develop other appropriate behaviors by using tokens, candy, and other extrinsic rewards in association with the target behavior. The basic tenet herein is that desire or motivation can be manipulated by simply applying the reward when the child performs the desired behavior and by withholding when the target behavior is not emitted. This conceptualization of motivation is considered reductionistic by MacMillan and Forness (1970). To support their contention these authors presented several motives which must be inferred from behavior—an inference that is unacceptable to the behaviorist who insists on the observable and quantifiable. These motives are curiosity, cognitive dissonance, exploration, and competence.

One of the most noted American psychologists, Harlow (1949, 1953), following a series of empirical studies, concluded that there may be an innate drive of curiosity. This drive usually operates only after the more primary needs are satiated (e.g., physiological needs, need for safety). In explaining how this drive operates, Harlow (1953) stated that children and monkeys can enjoy exploration for what it is. Put differently, the behavior itself need not result in the reduction of a biological drive or lead to obtaining some "payoff." Several findings which emerged from Harlow's (1949) research on learning sets are virtually impossible to explain from the operant position. For example, in one study monkeys were given a food pellet following each correct response. However, instead of immediately swallowing the food, the monkeys stored the pellets in their cheeks. To make things worse, occasionally, after making an incorrect response, the monkeys would swallow a food pellet, thus "reinforcing" the incorrect response. However, the monkeys improved in their development of learning sets despite their unsystematic reinforcement contingencies. Obviously something other than the schedule of reinforcement and the nature of the reinforcement accounted for the improvement in the development of learning sets. In most preschool-age children one can observe an almost insatiable curiosity (often to the dismay of their mothers), and educators might try to find out how to use it, or at least not suppress it, in the context of formal schooling.

From Festinger's "theory of cognitive dissonance" it is concluded that stimulation-seeking behavior reflects another intrinsic source of motivation for which there is no quantifiable or measurable payoff. Festinger contends that when incoming stimulation is contradictory to presently held conceptions or perceptions one is pushed to resolve these discrepancies. It is his belief, that in human beings cognitive incongruities are a primary source of motivation. A teaching technique that makes use of this notion is one whereby the teacher presents information or a point of view that is contradictory to the point of view held by a student or a group of students. When a student cannot accommodate the teacher's input within his (the student's) existing framework, he will be motivated to resolve the discrepancy by altering (either modifying it or discarding it) his framework. When used effectively the foregoing technique does appear to motivate students, yet there is no payoff that one can see.

Yet another source of intrinsic motivation is described in Piaget's equilibration process in which cognitive adaptation results from the dynamic interaction of assimilation and accommodation processes. Hunt (1961), in describing equilibration, stated that exploratory behavior is inherently interesting and rewarding to the child when it relates to his present schemata. This "match" between the task and the child's level of cognitive functioning is critical—it must be slightly ahead of where he is but within his grasp. When these two elements are present, one need not have a payoff for performing the task. This is where one gets into the artistry of teaching—how to select a task that achieves the match of which Hunt (1961) has written. Class assignments are usually unable to achieve it because within a class there is too wide a range of levels of cognitive functioning. It must be done on an individual basis, or at least with small groups.

Another framework within which one can consider intrinsic motivation was offered by White (1965) in his "concept of competence." Like Harlow's curiosity drive, White contended that it is in studying the satiated child that one can come to understand human nature. While his paper was critical of the traditional Freudian view of motivation, based on need reduction, his notions bear directly on the present discussion. White (1965) contended that human beings are motivated at all developmental stages to achieve mastery over their environment. In observing an infant at play or a one-year-old insisting on feeding himself, it is difficult to explain adequately such behavior in terms of need reduction or an observable payoff. If, for example, the one-year-old was principally concerned with obtaining food, he would get more food by letting his mother feed him. Rather, White (1965, p. 15) posited that the child wants to master his environment (the use of a spoon, for example). Regarding play behavior, he wrote:

> It is directed, selective, and persistent, and it is continued not because it serves primary drives, which indeed it cannot serve until it is almost perfected, but because it satisfies an intrinsic need to deal with the environment.

The goal of behavior, according to White, is to be effective in dealing with one's environment, to be competent, or to be autonomous. The individual is motivated or pushed to master various tasks in order to achieve a sense or feeling of competence—not observable and not quantifiable.

MacMillan and Forness (1970) argued that while one can acknowledge the usefulness of "pull" approaches to motivation, educators must also make use of whatever "push" sources of motivation are available. Curiosity, exploration, cognitive dissonance, and competence are motives not readily explained in behavioristic terms; nevertheless, they would appear to be useful in the context of education and should be used when possible.

According to Maehr (1968), one of the major selling points of teaching machines and programmed instruction is their "interest value." Regularly presented positive reinforcement increases attention, prevents extinction, and prolongs memory—in short, it solves education's most pressing problem, motivation. However, as Maehr (1968) pointed out, the assumption underlying this approach, that organisms cannot get enough reinforcement, appears invalid. Being right at a task can become "boring" to a student—the student apparently satiates. When there is no risk of being wrong, the student's attention wanes. The point emphasized by Maehr is that the schedule of reinforcement most appropriate for maintaining attention varies as a function of subject characteristics. For example, a child who has had little success with a task in the past will not satiate on feedback of success as rapidly as a child with a history of success, who will soon reject a 100 percent reinforcement schedule. Rather, the high achievement students appear to exhibit the highest motivation when the probability of success is moderate. He cited some of his own research which indicated that when subjects were right only 50 percent of the time they evidenced the greatest persistence on the task. He concluded that 100 percent reinforcement may be assuring, but not challenging; failure makes success meaningful and interesting.

Reinforcement

Reinforcement, according to behaviorists, is commonly defined as "a stimulus which increases the probability of a response." The reinforcement does not have to be related to the behavior; in fact, in many instances the separation is intentional. For example, the use of candy to reinforce reading behavior is unlike what occurs in the natural environment. The definition raises certain theoretical issues and has practical ramifications.

First, the definition of reinforcement, while appropriate for infrahuman subjects, may be limited in its applicability when applied to human subjects with a complex language system. Jensen (1968) described the verbal confirming response (V_c), which he contended is a type of self or symbolic reinforcement. It is extremely limited in lower forms of animals and young children, and according to Jensen, is more than a secondary reinforcement. A secondary reinforcer is a previously neutral stimulus that has gained reinforcing properties through being paired with a primary or effective secondary reinforcer. Secondary reinforcers are known to extinguish rapidly in animal studies, which is not true for V_c. However, the V_c has the effect of strengthening behavior despite the fact that it has no reinforcing properties in a biological sense. According to Jensen (1968, p. 124), "the V_c response is most often covert, especially in adults, and may even be unconscious. It consists, in effect, of saying to oneself *Good* or *That's right* or *wrong*." The function of language in the above manner has been demonstrated by several Russian psychologists

CONTROVERSIES SURROUNDING BEHAVIOR MODIFICATION

(Razran, 1959). The V_c response must be self-initiated. Hence to the extent that teachers provide extrinsic reinforcers which judge *right* and *wrong* for the child, are we precluding the need of the child to develop the V_c response? Should this be the case, the use of tangible reinforcers may be detrimental to the development of independent problem-solving behaviors.

Another potential problem in generalizing from animal studies to practice with human subjects has arisen in some pilot studies that I have run recently. The research to date has indicated that once a teacher begins to ignore a bit of inappropriate behavior in the classroom, he must be careful not to weaken and attend to it because that would put the child on an intermittent schedule, thus making the behavior highly resistant to extinction. This conclusion is supported by numerous investigations with animals; however, in the classroom with children with language and mediation abilities it needs systematic study. Luria (1961), the Soviet psychologist, provided extensive research pertaining to the role of speech in the regulation of behavior. This research indicated that once the child states the "rule" governing *when* to respond, that rule controls his behavior. Based on limited attempts, a similar phenomenon appears regarding the teacher's attending behavior. As long as the teacher "generally" ignores the target behavior, an occasional backsliding does not appear to alter dramatically the rate of extinction. The child seems to have stated a rule, "She will not attend to behavior X," and that rule regulates his behavior. This notion is extremely tentative and in need of experimental verification.

Finally, learning theory tends to ignore the differences between individuals whose behavior is being modified. Maehr (1968) stated that reinforcement is filtered through the perceptions and cognitions of the child, and that one must deal with how these perceptions and cognitions alter the reinforcement and thus ameliorate its effect. The example regarding 100 percent versus 50 percent reinforcement, given earlier in this chapter, applies here. Maehr (1968) pointed out that behaviorists must not ignore the subjective side of reinforcement. In keeping with this, MacMillan (1970) argued that one must not interpret the dictum "All behavior is learned" to mean that all children learn alike, in the light of the extensive evidence on individual differences in learning. For viewing reinforcement the internal frame of reference is as important as the external one.

Turning for a moment to a more applied aspect of reinforcement, Ferster's (1966) distinction between *arbitrary* and *natural* reinforcers must be considered by teachers. He noted arbitrary reinforcers differ from natural reinforcers in two ways: (1) When arbitrary reinforcers are used, the performance that is reinforced is narrowly specified rather than broadly defined. (2) For arbitrary reinforcers, the individual's existing response repertoire does not influence his behavior to the extent it does in the case of natural reinforcers. As a result, natural reinforcers are far more desirable because they lead to more integrated, general learning.

An example of the foregoing was given by MacMillan and Forness (1970, pp. 295–96):

> In the first case, a positive consequence is promised for a specific behavior, seat sitting, and a child can obtain that consequence only by conforming to specific demands. He sits in his seat to obtain the reward, but learning does not necessarily generalize to global behaviors, that is, adequate classroom behavior. In the second case, arbitrary reinforcers benefit the controller, not the controlled. The teacher who says, "If you sit in your seat, I'll give you five check marks" is arbitrarily reinforcing seat sitting, which is reinforcing to the teacher for employing the strategy. But the child is not being reinforced by a consequence that naturally exists in his environment. His natural environment has never reinforced his sitting in his seat with a check mark, nor is it likely to in the future. In fact nonsitting has probably been rewarded through satisfying the curiosity drive.

To elaborate, there will not be tokens provided outside the contrived environment, thus jeopardizing generalization of the new behavior. Therefore, MacMillan and Forness (1970) argued that arbitrary reinforcers may be justifiably used in the *acquisition* stage of a shaping program, but they must be supplanted by natural reinforcers during the maintenance stage. This topic, which will be dealt with again in the following section, seems to be one of the more easily overlooked problems in using behavior modification techniques.

PROBLEMS IN THE APPLICATION OF THE MODEL

Goals

Simmons (1970) described behavior modification as a delivery system. This may seem to be less than profound; however, it gets at the heart of a limitation of *omission*—that is, the behavior modification model provides the teacher with no direction whatsoever in determining goals for the student. This in no way suggests that behavior modification advocates claim that the model does determine goals, but in its inability to do so may lie the reason for its lack of acceptance by educators, in general. Hewett *et al.* (1969, p. 523) discussed the lack of balanced emphasis on goals and methods. They wrote:

> In general, selection of these goals is based on a desire to aid the child in changing maladaptive behavior to adaptive behavior. At best, these concepts of "maladaptive" and "adaptive" provide only the broadest of guidelines for selection of specific behavioral goals. In this sense the powerful methodology of the behavior modification approach is not matched by concern with goals in learning. Teachers are provided with an efficient means of taking emotionally disturbed children someplace but not substantially aided in the selection of where to go.
> It is this lack of balanced emphasis on goals and methods that may preclude the acceptance of behavior modification in the field of education, particularly in the public school, and thereby may greatly limit its usefulness.

As a result, in an attempt to answer the first question recommended by Ullmann and Krasner (1965, p. 1)—"What behavior is maladaptive, that is, what subject behaviors should be increased or decreased?"—a different question often gets answered (MacMillan and Forness, 1970, p. 292): "What behavior manifested by the child most annoys me as his teacher?" Sometimes, the behaviors emitted by a child which annoy a teacher may have no interfering effects on that child's learning or the learning of the rest of the class. It is the teacher's problem, not the child's, and probably should be left alone. In determining *what* should be taught, the teacher must use developmental theories (e.g., Erikson or Piaget) which suggest development tasks the child must master in order to achieve subsequent developmental levels. In the academic sphere, curriculum guides provide guidance for selecting *what* to teach. Lacking either of the above, the teacher can, and unfortunately often does, arbitrarily decide *what* the child must learn—this can have dire consequences.

Wood (1968) expressed concern over the possibility that teachers are provided a powerful tool (behavior modification techniques) without developing an understanding of its implications and potential misuse simultaneously. More specifically, one can only hope that teachers provided with the "how to" of behavior modification will exercise good judgment in selecting inappropriate and appropriate behavior. In the light of the evidence suggesting that teachers, in general, are more concerned with maintaining power over students than in transmitting knowledge and skill, this concern seems valid (Eddy, 1967; Henry, 1957; Landes, 1965; Moore, 1967).

The behavior modifier exerts tremendous control over his subjects. Wood (1968, p. 14) described this role as follows: Having defined the child's present behavior as inappropriate, *he* plans to shape it toward behavior *he* has defined as appropriate. In the following passage, he described the teacher most likely to misuse this power with disregard for the rights of the child to participate:

> These teachers may often be those against whose already abusive application of their authority pupils have the greatest need to be protected. Like many "tools," behavior modification techniques are themselves morally blind. Like a stout sword, they work equally well in the hands of hero or tyrant. Any person of mod-

erate intelligence can, with assistance if not independently, apply them with great effectiveness for good or ill.

As noted by MacMillan and Forness (1970) the danger is greater for exceptional children for whom many of their rights are abridged at the time of identification and labeling, thereby making them very susceptible to such abuses. Warren (1971, p. 2) echoed the same notions: "The behavior modification tool is called powerful, not perfect," and "Most powerful tools can be dangerous when improperly used."

Overkill

Throughout Part II of this book there is a recurring theme; namely that behavior modification is based on principles of learning and not on the gimmickry and trappings seen in some "behavior modification programs." To some teachers with limited exposure to the behavior modification field, the tokens, check marks, and M&M's are synonymous with behavior modification. As was noted earlier, this apparent seduction by some by the trappings of behavior modification has led to adoption of a program developed for one population (e.g., severely disturbed) for a group (e.g., regular third grade) that deviates little, if any, from the norm. MacMillan and Forness (in press) gave several possible explanations for this state of affairs. First, the original educational programs based on behavior modification (e.g., Birnbrauer and Lawler, 1964) were for children who deviated markedly from the norm, wherein low-level reinforcers were necessary. Some see such programs and adopt them lock, stock, and barrel to use with children who do not begin to resemble the original class on which it was used. A second reason for the use of low-level reinforcers may be the fact that the use of tokens precludes the necessity of identifying reinforcers that work for individual children. Finally, some may confuse a research design with recommended practice. In Hewett's (1968) Santa Monica Project, for example, all children in the experimental class received check marks at 15-minute intervals. What is often ignored is that the check marks served as a data collection device or a system of accountability. This was necessary in order to collect the kinds of data Hewett wanted, but nowhere did Hewett (1968) recommend putting all children on check marks regardless of their needs.

When to Use Behavior Modification

One danger inherent in advocating any one means of changing behavior is that one comes to function within the constraints imposed by that rationale. In the case of the teacher taught to use behavioristic techniques of shaping and modeling, that teacher may lack the flexibility to employ other techniques which may, in a given instance, be more appropriate. For example, one case I have seen (and apparently many similar occurrences have taken place in the light of the frequency with which it is mentioned) wherein after working over two years, a staff of teachers approached most behaviors in need of change by means of shaping. In one instance, a child was very disruptive. The teachers began taking baseline counts and devising intricate shaping procedures and the like, when their immediate supervisor stepped in and recommended that they first simply tell the child to stop the behavior. This nonscientific approach was tried and it worked. The obvious point is that time and energy can be wasted by inflexibility, and sometimes more direct approaches are more efficient.

Related to the above are the types of behaviors most amenable to behavior modification techniques. This was discussed early, so let it suffice to say that behaviors of limited topography (sitting, talking) are those where the probability of success is highest with the behavioristic approaches.

ETHICAL CONSIDERATIONS

The issue over whether the use of behavior modification techniques is ethical or unethical is bound to remain with us since it is a philosophical, not an empirical, question. Considerable attention and space have been devoted to this issue elsewhere; however, much of the criticism strikes me as creating a straw man to attack. No doubt, abuses in the name of behavior modification do exist; however, as Warren (1971) noted, one can also argue that if misused, damaging or an ineffective waste of time and money can result from penicillin, iodized salt, or education. Used by knowledgeable professionals, behavior modification can be a helping tool for children; misused by those with poor judgment or questionable motives it can be harmful. To date, I know of no screening devices for determining who should be allowed to learn the techniques derived from learning theory.

One question that commonly arises stems from the perceived evilness in manipulating or controlling the behavior of others. In education, one constantly attempts to control people, change their behavior, influence their attitudes, and so on—that is the nature of education and learning: "changes in behavior as a result of experience." What does pose a problem is the standard of judgment and the behaviors that are the target behaviors. Few would argue against changing a child's reading behavior to higher operations; however, most would question attempts to manipulate a child's attitudes toward political parties, toward religion, or against a minority group. This is true no matter what technique is being used to manipulate—independent of whether it is by means of behavior modification, nondirective counseling, reality therapy, or some other means.

Warren (1971) cited the use of punishment as *the* most controversial point, and the focus of the loudest criticism. With publication of an article in *Life* magazine (1965) concerning the use of punishment (electric shock) in the UCLA program with autistic children headed by Dr. O. Ivar Lovaas, harsh criticisms such as inhumane, sadistic, brutal were heard regarding this program and other programs like it. Is the use of electric shock with these children any more inhumane than allowing such a child to perform self-mutilations? Punishment is used everyday, as noted by Warren (1971); mothers spank, bosses scold, judges send men to prison, police give tickets, and on and on. The misuse, or abuse, of punishment is a result of the "Law of Least Resistance," or doing what is easy without serious consideration of what alternative approaches are the most likely to work.

For a high-level exchange on the issues of an ethical nature, the reader should consult the Rogers and Skinner papers published by *Science* (1956).

CONCLUSION

The use of behavior modification can be a great aid to the classroom teacher. In this book, an attempt has been made to present the learning principles on which such techniques rest; to present ways in which professionals have seen fit to translate these principles into practice; and finally to expose the reader to some limitations in the approach. Before closing, let one point be made which will counter some of the propaganda heard regarding behavior modification. In some circles, one hears advocates telling teachers that it is easy to use. To quote Warren (1971, p. 2):

> The simplicity of the techniques used is more apparent than real. The complexity and sheer hard work of developing behavior modification programs is far more real than apparent.

Like all other techniques, it is not a panacea. It is "a," not "the," tool (Warren, 1971, p. 2). I do believe it is a tool a classroom teacher will find advantageous to have at his disposal.

REFERENCES

Baumeister, A. A. More ado about operant conditioning—or nothing? *Ment. Retard.*, 7:49–51, 1969.

Birnbrauer, J., and Lawler, J. Token reinforcement for learning. *Ment. Retard.*, 2:275–279, 1964.

Coleman, J. C. *Psychology and Effective Behavior.* Glenville, Ill.: Scott, Foresman and Company, 1969.

Eddy, E. M. *Walk the White Line: A Profile of Urban Education.* New York: Doubleday Anchor, 1967.

Ferster, C. B. Arbitrary and natural reinforcement. Paper delivered at the meeting of the American Association for the Advancement of Science, Washington, D.C., 1966.

Festinger, L. A. *A Theory of Cognitive Dissonance.* Evanston, Ill.: Row, Peterson & Company, 1957.

Flavell, J. H. *The Developmental Psychology of Jean Piaget.* Princeton, N.J.: Van Nostrand Reinhold Company, 1963.

Forness, S. R., and MacMillan, D. L. Origins of behavior modification with exceptional children. *Except. Child.,* 37:93–100, 1970.

Gagné, R. M. Military training and principles of learning. *Am. Psychol.,* 17:83–97, 1962.

Harlow, H. The formation of learning sets. *Psychol. Rev.,* 56:51–65, 1949.

Harlow, H. Mice, monkeys, men, and motives. *Psychol. Rev.,* 60:23–32, 1953.

Henry, J. Attitude organization in elementary school classrooms. *Am. J. Orthopsychiatry,* 27:117–33, 1957.

Hewett, F. M. *The Emotionally Disturbed Child in the Classroom.* Boston: Allyn & Bacon, Inc., 1968.

Hewett, F. M., Taylor, F. D., and Artuso, A. A. The Santa Monica project: Evaluation of an engineered classroom design with emotionally disturbed children. *Except. Child.,* 35:523–29, 1969.

Hunt, J. McV. *Intelligence and Experience.* New York: The Ronald Press Company, 1961.

Jensen, A. R. Social class and verbal learning. In M. Duetsch, I. Katz, and A. R. Jensen (eds.) *Social Class, Race, and Psychological Development.* New York: Holt, Rinehart and Winston, Inc., 1968.

Landes, R. *Culture in American Education.* New York: John Wiley & Sons, 1965.

Life. Screams, slaps, and love, May 7, 1965, pp. 90-A–95.

Lovaas, O. I., Freitag, G., Gold, V. J., and Kassorla, I. C. Experimental studies in childhood schizophrenia: Analysis of self-destructive behavior. *J. Exp. Child Psychol.,* 2:67–84, 1965.

Luria, A. R. *The Role of Speech in the Regulation of Normal and Abnormal Behavior.* New York: Liveright, 1961.

MacMillan, D. L. Behavior modification: A teacher strategy to control behavior. *Report of the Proceedings of the Forty-fourth Meeting of the Convention of American Instructors of the Deaf.* Berkeley, Calif.: 1968, pp. 68–76.

MacMillan, D. L. Ground rules for behavior modification. Paper read at the Annual Meeting of the American Association of Mental Deficiency, Washington, D.C., May 7, 1970.

MacMillan, D. L., and Forness, S. R. Behavior modification: Limitations and liabilities. *Except. Child.*, 37:291–97, 1970.

MacMillan, D. L., and Forness, S. R. Behavior modification: Savior or savant? *Am. J. Ment. Defic.*, in press.

Maehr, M. L. Learning theory, some limitations of the application of reinforcement theory to education. *School Soc.*, 96:108–10, 1968.

Moore, G. A. *Realities of the Urban Classroom: Observations in Elementary Schools.* New York: Doubleday Anchor, 1967.

Rogers, C. R., and Skinner, B. F. Some issues concerning the control of human behavior: A symposium. *Science*, 124:1057–66, 1956.

Rotter, J. B. The role of the psychological situation in determining the direction of human behavior. In M. R. Jones (ed.) *Nebraska Symposium on Motivation.* Lincoln, Neb.: University of Nebraska Press, 1965, pp. 245–69.

Razran, G. Soviet psychology and psychophysiology. *Behav. Sci.*, 4:35–48, 1959.

Simmons, J. Q. The behavior modification model. Paper presented at the Ninety-fourth Annual Meeting of the American Association on Mental Deficiency, Washington, D.C., May, 1970.

Stafford, R. R., and Coombs, C. F. Radical reductionism: A possible source of inadequacy in autoinstructional techniques. *Am. Psychol.*, 22:667–69, 1967.

Ullmann, L., and Krasner, L. *Case Studies in Behavior Modification.* New York: Holt, Rinehart and Winston, Inc., 1965.

Warren, S. A. Behavior modification—Boon, bane, or both? *Ment. Retard.*, 9:2, 1971.

White, R. W. Motivation reconsidered: The concept of competence. In I. J. Gorden (ed.) *Human Development: Readings in Research.* Glenview, Ill.: Scott, Foresman and Company, 1965.

Wood, F. H. Behavior modification techniques in context. *Newsletter of the Council for Children with Behavior Disorders*, 5:(4):12–15, 1968.

Glossary

ADAPTIVE BEHAVIOR. That behavior which is considered appropriate for a given individual in a specific context. This term usually refers to behavior that is judged acceptable by authorities, such as teachers, and not in need of modification. These authorities are guided by developmental and societal norms for making such judgments.

AVERSIVE STIMULUS. Any stimulus to which, if given a choice, an individual would select a neutral stimulus in preference. Furthermore, the individual will select to terminate or avoid these stimuli if given a choice.

AVOIDANCE BEHAVIOR. Those responses emitted by the individual with the intent of avoiding or postponing an aversive stimulus.

BEHAVIOR. All observable and/or measurable activity of the individual whether elicited or emitted. Behavior can be segmented into responses and includes all activity which potentially can be measured and/or observed, thereby including even the most subtle activities.

BEHAVIORAL REPERTOIRE. This term refers to the total summation of all behaviors existent for a given individual. This usually refers to the individual's operant behavior but can also refer to respondent behavior.

CHAINING. The process whereby more complex behaviors are created by linking together of simple operant responses. Technically, the process includes the combining of operants which consist of discriminative stimulus-response-reinforcement sequences, in which a given stimulus in the chain serves both discriminative and reinforcing functions.

CONDITIONED STIMULUS. A stimulus that has acquired its power to elicit or reinforce behavior, since it initially lacked such power.

CONDITIONING. See Operant conditioning and Respondent conditioning.

COUNTERCONDITIONING. A technique for weakening a given behavior by establishing a stimulus-response connection (respondent) in which the new response elicited by the stimulus is incompatible with response formerly elicited by the same stimulus. In the operant paradigm, counterconditioning consists of reinforcing behaviors that are incompatible with the behavior one is trying to weaken.

CONTINGENCY. The conditions that must be met if a reinforcer is to be forthcoming. These conditions must be met fully prior to the presentation of the reward by the controlling agent.

DIFFERENTIAL REINFORCEMENT. A technique whereby certain responses are reinforced while other responses emitted are not reinforced. This procedure is particularly useful in establishing discrimination in responding to discriminative stimuli.

DISCRIMINATION. The process whereby the individual responds differently in different stimulus situations. This is developed through differential reinforcement of behavior in the presence of one stimulus situation and not reinforcing the same behavior in the presence of other stimulus situations. It is the opposite of generalization.

DISCRIMINATIVE STIMULUS. A stimulus which cues the individual that if he responds he is likely to be reinforced. The stimuli precede operant responses and come to exert control over these operants in that responses emitted in the presence of these stimuli are likely to be reinforced, whereas in the absence of these stimuli the same responses will go unreinforced. Hence discriminative stimuli exert control over the probability that operants with which they are paired will be emitted.

ESCAPE BEHAVIOR. A response that is negatively reinforced, or strengthened, by the avoidance or termination of an aversive stimulus.

EXTINCTION. A process for weakening behavior to its preconditioning level. In the respondent model, it consists of continuous presentation of the conditioned stimulus without the unconditioned stimulus. In

GLOSSARY

the operant model, it consists of withholding reinforcement after the response is emitted.

FADING (of stimulus control). A technique for errorless learning whereby the teacher cues the child with multiple stimuli to make the correct response. Gradually, the number of cues are reduced, or "faded," until only one stimulus comes to exert control over the responding.

GENERALIZATION. The occurrence of a response in the presence of other stimulus situations following its reinforcement in the presence of one stimulus situation. Usually, the more the other stimulus situations are like the one in which the behavior was reinforced, the higher the probability that the response will be emitted.

INCOMPATIBLE RESPONSE. Any combination of responses which cannot occur simultaneously: in-seat behavior is incompatible with out-of-seat behavior.

INTERMITTENT REINFORCEMENT. Any schedule of reinforcement in which some responses are not followed by reinforcement.

INTERVAL SCHEDULES OF REINFORCEMENT. Those intermittent schedules of reinforcement in which the contingency is based on the passage of time since the last reinforcement. In general, the overall rate of responding on interval schedules is low compared to ratio schedules.

MALADAPTIVE BEHAVIOR. Those behaviors judged as inappropriate or ineffective in a given context, such as the classroom. In general, such behaviors interfere with a child's learning or social interaction and lead to discomfort.

MEDICAL MODEL. This model holds that inappropriate behavior is a symptom of some underlying *cause*. In thus conceptualizing of the problem, it follows that the individual exhibiting such behavior is "sick" or disordered—the problem resides within the child. In order to treat such behavior, it is judged necessary to identify the underlying cause and treat that entity rather than the behavior, since the behavior is simply symptomatic.

MODELING. A procedure for learning in which the individual observes a model perform some task and then imitates the performance of the model. This form of learning accounts for much verbal and motor learning in young children.

NEGATIVE REINFORCEMENT. A procedure for strengthening behavior

GLOSSARY

when the consequence of that behavior is the termination or avoidance of an aversive stimulus. That is, the response is followed by the avoidance or termination of some event noxious to the individual.

NEUTRAL STIMULUS. Those stimuli which precede, accompany, or follow a response but exert no control over the response.

OPERANT BEHAVIOR. Those behaviors which act on the environment, and hence are controlled by their effect on the environment (their consequences). These behaviors are emitted, voluntary, and involve primarily the skeletal musculature. Most daily activities of human beings are operant in nature.

OPERANT CONDITIONING. The process whereby reinforcing stimuli follow emitted responses, and thereby increase the probability of those responses occurring in the future.

POSITIVE REINFORCEMENT. Any stimulus which when made contingent upon a particular response will strengthen that response. The acid test of which stimuli are positively reinforcing to a given individual is whether or not it does strengthen a given response.

PREMACK PRINCIPLE. This principle states that when any behavior A is more probable than behavior B, then behavior A can be used to reinforce behavior B by making A contingent upon B.

PRIMARY REINFORCER. Those stimuli that can strengthen behaviors they follow without prior learning. These reinforcing stimuli derive their reinforcing power from the fact that they satisfy physiological needs of the organism (e.g., food, water).

PSYCHOLOGICAL MODEL. This model is based on the notion that almost all behavior is learned, adaptive, or maladaptive. Behaviors judged as maladaptive are not considered symptomatic, but rather are approached as learned behaviors. Modifications of these behaviors are approached through the manipulation of environmental stimuli, which are seen as supporting the maladaptive behavior.

PUNISHMENT. A process for weakening behavior which can take one of two forms. First, an aversive or noxious stimulus can be made contingent on the response to be weakened. Second, a positively reinforcing stimulus can be withheld or removed contingent on the response to be weakened.

RATIO SCHEDULES OF REINFORCEMENT. Those intermittent schedules of reinforcement in which reinforcement is contingent on the number of responses emitted. Such schedules differentially reinforce rapid responding, and behaviors on such schedules are characterized by high response rates.

GLOSSARY

REINFORCEMENT. An operation that will increase the strength of a response. In the respondent paradigm, this operation is the pairing of the neutral stimulus with the unconditioned stimulus. In the operant paradigm, the operation refers to a stimulus event which follows the emission of a response, which is thereby strengthened.

REINFORCER. Any stimulus event that can be used to strengthen a behavior it follows.

RESPONDENT BEHAVIOR. Those stereotyped behaviors that are elicited by stimuli that precede them. These behaviors are involuntary, and are mediated by the autonomic nervous system.

RESPONDENT CONDITIONING. A procedure for pairing a neutral stimulus with an unconditioned stimulus, with the result of establishing the neutral stimulus, through pairing, to elicit the same response as the unconditioned stimulus.

RESPONSE. This term refers to the units into which behavior can be segmented. In the behavioristic model, responses must be observable and/or measurable. Responses, in this book, are subdivided into respondent and operant responses, depending on whether they involve the autonomic nervous system or the central nervous system.

RESPONSE STRENGTH. This is a descriptive term which can be inferred from the frequency of a response, its latency, and/or its magnitude.

SATIATION. A procedure for weakening behavior, whereby the strength of a response can decrease as a result of continued reinforcement. The individual gets "sick of" the stimulus that was initially reinforcing and ceases responding in order to obtain that particular consequence.

SCHEDULES OF REINFORCEMENT. A general term which refers to the specification of which responses, of those emitted, will be reinforced. The schedules considered in this book are: *continuous schedules* in which every response is reinforced; *fixed ratio* in which reinforcement is forthcoming after a constant number of responses are emitted; *fixed interval* in which reinforcement is presented following the first response following the passage of a constant period of time; *variable ratio* in which varied numbers of responses have been emitted before reinforcement is presented; and *variable interval* in which the first response emitted is reinforced following the passage of varied time intervals.

SHAPING. A procedure for developing new, or more complex, behavior through the reinforcement of successive approximations to the goal

GLOSSARY

behavior. This procedure uses both positive reinforcement and extinction procedures to develop these closer approximations.

STIMULUS. This term generally refers to the units into which the environment can be segmented, but can include events internal to the individual. Stimuli can be divided further into the functions they serve as eliciting stimuli, reinforcing stimuli, discriminative stimuli, or neutral stimuli. They can also be reclassified according to whether they develop their functional qualities through learning into unconditioned or conditioned stimuli.

TIME-OUT. This procedure is a mild form of punishment based on the withdrawal of reinforcement, which has been used effectively in education. It consists of removing the child from the setting in which reinforcement is provided for some specified length of time. Hence, the term "time out from reinforcement."

TOKEN ECONOMY. An economy in which a common "medium of exchange" or currency is used as the form of immediate reinforcement, which can later be exchanged for "backup reinforcers" such as candy, trinkets, or privileges. The currency is some form of token (chips, check marks) which serves the same function as money in the larger society in that the tokens have purchasing power.

TOPOGRAPHY OF THE RESPONSE. The physical nature of the response such as the forcefulness, the duration, and the exact form of the response.

Index

Antecedent behavior
  identification of, 132
  recording of, 132
Ayllon, T., 29, 36, 74, 111, 128
Azrin, N. H., 26, 75

Baer, D., 26, 27, 28, 54, 70, 80, 95, 105, 106, 109, 110, 162
Bandura, A., 4, 30, 57, 58, 59, 60
Becker, W. C., 152, 155, 158, 176, 178, 179, 180, 181, 182, 183, 186, 187, 190, 191, 196, 199, 200
Behavior modification
  assumptions underlying, 41–42
  controversies surrounding its use, 207
  defined, 7–11
  in the regular class, 175–205
  in the special class, 145–174
  in the context of education, 138–142
  popularity of, 208–209
Bijou, S., 54, 70, 80, 95, 105, 106, 109, 110, 123, 130, 147

Birnbrauer, J., 36, 111, 124, 126, 128, 129, 137, 138, 147, 149, 151, 158, 221

Chaining, 82–85, 90
Charting of behavior, 122
Consequences. *See also* Reinforcing stimuli; Punishment
  identification of, 133
Contingency management, 57, 81
Contracting, 200–204
Controversy. *See* Behavior modification
Counterconditioning, 72–73, 79, 135

Desensitization, 52

Environmental determinants of behavior, 44
Extinction, 69–72, 79, 135, 193–194
  on fixed interval schedule, 103–104

235

INDEX

Extinction (*cont.*)
  on fixed ratio schedule, 100–101
  on variable interval schedule, 108–109
  on variable ratio schedule, 106–107
Fixed interval schedule of reinforcement, 107–110
Fixed ratio schedule of reinforcement, 99–101
Forness, S. R., 11, 111, 120, 122, 129, 132, 133, 138, 139, 161, 162, 171, 175, 207, 208, 209, 210, 211, 212, 215, 218, 220, 221

Generalized reinforcers, 67
Goal behavior, section of, 127–129

Haring, N. G., 36, 112, 124, 126, 136, 161, 163
Hewett, F. M., 3, 4, 10, 35, 36, 37, 51, 76, 112, 113, 121, 138, 141, 146, 147, 154, 155, 156, 158, 159, 160, 163, 165, 168, 170, 202, 210, 221, 222
History of behavior modification, 11–37
  ancient, 11–14
  early 1900s, 14–18
  1930s and 1940s, 18–23
  1950s, 23–28
  1960s, 28–37
Homme, L., 110, 111, 140, 153, 165, 185, 186, 200, 201, 202, 203

Intervention program, 134–136

Jones, M. C., 15, 16, 17, 18, 52, 53

Keller, F., 42, 46, 70, 102

Learning concepts, 41
  contingencies, 48
  explanations of behavior, 42–44
  responses, 46
  stimuli, 46
Learning models, 49
  operant model, 54–56
  respondent model, 50
Limitations of behavior modification
  ethical considerations, 222
  in the application, 219–222
  of the model, 209–218
Lindsley, O., 26, 28, 32, 125, 146, 160
Lovaas, O. I., 35, 111, 223

MacMillan, D. L., 5, 10, 11, 53, 111, 113, 114, 125, 126, 127, 132, 138, 139, 148, 149, 161, 162, 171, 207, 208, 209, 210, 211, 212, 215, 218, 220, 221
Maehr, M. L., 209, 210, 211, 215, 217
Medical model, 4–7
Modeling, 57–61, 89, 90, 135, 191–193

New behaviors, development of, 189–193

INDEX

O'Leary, K. D., 151, 152, 154, 155, 158, 164, 166, 167, 169, 172, 200
Operant conditioning. *See* Learning models

Premack principle, 185
Probability of behavior, 45
Psychoanalytic approach to behavior disorders, 3
Psychological model, 7–11
Punishment, 76–79, 135, 194–200. *See also* Time out

Reese, E. P., 76, 78, 88, 194, 198
Regular classroom procedures, 175
   contracting, 200–204
   developing new behaviors, 189–193
   general procedures, 178
   population in the regular class, 177
   strengthening behaviors, 180–189
   weakening behaviors, 193–200
Reinforcing stimuli
   activity reinforcers, 181, 185–187
   conditioned reinforcers, 66
   continuum of reinforcers, 110–114
   negative reinforcers, 55–56
   positive reinforcers, 122
   primary reinforcers, 66
   social reinforcers, 181–185
   symbolic reinforcers, 181, 187–189

Reynolds, G. S., 44, 70, 71, 84, 99, 101–102, 105, 107, 108, 109
Reversal of contingencies, 136–137

Satiation, 73–75, 79, 135
Schedules of reinforcement, 93, 163
   continuous schedule, 94, 95–96
   effect of schedule of reinforcement on extinction, 71
   fixed schedules, 97. *See also* Fixed interval; Fixed ratio
   intermittent schedules, 94
   interval schedules, 94, 97. *See also* Fixed interval; Variable interval
   ratio schedules, 94, 96. *See also* Fixed ratio; Variable ratio
   variable schedules, 97. *See also* Variable interval; Variable ratio
Sensory-neurological approach to behavior disorders, 3, 4
Shaping, 85–89, 90, 135, 189–191
Skinner, B. F., 8, 23, 67, 77, 99, 109
Stimuli
   discriminative, 48, 64, 65
   eliciting, 46–47
   neutral, 48
   reinforcing, 47, 55, 56, 65, 90
Stimulus control of operants, 63
Strengthening operants, 79

Target behavior
  graphing of, 131
  recording of, 129–132
  selection of, 126–127
Teacher
  as a behavior analyst, 124
  role in analyzing behavior, 125
Thorndike, E. L., 54
Time out, 194–197. *See also* Punishment
Time sampling, 130

Ullmann, L., and Krasner, L., 4, 5, 6, 8, 125, 146, 219

Variable interval schedule of reinforcement, 107–110
Variable ratio schedule of reinforcement, 104–107

Watson, J. B., 15, 18, 50
Weakening behavior, 69–79, 193
Whelan, R., 36, 112, 161, 163

Zigler E., 112, 113, 148